Jeanne Guyon's Interior Faith

Jeanne Guyon's Interior Faith

*Her Biblical Commentary on the Gospel of Luke
with Explanations and Reflections
on the Interior Life*

JEANNE DE LA MOTHE GUYON

INTRODUCTION AND TRANSLATION
FROM THE ORIGINAL FRENCH BY NANCY CAROL JAMES

Foreword by William Bradley Roberts

☙PICKWICK *Publications* • Eugene, Oregon

JEANNE GUYON'S INTERIOR FAITH
Her Biblical Commentary on Luke with Explanations and Reflections on the Interior Life

Copyright © 2019 Nancy Carol James. All rights reserved. Except for brief quotations in critical publications or reviews, no part of this book may be reproduced in any manner without prior written permission from the publisher. Write: Permissions, Wipf and Stock Publishers, 199 W. 8th Ave., Suite 3, Eugene, OR 97401.

Pickwick Publications
An Imprint of Wipf and Stock Publishers
199 W. 8th Ave., Suite 3
Eugene, OR 97401

www.wipfandstock.com

PAPERBACK ISBN: 978-1-5326-5868-6
HARDCOVER ISBN: 978-1-5326-5869-3
EBOOK ISBN: 978-1-5326-5870-9

Cataloguing-in-Publication data:

Names: Guyon, Jeanne Marie Bouvier de La Motte, 1648–1717, author. | James, Nancy Carol, introduction writer and translator. | Roberts, William Bradley, foreword writer.

Title: Jeanne Guyon's interior faith: her biblical commentary on Luke with explanations and reflections on the interior life / Jeanne Guyon, introduced and translated by Nancy Carol James.

Description: Eugene, OR: Pickwick Publications, 2019 | Includes bibliographical references.

Identifiers: ISBN 978-1-5326-5868-6 (paperback) | ISBN 978-1-5326-5869-3 (hardcover) | ISBN 978-1-5326-5870-9 (ebook)

Subjects: LCSH: Guyon, Jeanne Marie Bouvier de La Motte,—1648–1717 | Bible—Luke—Meditations | Bible—Luke—Devotional literature | Spiritual life—Catholic Church | Quietism

Classification: BX4705.G8 A25 2019 (paperback) | BX4705.G8 (ebook)

Manufactured in the U.S.A.   04/05/19

Dedicated to my grandmother Priscilla Culbert James
A musical woman filled with faith and wonder

Contents

Permissions | ix

Foreword by William Bradley Roberts | xi

Preface | xv

Acknowledgements | xvii

Introduction | xix

Jeanne Guyon's Interior Faith | 1
Her Biblical Commentaries on the Gospel of Luke
with Explanations and Reflections on the Interior Life

Bibliography | 177

Permissions

Scripture quotations are from New Revised Standard Version Bible, copyright © 1989 National Council of the Churches of Christ in the United States of America. Used by permission. All rights reserved worldwide.

Foreword

NANCY CAROL JAMES STANDS firmly at the forefront of Madame Guyon scholarship. This is in fact her eighth book either describing or translating the work of Madame Guyon. Being a seasoned scholar of Guyon allows James to write with the kind of penetrating insight only possible after years of exposure to her subject. Dr. James has lived with this fascinating mystic long enough that she can speak in Guyon's voice, nearly anticipating what Guyon will say.

What the reader craves in a translation is for the prose to flow as smoothly as if this were the first writing and the first tongue. In the case of James' translation this is exactly what is offered: smooth, flowing sentences without oddly-placed prepositional phrases, jarring syntax, or stilted language.

The reader quickly discovers the truth that both Guyon and James care deeply about the Bible. As unusual as this is in contemporary society, it was even rarer in Guyon's day, especially for a woman, because women were frequently barred from education. This stricture was even more pronounced when it came to the study of sacred texts.

Their love of holy writ—Guyon's and James's—arises not primarily from their love of scholarship, as ardent as that is. Instead, both author and translator share a deep passion for God as revealed in scripture, and this passion shines through their words, revealing hearts both devoted and consecrated.

The writer of Luke asserts from the outset that several accounts have been written of the life of Jesus Christ. Since we know only three others in the biblical canon, one is intrigued to imagine what might be learned from access to the other witnesses. Perhaps our passion would be stoked by going deeper into the spirit, the psychology, and the life of this singular man. Guyon, through James, does lead us to a profound depth in the scriptural text.

Guyon's passion is everywhere in evidence. Believing fervently in the prophetic word, she states that "God's word in us triumphs over everything." At the same time "doing the will of God and tending to the perfection that God wants for us" is crucial.[1] This calls to mind the admonition of James 1:22, "Be ye doers of the word, and not hearers only, deceiving your own selves." She understands that action is the evidence of revelation received.

Guyon is well aware that God's revelation comes to the community and not just to individuals. A deeply committed devotee of the Church, her faith in it is especially remarkable in light of the unjust treatment she experienced at its hands. Earlier books of James explore that treatment. In *Standing in the Whirlwind*, James explores Guyon's long and violent incarcerations and yet Guyon's forgiveness of those who abused her. One might call Guyon's faith "blind faith," but then faith by its very definition is, in a sense, blind. ("Now faith is the substance of things hoped for, the evidence of things not seen." Hebrews 11:1) Even after a personal inquisition by the Roman Catholic Church, Guyon concludes, "People are blessed who are in the Church of God."[2] Indeed, Guyon sees the church as a bestower of gifts, specifically designed for each believer.

Jeanne Guyon believes ardently in the Church's laws and refutes those who place tolerance above Law. She views the practices the Church gives us—e.g., holiness and salvation—as stairs that lead us to God. It is union with God, relationship with God, that Guyon sees as the goal of the practices we receive from the Church.[3]

For Guyon scripture is the dependable revelation of God. It is also true, however, that our spirits, animated by the Holy Spirit, enlighten us. African American Lukan scholar Brian K. Blount in his ironically titled essay "The Last Word on Biblical Authority" asserts that there is no such thing as "the last word" on biblical authority, because the Bible is a living word. As an example he relates a story from Howard Thurman about his grandmother, a slave. Upon occasion the master's minister would hold

---

1. Guyon, *Commentary*, 3.
2. Ibid., 105.
3. Ibid, 2.

services for the slaves. At least three or four times a year, he used as his text, "Slaves be obedient to them that are your master..., as unto Christ." (Ephesians 6:5) But Thurman's grandmother was steeped in the Bible, and she knew instinctively that there was something wrong with using the passage to justify slavery.[4] Guyon's symbolic, scriptural interpretation supports leaving behind superficial literal understandings and instead substituting the profound thoughts of scripture as symbols guiding the interior faith.

What is the theme of Luke? Joel B. Green, in his book on Luke, declares that, "among the New Testament writers, none is more concerned with *conversion* than Luke-Acts."[5] For the author of Luke, conversion is less about accepting a particular set of faith claims and more about participating in the unfolding of a particular story. "Conversion also involves an orientation toward God's eschatological purpose." It is "about God's restoration of God's people" and finally involves participation in the practices of God's restored people. Throughout Green's treatise on conversion, we're made aware that, unlike modern evangelicalism, the principles of conversion are firmly rooted in the community of the faithful.[6] Madame Guyon was deeply committed to the Church, a church that mistreated her, but where she nonetheless found herself grounded in faith.

We see in Guyon, as, indeed, in scripture, a dynamic tension between personal salvation— conversion of the individual—and God's saving acts in the community. Luke Timothy Johnson emphasizes that Luke affirms the value of human culture, citing as an example Luke's use of forms of Hellenistic literature, which he does with skill and creativity. The author of Luke implies the compatibility of Christianity and culture, as opposed to those who find culture evil and contrary to the Reign of God. Johnson agrees with Green that conversion means the acceptance of the prophetic critique and the "turning" of one's life. Those who enter the "people that God forms around the prophet" must turn around, the most impressive example of which is the "turning" of Paul from persecutor to apostle.[7]

In Madame Guyon's epistemology, great importance is given to the relationship of the believer to Jesus, grounded in the community of the Church. The presence of Jesus is so assured by the person of the Holy

---

4. Blount, *Biblical Authority*, 58.
5. Green, *Conversion*, 161.
6. Ibid., 162.
7. Johnson. "The Gospel of Luke," 22–23.

Spirit that she is led to say, "in losing his presence from their senses, they had the steady presence of his Spirit that filled them with great joy."[8] "This substantial stream of the Spirit of the Word causes a profound joy which will never be lost.[9]

Amen.

The Revd William Bradley Roberts, D.M.A.
Virginia Theological Seminary
Alexandria, Va.
May 24, 2018

---

8. Guyon, *Commentary*, 175.

9. Ibid., 176.

Preface

Jeanne Guyon understood the gospel of Luke as the revelation of the compassionate words and actions of Jesus Christ. In his Sermon on the Mount, he says, "Blessed are you who are poor, for yours is the kingdom of God" (Luke 6:20). Jeanne Guyon experienced these words of spiritual consolation in the midst of profound spiritual poverty and lived his presence through an unhappy marriage, deaths of two children, unjust incarcerations, and physical abuse. She wrote this biblical commentary to help others understand that Jesus Christ's words are true and to be trusted. I have translated this commentary to offer again the strengthening and consoling power of the interior Christian faith lived within the human heart, mind, and soul.

I offer this volume to all those who wish to live the profound Christian faith. Jeanne Guyon lived this and has helped many throughout the centuries find the path to hope and salvation.

These are the first English translation of Guyon's French commentaries of Gospel of Luke. For the Bible translation, I chose the New Revised Standard Version.

I pray that this short volume be a place of spiritual refreshment for all who long for the living Word of Jesus Christ within our heart, the interior faith, as Jeanne Guyon called this.

Acknowledgements

MANY PEOPLE HAVE CONTRIBUTED to this volume. I am grateful for the support of Dr. Carlos Eire during my dissertation work on Jeanne Guyon. I thank the Revd William Roberts for his understanding of Jeanne Guyon's theology and his foreword which makes a substantial contribution to this book.

I want to thank the parishioners of St. John's, Lafayette Square, Washington, DC for their dialogue about Jeanne Guyon and her rich theology.

Many thanks go to my family who shares my passion for the work of Jeanne Guyon. Roger, Hannah, and Melora have read, explored and researched Jeanne Guyon along with me. I am grateful that we share this love.

Above all, I think my readers who share a love for Jeanne Guyon and her ideas about interior faith. Guyon's books have been kept alive by those who continue to seek a profound interior life where Jesus Christ lives and moves and has his being. I hope that Guyon's Christian interior faith lives for centuries yet to come.

Introduction

IN FRANCE IN 1664, the parents of the fifteen-year-old Jeanne Guyon forced her into an arranged and unhappy marriage with an older man. In 1668 when pregnant with her second child, Jeanne, tempted by thoughts of despair and suicide, sought spiritual counsel from a wise monk. He told her that she could find God within her heart and immediately she felt Christ filling her with love. She wrote about this saying, "O my Lord, you were in my heart and you asked from me only a simple turning inward to make me feel your presence. O infinite Goodness, you were so near."[1]

This began Guyon's adventure into the interior life and her great passion to know Jesus Christ within. She wanted to know and love Jesus Christ as her intimate Lord and Master. She wrote about Jesus Christ with adoration. "I loved Him and I burnt with love, because I loved Him I loved Him in such a way that I could only love Him; but in loving Him I had no motive but himself."[2]

While researching Guyon at the University of Virginia, I became fascinated by her ideas and have tried to live her ideas of abandonment to God which creates an interior life of encounter with God. I have found what she says is trustworthy and deserving of our attention. Her radical theology frees us from pedestrian and petty concerns and substitutes in their place the ultimate concern, to use a phrase from Paul Tillich. Instead of focusing on self, we focus on God. Instead of concern only about material reality, we ponder the mysteries of the spiritual universe. We see all people as made in the image of God and because of this, we live in this world in a way that gradually unites us with loving power of Jesus Christ. The Christian faith proclaims the possibility of spiritual life within while living in the world of the flesh. Guyon understood this truth

---

1. James, *Pure Love*, 27.
2. Guyon, *Autobiography*, Vol. 1, 96.

beyond others and her life of afflictions allowed a testing and proving ground for her radical ideas. I have been blessed, and continue to be filled with wonder, at the trustworthiness of her thinking and theology.

Guyon lived in abandonment to Jesus Christ. She said that the Kingdom of God is within our being, yet the way to the kingdom is a long and arduous journey. She believes that all scripture is given to aid and guide on this long yet crucial path.

Her commentary on Luke reveals to us the profound and satisfying relationship with Jesus Christ. She said that she found happiness and joy, even in the midst of her experience in violent prisons and conflicted courtroom battles. Because of her profound encounter with the living Lord, she expressed the gospel faith in ways that no one else has. Guyon testifies to us that as we trust Jesus Christ, he dwells within our very being in the foundation of our soul.

Guyon's Theology of Interior Faith

In her commentary on Luke, Guyon passionately describes the life of interior faith. Guyon says that Luke as an eyewitness wrote this gospel for us to see what the apostles saw and witnesses that we too can see Jesus Christ and know the joy and fulfillment of being an apostle. Through this apostolic spiritual disposition, we have interior eyes to see what the apostles saw. This complete and satisfying interior vision of Jesus Christ and his kingdom brings us contentment and happiness.

Time and time again Guyon pours out her own interior being as she sweetly proclaims her love for Jesus Christ and the grace he has poured out upon her and all sinners. She writes with wonder about those to whom the kingdom is revealed and the sudden impact the kingdom may have on the faithful. For example, she describes the dying thief on the cross who sees and believes in Jesus Christ. Guyon proclaims, "A crucified sinner becomes in one moment a convert who confesses his crime and sees the goodness of God. He instantly becomes an apostle, a Preacher, and a Martyr!"(158)

With the glory of these sudden insights, our interior life brings an indestructible union with God that floods and storms may attack but cannot break (Luke 6:47–48). In our spiritual foundation we receive and live in God's will. Then the sweet, small breeze of God blows through our dusty soul and, in love with Jesus Christ, we receive his Word. He calls to us and our hearts leap with joy. Guyon writes, "When we remain in God, he fills our emptiness easily, but if we do not remain in God, he empties our fullness." She adds, "When we understand this secret, that in remaining we are filled and in leaving we are empty, there is no more difficulty in the interior life." (19) The Word lives inside of us. Guyon says, "Let God rule and command his kingship in us." (50)

God's interior kingdom is always powerful and efficacious. To create this interior kingdom, the Holy Spirit falls upon us and shelters us as the kingdom grows within. The Holy Spirit acts as a shadow that holds us in obscurity until the right time. Guyon describes Mary Magdalene's soul growing within, describing this as a valuable alabaster vase. "After Jesus Christ regards us favorably, our dirty earthen vessel, as hers was, becomes an alabaster vase, ready to hold the most excellent perfume of grace." (63) Guyon writes, "Collect yourself in your love for Jesus Christ, who will fill you with superabundance." (64) Guyon describes Magdalene as having found this. "Magdalene's heart is abandoned and is no longer only her heart. Her heart is in Jesus. He does not need to search for the heart of Magdalene in Magdalene. Jesus searches for her heart in him. So she finds in him an advocate, a defender, a doctor, and a lover. Jesus does all these services for Magdalene, and he does this for all souls who forget themselves for him." (67) Mary Magdalene received this interior kingdom with abandon and passion.

Interpretation of Symbols in the Bible

Guyon interprets the symbolic meaning of the biblical stories. She takes the literal words of the scriptures and interpret them symbolically as a guide into the kingdom of interior faith. She says that we live these events and stories in spiritual dispositions or states of being and they lead us into the glories of the apostolic state. Guyon offers maybe examples of how we live these biblical symbols and puts them in a consecutive order of human spiritual growth. At the beginning of the journey, Guyon uses the ideas of John the Baptist who preaches to us about needed tears of repentance that introduce us to into interior heart and mind. Other examples of her symbolic interpretation abound. Like Jesus, we rest in spiritual swaddling clothing similar to a repose in a disciplined circumstance so that we experience the sweetness of God within. After the disposition of swaddling, the Holy Spirit circumcises our interior lusts and indulgences of the flesh. In a consecutive stage, the Holy Spirit drives out the money-changers from our soul within that could lead us into corruption. In times of interior solitude, our interior life becomes strong. Later in our interior journey, we may live in a conflicted circumstance such as in the Garden of Gethsemane and we pray, "Not my will but your will be done."

Guyon interprets the Mary and Martha story as preeminent for the interior faith. Mary, sitting at the feet of Jesus, has chosen the better part. Guyon writes, "All that has been said in the Old and New Testament is almost all contained in these words: leave multiplicity, care, worry, and distractions and enter into simplicity, unity, abandon, surrender, peace, tranquility, and silence. . . . Jesus Christ, the perfect model that we follow, had to spend thirty years hidden before he was given an exterior life. Like him, we must be entirely established in the interior, before we are given an exterior." (84) Like Mary, we must listen to God and repose in him within our heart, mind, and soul.

Guyon's symbolic interpretation adds an entire level of biblical meaning never written before. Guyon's brilliant connection between the Law, the Prophets, and the Gospels creates a consistent and powerful vision of God reaching out to suffering humanity through the mediation and reconciliation of his Son Jesus Christ. As an example, Guyon writes about the prophet Anna in Luke 2:36–38 saying, "A woman who is a prophet and an apostle speaks so that we see that the Lord's hand is not too short to save (Isaiah 59:1)." (36) In this example, Guyon connects Isaiah's prophecy with the fulfillment of this prophecy spoken through Anna. Guyon's connections between differing scriptures creates a unified meaning from the biblical message.

Guyon also reveals the biblical symbols of sin and degradation. She says this dwells in inauthentic people, such as the Pharisees, and calls this propriety. In this sin, we consider ourselves as are our own property and a thing to be manipulated to bring ourselves fleshly pleasures. We believe in our self-ownership and do not abandon our lives to Jesus Christ. Indeed, propriety is to live in the original sin of Adam and Eve. For Guyon, propriety is the opposite of grace. She writes, "But if we are attached to the exterior and the exterior rules us, while the interior is full of propriety, (signified by *greed* and *wickedness*), we are claiming for ourselves the righteousness of God. To not attribute to God justice in all things is propriety." (90) The biblical person who personifies propriety is the critical elder son looking disdainfully upon the conversion of the sinning prodigal son. Yet even here Guyon proclaims hope. Our awareness of our self-adulation and propriety may lead us to repentance and the fresh air of grace.

Stages in Interior Growth

What is Guyon's journey into interior faith? Through the fall of human beings, the life of Adam has become our interior life and destroyed the divine life within. Our conversion begins the annihilation of this life of Adam and brings the resurrection of Jesus Christ within. Guyon describes this interior life in three stages.

In the first stage of conversion, the person lives in the graces of God. Jesus Christ begins to be formed within us and brings the peace and joy of intimacy with the Holy Trinity. The interior life brings a profound communion with Jesus Christ's generous grace. Guyon writes, "The Holy Spirit communicates these ineffable communications. Those that experience them have a germ of life given to them that they cannot fully distinguish." (14)

In the second stage, the person is annihilated through the power of overwhelming and abundant grace. Jesus Christ retraces the image of God within us and heals the wounds of the Fall. This is a stage of radical transformation. Guyon writes, "O souls who are happy to be the stigma of people, the abjection of all people, the subject of their contradiction, rejoice to be treated like your Master!" (155) We are happy to be treated like this because Jesus Christ lives in the depths of our souls. She describes this annihilation as the face of Jesus Christ within. "This face is no other than the Divinity of Jesus Christ, which is imprinted in all human beings. But they wiped away the face by their sins, and the image cannot be repaired except by Jesus Christ." (151) In annihilation, the believer receives the abundant grace that retraces the image of God within our soul. Jesus Christ says, "You are those who have stood by me in my trials" (Luke 22:28). As believers stand by Jesus Christ in his trials, they are honored to be there with him, even though despised and rejected by others.

In the third stage, the annihilated soul no longer lives alone but Jesus Christ lives within us and works through us. As Paul proclaims, "It is no longer I who live, but Jesus Christ within me" (Galatians 2:20). Jesus Christ is then perfectly formed within us. Guyon declares that Jesus Christ infuses abundant grace within us and when we receive and treasure this, we have an interior home formed within. This place is a place of the holy resurrection of Jesus Christ. This grace makes us cry out that we have a powerful Savior who promises to be with us always. Guyon writes, "O secret of the interior! It is in weakness that we find your power. It is in captivity that we find your freedom. It is in the exterior of an infant that we find the hidden truth of God. There we may find the truth of the mystery and discover how Jesus Christ begins to be formed in the interior. We find an infant in simplicity and innocence where we may be formed in the will of God." She writes, "O divine infant! You are born within hearts that do not oppose you." (27) In the most profound center of our soul, our savior Jesus Christ is born. The believer dwells in the midst of the fiery love of the Trinity.

The Invitation to the Interior Banquet

Guyon invites everyone to this interior banquet in her symbolic interpretations of Luke. One example of this comes from the bent-over woman in Luke 13:13. She describe this healing operation of God in the following quote.

> First, Jesus Christ calls her. Then he delivers the soul from the ties and ropes that attached her to things of the earth and to herself, that kept her bent over and turned away from God. Following this, he lays his hands on her that is an application of power and she turns toward him, taking a posture entirely different that the one she had. This great good only comes to this soul because she is exposed and open before God. (100)

As the soul finds love transporting her out of her propriety and self-ownership, she stands upright, and leaving behind the things of the earth, she finds her gaze staying on Jesus Christ. As her soul keeps him in sight, Jesus Christ works and operates in her life, removing self-destructions and addictions, adding strong passions and dreams, and finally uniting completely with her. She lives in Jesus Christ and Jesus Christ lives within her. This tender union will carry her to fulfillment and consummation in God.

In her commentary on Luke, Guyon invites us to a place of blessing, wonder, and love. Jesus Christ creates the fountain of divine grace within our interior being of heart, mind, and soul. This fountain sweetly and gently caresses us with living water in our interior being where the

Trinity of God, Father, Son, and Holy Spirit dwells and makes a home with us. In this place of interior faith, we see Jesus Christ within and then live his actions without. The Holy Spirit flows within and without us and makes us living apostles, even though separated in earthly time from him by many centuries. Still, through the interior fountain of living grace, we see, live, and know Jesus Christ and become united to him through the indwelling of the Holy Spirit.

Guyon yearns to share her spiritual revelations with others, especially the afflicted and suffering. She describes how God operates on the human being and creates an interior life where Jesus Christ becomes our Savior. Our interior being seeks union with God, the greatest of all possible gifts.

Nancy Carol James
July 22, 2018

Jeanne Guyon's Interior Faith
Her Biblical Commentaries on the Gospel of Luke with Explanations and Reflections on the Interior Life

> Since many have undertaken to set down an orderly account of the events that have been fulfilled among us, 2 just as they were handed on to us by those who from the beginning were eyewitnesses and servants of the word, 3 I too decided, after investigating everything carefully from the very first, to write an orderly account for you, most excellent Theophilus, 4 so that you may know the truth concerning the things about which you have been instructed. (Luke 1:1–4)

THIS BEGINNING OF THE Gospel appears but a prelude and an introduction, yet it shows us why this gospel was written. Both Luke and Mark have written their gospels based on the words of the apostles. Why wouldn't we believe in these reports from the saints? We must be self-deceived if we reject these reports coming from the apostles that are written in the Gospels of Luke and Mark and that the church holds to be true. Luke and Mark have written these gospels for us to see what the apostles saw.

Luke assures us that there are several others who have written what happened from the beginning about the state and life of Jesus Christ. It is evident, therefore, that others also wrote scriptures about this, yet there are only four gospels recognized by the church. The church judged this gospel as accurate and if I reject this tradition that the church approves, than I have doubted the truth of this gospel. In the true church, as we look at scripture and its witness, we see rapport with truth in perpetuity, as it lives from century to century going back to Jesus Christ. But when we find a church following scripture, we know this church to be true. The nobility and truth of a church needs the tradition presented in scripture.

We have this truth and justice in the church of God. The church must be *the pillar and bulwark of the truth* (1 Timothy 3:15) and also the perfect rule of our faith. In following the church whose foundation is truth, we cannot be mistaken.

The church interprets church laws with counsel and tolerance. There are people, though, who reverse the order of things and put tolerance in the place of Laws. Some now practice spiritual ceremonies not supported by scripture. The church as the body of Christ, though, is a good mother and has many children of all ages. The church gives the nourishment of bread and milk yet does not have to tolerate all the unwise practices. Instead, the church needs to follow laws and give gifts to everyone to fill her needs.

For example, as scripture tells us, the church wants us to be united and attached to God and this is the indispensable law. This is a positive commandment that *all Christians are to be united to God and Jesus Christ, as members of their head.* The church tenderly shows them the way to God, so when we arrive, we leave our sins with him. I need to use the ways the scriptures of the church teach to practice of holiness and salvation. But when I arrived in union with God and when I have been habitually united to God with a constant, durable, and permanent love, the intention of the church is that I rest in this union, so that nothing may turn me away from this, and I avoid what can pull me away from God. Therefore, I remain content in what the church wishes for me in this state. I am not attached to scrupulous practices that pull me away from my tender union with God. These practices do not help my union with God, and actually create distance between God and me. For example, I walk up the stairs to arrive at a room. I leave the stairs after I arrive at the room. I do not continue advancing on the stairs but it is necessary that I rest in the room so that I can find the rest I need. He who made the stairs did not intend them as a lodging or a place of rest. Instead, I go into the chamber to rest.

The church recommends good practices to carry her children to union with the Bridegroom. Yet the children need to leave these practices if and when they find union with God. The church also has certain prayers to raise the soul to God. Yet many are not raised to union with God and neither do they serve God. Yet there are souls in a very close union with God; how did they the way to God? There are people doing spiritual practices that see others not using the practices and so they accuse them of being in error. Yet far from being in error, they are in the true spirit of the church, and in the interior states of Jesus' church.

The Gospel reveals the true spiritual practices. Those who are close to Christ believe with a strong faith. They do what Christ commands. They participate in the sacraments, and take care to repent when needed. They take communion. This life of the soul protects our union with God while increasing it and providing armor against corruption. The church distributes these treasures of the commandments of Christ, repentance, forgiveness, baptism, and communion to all the faithful. Because of these, we do well. They are signs of the mercy and kindness of God.

God's Word in us triumphs over everything. We all must live in the will of God in our lives but not all do this. Catherine of Genoa was placed in a love so pure, she wanted to use this pure love for the cause of justice. It turns out that today, through some unwise practices, many find torments, rather than win God's mercy and kindness.[1]

Faithful people who still follow unnecessary practices are in error. They are far from the kindness of God and are not using God's strength. They have a respect for the church and would die to support it. But they do not choose the way of living in the will of God, to which they will be at the end united in a perfect way. Vocal prayers are not an absolute obligation. The prayer books given to priests are an example of a way given to them to unite them to God. When the soul is united to God, it is necessary that they remain in union with God and not return to their previous ways that were good and holy in their time. Vocal prayers are no longer good for the soul, because God asks other things from them. It is the same with all other devotional practices. Therefore we do not need to accuse others of errors because they are in the state that the church wishes for its children. They might need to stay there because of their weakness. All things have their season. Even when the counsel is holy and good, it is not for all. We must do everything that is holy. This means *doing the will of God* and *tending to the perfection* that God wants for us, each to her own state. The religious orders are good but they may prevent a person from entering into the will of God.

This is said to let those know who live in the Will of God that there are ignorant people who will condemn them. If the believer remains in repose and holds on to their path, they will find the contentment that God chooses for them.

---

1. Guyon frequently says that devotions not dedicated to finding the will of God are a form of peculiar torment. Guyon's Protestant theology is clearly seen in this passage.

> In the days of King Herod of Judea, there was a priest named Zechariah, who belonged to the priestly order of Abijah. His wife was a descendant of Aaron, and her name was Elizabeth. 6 Both of them were righteous before God, living blamelessly according to all of the commandments and regulations of the Lord. (Luke 1:5–6)

This scripture describes well the grandeur of the holiness of the parents of John the Baptist and his extraordinary birth. John originates from the priesthood and this scripture shows all priests that they should be engaged like John the Baptist, *a voice crying in the wilderness*. The priest should *prepare a way for the Lord* so they may learn about Jesus Christ: *Behold, the Lamb of God*. John the Baptist cried in the wilderness, which is to say in the desert of people's souls.

John the Baptist is the model that priests must imitate so they may lead souls to Jesus Christ, without losing any of them. The holy parents of this forerunner of Jesus Christ *were righteous before God* and conformed to God in holiness and justice. God revealed their justice before humans. They had no self-will which is the principle character of justice. They were *living blamelessly according to all of the commandments of the Lord*. They lived in God's will as revealed in scripture and were justified like God has for every individual person. Like the parents of John the Baptist, all priests must follow God and have morals beyond reproach.

Jesus Christ does not have priests for his parents and was born into a family of more common origin. He is to be imitated by everyone.

> But they had no children, because Elizabeth was barren, and both were getting on in years. 8 Once when he was serving as priest before God and his section was on duty, 9 he was chosen by lot, according to the custom of the priesthood, to enter the sanctuary of the Lord and offer incense. 10 Now at the time of the incense offering, the whole assembly of the people was praying outside. 11 Then there appeared to him an angel of the Lord, standing at the right side of the altar of incense. 12 When Zechariah saw him, he was terrified; and fear overwhelmed him. 13 But the angel said to him, "Do not be afraid, Zechariah, for your prayer has been heard. Your wife Elizabeth will bear you a son, and you will name him John." (Luke 1:7–13)

The circumstances that happened before the conception of John the Baptist are amazing. First, God shows his favor with light. The birth is known throughout the world and nothing is hidden because the priest must tell what happened outside. For the one who must announce Jesus Christ must have light, not for himself, but for the others. He must not be ashamed of preaching and confessing Jesus Christ. The promises given for John the Baptist were announced to Zechariah because as a child John must remain strong in him. Promises about Jesus were given to Mary and not to Joseph, because she had to ponder what was necessary for the formation of Jesus Christ. John comes from parents who were sterile and advanced in age so that we see the grace and miracles surrounding his birth, and also to see the purity that he had for the ministry of the Word. John's name is given by heaven before his birth to mark his vocation as an apostle.

> "You will have joy and gladness, and many will rejoice at his birth, 15 for he will be great in the sight of the Lord. He must never drink wine or strong drink; even before his birth he will be filled with the Holy Spirit. 16 He will turn many of the people of Israel to the Lord their God." (Luke 1:14–16)

John's proclamation of repentance brings joy to the world because that which afflicts the body, fills the spirit with contentment. Discipline gives us a strong and powerful support. John's coming, though, brings ruin to some and yet the resurrection of many. John's repentance brings ruin followed by resurrection. He *will be great in the sight of the Lord* because repentance brings faith and wonderful gifts. *He must never drink wine* because repentance brings all pleasure to the soul. Repentance also creates life in a community.

After the angel tells Zechariah of John's gifts as a person of repentance, he says that John will announce the eternal Word. John will be *filled with the Holy Spirit* of the new birth while in the womb of his mother so he may serve as the bearer of the Word. And to show that John has the quality of a preacher and a voice full of the Holy Spirit, the angel continues to say, *He will turn many of the people of Israel to the Lord their God*. This apostle will convert souls away from sin to grace, both in the exterior and in the interior, so they return to the kingdom of the Lord their God. This is why all the preaching of John announced that the kingdom of God is near.

> "With the spirit and power of Elijah, he will go before him, to turn the hearts of parents to their children, and the disobedient to the wisdom of the righteous, to make ready a people prepared for the Lord." (Luke 1:17)

John was sent to prepare the way for the Lord in the zeal, power, and virtue of Elijah. He was like a wind purifying the air in the places that Jesus Christ would pass. He must *go before Jesus Christ* to prepares the repentance before Jesus Christ. If a soul repents entirely, then she follows Jesus Christ who is the way and he leads the soul. Repentance is *a reconciliation of the heart* that heals our mistakes and lack of belief. This leads us to abandon ourselves to the way of God that is the *wisdom of the righteous*. If folly causes faithlessness, true faith and trust bring wisdom. Finally, John was to *make a people prepared for the Lord*. This involves the perfect conversion of both the interior and the exterior. When souls entirely turn to God, a people is prepared. The soul experiences the consummation of perfection.

Zechariah said to the angel, "How will I know that this is so? For I am an old man, and my wife is getting on in years." The angel replied, "I am Gabriel. I stand in the presence of God, and I have been sent to speak to you and to bring you this good news. But now, because you did not believe my words, which will be fulfilled in their time, you will become mute, unable to speak, until the day these things occur" (Luke 1:18–20).

The archangel Gabriel announces the mystery of the incarnation. Always standing before God, Gabriel's ministry is of the Word and he announces this Word in souls. The archangel Michael comes to destroy self-love and all that opposes the reign of God through the movement of the Word into the soul. Yet when Gabriel speaks, Zechariah asks, *How will I know the truth of these words*? He asks for a testimony contrary to faith. Mary does not ask for this testimony when Gabriel announces to her, because she is not in defiance. Instead, she asks, *How will this happen?* She does not doubt or defy but wants to be instructed in the will of God so that she may do this, even at an expense to her. Had God wanted something more, she would have consented. But Zechariah does not ask, *How will this happen?* He wants a testimony to the truth that is announced to him. This is offensive to God.

Gabriel assures him that he is the angel that *stands in the presence of God* and brings *this good news*. It as if he says, "The truth of my words cannot be better manifested than by the continual presence of God that I possess. If you had the same advantage of the presence, you would have more faith. I bring you the news that you will be given the divine presence. This is why you will *become mute, unable to speak*. With the cessation of words, you will be in a state where you will hear. You will be mute until the voice is given to you and this voice brings light." This voice is

John in an apostolic state who brings the Word of his Father. The voice is given to the apostles, who will speak of Jesus Christ coming to the hearts as the Word. God the Father chose John to announce and serve Jesus Christ. *I am*, he says, *the voice of one crying in the wilderness.*

But why does the angel speak to Zechariah as if his silence is a punishment for his lack of faith, since this silence brings an advantage to him? We need to know that there are two silences, one exterior and the other interior: the exterior is a punishment and the interior one a grace. Ministers are placed in their place to announce the reign of God. Their mission is hurt by their faults but the words they announce do not fail to accomplish their mission in the right time. Their words are necessary to teach all persons these extraordinary things. Minister should not be anxious about the interior words. Neither should they try to make them happen, but to trust everything to divine providence, who will bring this about in the right time. These words are accomplished in the time that God destines. Sometimes God promises many things that are not accomplished for a long time. The promises to Abraham are an example of this.

> Meanwhile the people were waiting for Zechariah and wondered at his delay in the sanctuary. 22 When he did come out, he could not speak to them, and they realized that he had seen a vision in the sanctuary. He kept motioning to them and remained unable to speak. 23 When his time of service was ended, he went to his home. 24 After those days his wife Elizabeth conceived, and for five months she remained in seclusion. She said, 25 "This is what the Lord has done for me when he looked favorably on me and took away the disgrace I have endured among my people." (Luke 1:21–25)

All the people witnessed this miracle that Zechariah had in his ministry. Through grace of God, Gabriel had witnessed to Zechariah, but he was forbidden to speak words about this. God gives grace at times and wants this hidden until certain times. Because Elizabeth heard the Lord's voice at the time of her conception, she hid herself as much as possible. She learned as a newly interior soul that God creates the interior, and the person must be hidden as much as possible to receive this manifestation of God. This is the work that God does within the soul, and this operation is preserved and heightened by silence. This is why Elizabeth says, *"This is what the Lord has done for me when he looked favorably on me."* It is known that if the soul turns toward God as if God is the sun, and the soul exposes herself to the Sun with a steady gaze, as an atom or small ray is attracted by the Sun, then God looks steadily also at the soul. A consequence of the soul exposing herself to the divine gaze is that in a very short time the formerly sterile soul becomes very fertile.

> In the sixth month the angel Gabriel was sent by God to a town in Galilee called Nazareth, to a virgin engaged to a man whose name was Joseph, of the house of David. The virgin's name was Mary. (Luke 1:26–27)

After Gabriel announces the conception of the child who will prepare the way for the Word, he also announces the incarnation of this same Word. John arrives six months before Jesus Christ. He has this short amount of time to prepare the way, and when this is done, Jesus Christ comes quickly. The angel was sent to a virgin because what the Word was producing in the world. She was a virgin of both soul and body. This virgin was engaged to a man, but she had not known a man. This is to show the union that must happen between the Word and the Virgin to better hide this grand mystery. The conception of John was announced with light but the incarnation of the Word was hidden with care. God hid his grand and marvelous ways under the ordinary and natural. Joseph was of the house of David, because Jesus Christ must be born of David according to the flesh. And this virgin's name was Mary because she must produce a fruit of both joy and sorrow.

> And he came to her and said, "Greetings, favored one! The Lord is with you." (Luke 1:28)

This heavenly ambassador enters into the presence of the holy virgin. She still lived bodily on earth while being transformed into God. As this was the message that would astonish both human beings and angels, God took all the necessary measures, so that this would be hidden from humanity for a time. This message to Mary carried the blessing of reconciliation of God with humanity by receiving within herself the Mediator who reconciles all of humanity. As Eve had been the mediator for sin and division, Mary would serve as the mediator for grace and reconciliation. Therefore, Mary consented to peace on behalf of the entire human race.

In close rapport with God, the angel with his pure spirit and intelligence brings the message of a real marriage between God and the humanity. He chooses words that show this mediation. "Greetings, Favored One!" he says. He shows his respect and at the same time declares the secret of his mission. He salutes her with grace. Because of this, she knew a perfect fullness of grace without any emptiness. God continually increased both the fullness of grace and her capacity to receive grace through all her days. A perfect annihilation brings an absolute emptiness and a capacity for this emptiness: this excessive emptiness through grace becomes an excessive fullness. The measure of emptiness in the self brings the measure of fullness she will know because God never lets the emptiness stay open without filling it. This brings strength and not sin. Being empty inside without faith causes anger and wrath but emptiness with grace brings generous love. Mary was entirely filled with love.

But, Mary, if you were so full, how did you receive the Word? Oh, it is the fullness of God that always causes both the emptiness and then the gift of reception. God made Mary a pure creature. She received the fullness of the Word but she was not herself the incarnation. She received the Word mystically. O wonderful interior of Mary with its perfect grandeur! What can we say about this? Because God is outside of all that we can comprehend, we can say little about God except what God says, "I am who I am." We may say nothing about Mary except that you are the mother of God and in saying that, we say all that we can say. If we say more than that, we weaken the Word. O the interior heart, mind, and soul of Mary! No one can understand you and what is happening! *The Lord is with you.* You are united to the Lord in a perfect way, although you do not have the incarnation yet. *Blessed are you among women!* Your production is worth infinitely more than all others. O infinite and fruitful virgin! O fullness of infinity! O immense emptiness of Mary! Who can comprehend this?

> But she was much perplexed at his words and pondered what sort of greeting this might be. (Luke 1:29)

Mary was troubled by his greeting. Her hidden interior of heart, mind and soul was ready to accept the meaning of these words, yet her senses caused her perplexity. Mary could well experience this, since Jesus Christ also experienced the same. Jesus says, *Now my soul is troubled* (John 12:27). He too knew astonishment in his senses.

> The angel said to her, "Do not be afraid, Mary, for you have found favor with God. And now, you will conceive in your womb and bear a son, and you will name him Jesus. He will be great, and he will be called the Son of the Most High, and the Lord God will give to him the throne of his ancestor David. He will reign over

the house of Jacob forever, and of his kingdom there will be no end." (Luke 1:30–33)

The angel says, *Do not be afraid, Mary*. What do you fear, Mary? The approach of this angel? Yet the virgin is not afraid. To the contrary, she is very welcoming, because she is not filled with scruples that would make her sin against the will of God. The angel says not to be afraid because she has *found favor with God*. He says this for two reasons. First, to show her to what a high degree that she has been elevated for all humanity and that this gift is freely given to her. This is done to her by the grace of God and not for any proper merit of her own. God out of his goodness and kindness has chosen her out of many. God raises Mary in a wonderful way. This is the truth that she confirms when she says, *The Lord has done great things for me*. "This is why the nations will call me blessed. I am blessed only because of what the Lord has done in me and nothing that I have done myself."

Secondly, the angel told Mary not to be fear because of God's great grace which is entirely pure of the malice and corruption of Adam.

Finally, she has nothing to fear even in these most dangerous things because of her innocence. And to increase her astonishment, he says something even more surprising that the virgin cannot even comprehend: *You will conceive in your womb and bear a son, and you will name him Jesus*. The angel does not say that the child is the Son of God whom she will conceive and bear. Gabriel preserves her in the will of God because in this moment, Mary is entirely present, without imperfections and self-will. The angel tells her that she will bear the Son who will be great, but he does not say that he is the Christ, but he *will be called the Son of the Most High*.

The angel tells her also about the Son's life in time and history: *he will reign on the throne of David forever*. To take these words and promises literally, Mary must believe that she will be the mother of the king of Israel and of Judah, and that Jesus will truly reign as David did in an external way. The words of God must be interpreted in an interior and spiritual way, otherwise we would see Jesus in his poor and afflicted state and think that the promises of the angel were not true. Though David was the father and ancestor of Jesus Christ, he showed the future image of Jesus Christ as King and Pastor. God gives Jesus Christ the throne of David and the rights of a legitimate pastor who must lead his flock Israel to green pastures. This excellent pastor leads with strength. He has the right *to reign* over the *house of Jacob* over abandoned souls, like David did in an external way. Jesus Christ reigns in an interior way. We must let Jesus Christ rule as King over our hearts and to let him lead as a Pastor because it is for this that he came into the world. His *reign is forever* because he will reign through eternity with strength. He holds us in the present and we begin eternity already. It is so easy to let Jesus reign; we only have to stop ruling ourselves.

> Mary said to the angel, "How can this be, since I am a virgin?" (Luke 1:34)

The question Mary asks is not one of doubt or refusal because she wants to be ready to do the thing that God asks of her. She wants to know if her way of life must change. She is ready to accomplish the will of God and wants to know if she needs to do something differently.

The angel said to her, "The Holy Spirit will come upon you, and the power of the most high will overshadow you; therefore the child to be born will be holy; he will be called Son of God" (Luke 1:35).

The angel tells Mary that she has nothing to do on her part to accomplish this great mystery. *The Holy Spirit will come upon you*, says the angel to Mary. But how is this to be done? It will come in a specific way and will not commune with any other. *The Most High will overshadow you*. But does the angel talk about light? Oh, it is because this light is so excessive, the light will appear like a shadow. Mary will be covered with this shadow and this shadow will make her fertile. These will be virtues of the Most High and the work of the all-powerful God. This is why Mary speaks of the mystery that God will accomplish with all the power of divine arms. It is necessary that this be done through the operations of the virtues and power of God. This holy one, in whom all holiness and righteousness is found, will be called the *Son of God*. For this is not the work of human beings, but is the production of the Holy Spirit.

The mystical incarnation comes from God's strength and not from human beings. *The Holy Spirit comes* in her soul with the infinite fullness and fertility of the Trinity. The Holy Spirit is always fertile. As the Bible says, God rested on the waters and they became very fertile. Genesis 1:2 reads, *The earth was a formless void and darkness covered the face of the deep, while a wind from God swept over the face of the water*. Genesis 1:20 reads, *And God said, "Let the waters bring forth swarms of living creatures, and let birds fly above the earth across the dome of the sky."* The Father and the Son communicate life through their life-giving warmth and give fertility to all things. God gave fertility to Mary by the Word present in her to do his work. The Holy Spirit produces the Word in souls and makes them fruitful. The Holy Spirit comes into an annihilated soul and by his life-giving fire, he sows the life of the Word in the soul, making a mystical incarnation, which takes place only when the power of the Most High covers the soul with its shadow. This soul loses all her own proper self-virtue, but she is under the shadow of divine virtue, that covers, guards, and defends her. The Holy Spirit acts as a shadow holding her in obscurity as everything happens within her. This is why all of God's operations born in the soul are done in a particular manner making her good and holy. This is also how Jesus Christ is *formed* in her by the operation of the Holy Spirit in a mystical manner. Paul also assures us of this, *My little children, for whom I am again in the pain of childbirth until Christ is formed in you* (Galatians 4:19).

> "And now, your relative Elizabeth in her old age has also conceived a son; and this is the sixth month for her who was said to be barren. 37 For nothing will be impossible with God." (Luke 1:36–37)

How poor, blind, and confused we are when we want to set and give limits to the divine power! If something surpasses human understanding, we declare it impossible. We want to regulate the will of God and his power by a science that is truly ignorant. *Nothing is impossible to God.* This is why a soul with the profound light of God is surprised by nothing; she judges and condemns nothing. Because she believes that in an instant *God is able from these stones to raise up children to Abraham* (Matthew 3:9). True faith never doubts or hesitates because she knows that God would not be God if he depended only on human understanding.

> Then Mary said, "Here am I, the servant of the Lord; let it be with me according to your word." Then the angel departed from her. (Luke 1:38)

Here God does a wonderful thing! God is so powerful that nothing may resist his will. However, he does not first ask for anything particular and extraordinary from the creature, but he only asks for their contentment. God considers the freedom of the human being and never violates this standard. God works freely and infallibly. God wants to operate the mystery of the incarnation in Mary for the salvation of all humanity through the contentment of Mary. In this particular person, God works his mystery and reconciles the affairs of the whole human race. She expresses her contentment: *Here am I, the servant of the Lord*, she says, and I will obey him without resistance. He will be pleased with me and he will care for the salvation of humanity, by accomplishing his Word and the promises given for our favor. Contentment is absolutely necessary for the freedom of the human being because God wants his salvation accomplished as a free and voluntary choice. Although we are not meriting or making this salvation, we must consent that the Word is formed within us. He lives within us; he governs, acts and operates within us. There are some who say, "Why does God not do all these things in all souls, since he is all-powerful?" It is true that God is all-powerful and He could do this, but he never does anything without our consent. All souls do not enter into the disposition that he requires. All souls that advance understand one thing: that God wishes for them to be a new sacrifice. If God wishes to give them extraordinary grace, he gives them contentment before he introduces them into the new state.

The angel's announcement about these extraordinary things is now finished. The Word will produce this operation. Now Gabriel no longer addresses Mary but Joseph.

> In those days Mary set out and went with haste to a Judean town in the hill country, where she entered the house of Zechariah and greeted Elizabeth. When Elizabeth heard Mary's greeting, the child leaped in her womb. And Elizabeth was filled with the Holy Spirit. (Luke 1:39–41)

As soon as Mary conceives the Word in her being, then she leaves to do the work of an apostle. The infant God from the womb of Mary will work here the great mystery of sanctification in John the Baptist while still in the womb of Elizabeth. Oh, if we knew the great things going on in the communications between the faithful and God! When a person who has Jesus Christ formed within her approaches another who is well disposed, she communicates a certain life-giving principle that fills the other person's soul with joy and contentment. There operates in the person a grace that is not understood, but experienced as good. This is the communication of the Word with John. He receives the sanctification of the merit and courage of future repentance. Mary *greets and embraces* Elizabeth and in this chaste embrace John becomes sanctified. Oh, the wonderful communion that happens among Mary, Elizabeth, Jesus Christ, and John, during the three months that they remain together! It was a communion of quiet but a profound and efficacious quiet. From afar Jesus Christ instructs John during these three months. John learns while in the womb of his mother this intimate and interior communication with Jesus Christ. In his life John the Baptist went to tell others about Jesus Christ and yet in the world he did not look for Jesus Christ. Did he not know that Jesus Christ was there, John who taught this to others? If John knew, why did he not go look for Jesus Christ? Was this a mistake? Who would believe that? Was John the Baptist indifferent to Jesus Christ? No, it was because he did not need human communication with Jesus Christ. They already had a profound and ineffable communication. John had to do only one thing and that was the will of God. John did not need to go find Jesus Christ, because Christ had already given him his movements. John was content with his life, as he worked at the ministry and office that Jesus Christ had given him. John with his state and dispositions was already united with Jesus Christ and even more, he had already been with Jesus Christ. So it was not a new thing to see Jesus Christ. John knew Jesus Christ first, not in the exterior, but in the secret virtue that Christ communicates within. This pure and sublime communication is experienced within. Oh, the experience of this! The Holy Spirit communicates these ineffable communications. Those that experience them have a germ of life given to them that they cannot fully distinguish.

> Elizabeth exclaimed with a loud cry, "Blessed are you among women, and blessed is the fruit of your womb. 43 And why has this happened to me, that the mother of my Lord comes to me?" (Luke 1:42–43)

When the soul receives the impression of the Word, she cries out to the one who communicates this, as does Elizabeth when she receives the Word, *Blessed are you among women!* Oh, the great blessing we have when Jesus Christ is communicated to us! Oh, wonderful fertility for that which was sterile is now fertile! Mary is blessed among women, because she was destined not only to bear the mystical Word in her as a chosen soul, but also in reality and in the body. This is why Elizabeth said to her, *Blessed is the fruit of your womb!* This is the blessing of a double benediction. Not only does she contain the treasure of divinity, but because this fruit extends from infinity and communicates infinity, all creation is blessed in him. The other souls in whom Jesus Christ is formed and carried in their hearts will also bless others through the fruit of their heart. Mary's heart is made fertile so the Word can be produced in other hearts.

Mary has a double fertility of both her heart and her womb in bringing Jesus Christ to the earth.

Elizabeth cries again, *And why has this happened to me, that the mother of my Lord comes to me?* Mary who produces the Word in hearts has come to see Elizabeth in the flesh. Oh, the great advantage that the souls in whom Jesus Christ is formed communicate to others! If we knew the blessing that they give, we would be charmed. Oh, great and admirable things that they express to us!

> For as soon as I heard the sound of your greeting, the child in my womb leaped for joy. 45 And blessed is she who believed that there would be a fulfillment of what was spoken to her by the Lord. (Luke 1:44–45)

Elizabeth discovers a great mystery that proves the communications between interior souls. If a person in the apostolic state speaks to another one, grace produces a *certain thrill of joy in the heart*. This is the communication of the Word that expresses and imprints this in the apostolic soul who speaks. The marvelous effect in the heart and these words are immediate. God touches John in this moment. O wonderful impact of these communications! So different from what we imagine! They are the conversions that surprise the world and we do not know the cause of them, but these grand things come only by faith. The promises of God are infallible when faith is made without hesitation and defiance. Mary was *very happy when she first believed*. Her happiness came from her faith.

> And Mary said, "My soul magnifies the Lord, 47 and my spirit rejoices in God my Savior." (Luke 1:46–47)

Mary loses herself in this immense happiness and does not defend herself from this joy. That would be propriety and contrary to truth and simplicity. Propriety deprives God of his very great glory. We must know God's goodness and publish this, when God moves us to do this. The truth moves Mary to speak without excuse or embarrassment, without hiding what God out of his mercy has done for her. She says, *My soul magnifies the Lord* and publicize the effects of his goodness and power. *My spirit rejoices*, not only in that which is ordinary. My spirit is always ravished by God and passes into him. The joy that I have causes me ecstasy and this joy is *in God my Savior*. I am his child and he is within me; he is my Savior. And as my Savior, he gives me powerful and abundant redemption. Annihilated souls know not to defend themselves from his glory or to hide from others the mercies of God.

> "For he has looked with favor on the lowliness of his servant. Surely, from now on all generations will call me blessed." (Luke 1:48)

Following this, Mary says that God has given her justice. She confesses that God has *looked* with favor on her, not because of her qualities, but because of his mercy. God sees the depths of Mary's humiliation and pours mercy on her. God's mercy forms Jesus Christ within the soul and this annihilates Mary. This annihilation is profound because of the great plenitude of the Word within the soul. God is pleased to fill this valley. No one else will ever be as annihilated as Mary. Oh, the profound wonder of the annihilation of Mary, which can never be comprehended except by contemplating the graces that God has given her! Mary does not say that God looks upon her purity, or her saintliness, or her virtues, but her *lowliness* and humiliation. She has nothing of her own but her lowliness and humiliation. That is why she adds, *all generations will call me blessed*.

> "For the Mighty One has done great things for me, and holy is his name." (Luke 1:49)

With strength Mary explains this. She says that the *Mighty One has done great things*. And she adds, *His name is holy*. Mary says that God has raised her to this eminent grace, yet she claims none of this holiness as her own. God is holy within her. It is as if she would add, "For me I am in the most profound annihilation that a creature can be in." We are astonished when we see certain interior souls who have no difficulty confessing and publishing the mercies of God. Confessing that everything is of God, they give God all the glory and keep nothing for themselves. God is all and in all. The soul is then exempt from propriety. This is why she is in a state to publish the mercies of God without attributing anything to herself and stealing anything from God. If she does not do this and hides what God does, then she becomes proprietary.

> "His mercy is for those who fear him from generation to generation. 51 He has shown strength with his arm; he has scattered the proud in the thoughts of their hearts." (Luke 1:50–51)

The moment that the soul enters into the *fear* of displeasing God, He acts and fills and blesses her with mercy, as one sees a father soothing a child with caresses after a moment of displeasing him. The father fills the child with goodness and caresses, so that she loses the fear but keeps a loving respect. There are some souls who filled with respect and love do not fear. Their generous love banishes all fear, and gives them a strong and vital boldness.

These souls speak of his rigorous mercy. Justice is their portion and God is pleased when they exercise the courage that he has given them. He *shows* them, *the strength of his arm*. But, I say O God! You content some souls with the simple touch of your justice. You touch them with your hand like a father and caress them like a tender and timid infant. Yet God places on his strong and courageous children a heavy weight. Does this mean that he loves them less? No, to the contrary God will give them a whole other part of an inheritance. The mercy and caresses are for the weak and timid infant. God pours *his mercy* on those who fear but he is pleased to extend *his power* on those who love him with a strong love, vigorous and pure. God leads these devoted and strong souls. God also scatters *the proud in the thoughts of their hearts* who would limit divine power and prevent his arm from being heard.

Mary speaks here of our Savior who pours out his favor on all people, extending his mercy *from generation to generation*. God's salvation passes in succession through all centuries, as Adam passed his sin down through all the ages. The Savior came to bring salvation to all those who have the sin of Adam. Mary sees that God sent Jesus Christ with all the *strength of his arm* who is the Word, Jesus Christ, the Son with all the strength of the Father. The Father's power is incarnated and deployed in Jesus Christ the man. God is all in his Word, as his Word is all in him. God in this incarnation has sent Jesus Christ with all the strength of his arms.

God extends justice through Jesus Christ with all his strength and power to suffer for the sins of the whole world. What courage God has given one human and what strength he has placed in him. Divine justice touches simply. The souls with the purest love also have divine justice. Jesus Christ was entirely devoted to divine justice, because he was entirely devoted to the glory of God the Father and only to God's interests. This is why God deploys Jesus with all the strength of his arm and his character, to support all the weight of a just God. The excessive suffering of Jesus Christ was so extreme because he presented this justice. Therefore God's arms were outstretched, enough to consume and carry millions of worlds for God.

When bearing divine justice, all torments are sweet with the prize of divine justice. The justice of God contains all his attributes and character. Therefore it is jealous because all the attributes look at God alone. The greatest glory that God can have is when the person with contentment enters into this justice. Humanity alone can never enter into divine justice because humans are small and weak creatures, and they may not carry the weight of divine justice. This is the weight of God. This weight is given more or less according to the gradations of strength of the human being. This justice is given to a few souls by a simple touch of God. It was necessary therefore that Jesus Christ contain all justice as he glorifies his Father. This is how souls in whom Jesus Christ lives and operates are the souls devoted to divine justice in a particular manner. They do not serve any particular self-interest, not even for their own salvation and perfection. Instead, they remain in God to exercise for him his justice in a way that pleases him. He does not spare them: to have mercy on them would be painful for them. Though human nature trembles and agonizes at the sight of divine justice, they continue to pray that they will not be spared. O God! They say, change me and reduce me to dust and do not spare me.

God extends justice only to accomplish the designs for the soul. The door to the justice of the Father is Jesus Christ. Mercy is for sinners and for mercenary souls. But justice is for the souls devoted only to the interests of their Father. O divine justice, you have been fully sent in Jesus Christ. You have put all glory into Jesus Christ. A heart freed from all propriety loves only divine justice and cannot fail to suffer. This person will be in him and with him throughout all eternity. Those overwhelmed with divine justice do not have the ire and wrath of God but unrepentant sinners do. But divine justice is for chosen souls in whom Jesus Christ lives and reigns. God takes pleasure in removing their pride and propriety, and then he executes the power of his will by leading these simple and abandoned souls, who have no other design but to remain in perfect abandonment in God.

> "He has brought down the powerful from their thrones, and lifted up the lowly." (Luke 1:52)

Mary describes here in a few words the way of Jesus Christ. *He has brought down the powerful.* He removes those who appear extraordinary *from their thrones* where they believe they are established forever. *He lifted up* those who are *the lowly* who are low and annihilated. God is pleased to lower those who are raised and to raise those who are lowly.

> "He has filled the hungry with good things, and sent the rich
> away empty." (Luke 1:53)

When the soul is empty, God *fills* it with himself. God alone, the sovereign good, has goodness. God brings a perfect refinement of goodness to those have suffered *hunger* and strange deprivations. God *sends the rich away empty*. His strength in doing this explains the economy of the spiritual life. God gives hunger to those who are full and fills those who are hungry. These two words contain all that we need to say about the interior life. We remain in God to fill the emptiness and to empty the fullness. When we remain in God, he fills our emptiness easily, but if we do not remain in God, he empties our fullness.

When God fills those who are empty, what is he doing? He fills them with himself. But when he empties those who are filled with their own richness, he seems to send them away from him and this distance from God causes little by little their emptiness. When we understand this secret, that in remaining we are filled and in leaving we are empty, there is no more difficulty in the interior life.

> "He has helped his servant Israel, in remembrance of his mercy,
> 55 according to the promise he made to our ancestors, to Abraham and to his descendants forever." (Luke 1:54–55)

Israel is an abandoned soul, who God *helps with his protection* in a totally special way. When we abandon ourselves to God, he cares for the soul in a way not done for those in the world. God does this *in remembrance of his mercy*. He exercises his justice. The soul is never in a moment without feeling the effects of his particular and special protection. God grants his protection in favor of the person's faith and abandon, *according to the promise he made* never to abandon those who trust in him.

> And Mary remained with her about three months and then returned to her home. (Luke 1:56)

Oh, the advantages of Mary's stay with Elizabeth! It is inconceivable. Oh, the wonderful exchange they had! The sweet communication! It was at this time that this holy family was united in wonderful holiness.

> Now the time came for Elizabeth to give birth, and she bore a son. 58 her neighbors and relatives heard that the Lord had shown his great mercy to her, and they rejoiced with her. 59 On the eighth day they came to circumcise the child, and they were going to name him Zechariah after his father. 60 But his mother

said, "No; he is to be called John." 61 They said to her, "None of your relatives has this name." Then they began motioning to his father to find out what name he wanted to give him. 63 He asked for a writing tablet and wrote, "His name is John." And all of them were amazed. (Luke 1:57–63)

God gives the name to John, to the voice who will announce his Son to all humanity. God will also give the name to Jesus Christ. When the soul is consummated and arrives in God, before entering into the apostolic state, she is given a new name, which confirms and establishes her in this state. John receives a new name as soon as he is born to mark that he is sanctified, he was drawn out of propriety, not like other infants, but by losing all of Adam's sins and propriety. This grace was given him because of the approach of Jesus Christ, as this is only given to the soul whom Jesus Christ approaches. The soul, though, that lives in propriety lives in Adam and has no newness, and has not entered into new life. Before this, John was in the life of Adam. At the beginning of this new life, John entered into the new life that was purely divine. This is why the new name and the confirmation of this state was given after his birth. To mark at this moment he was established as an apostle. At this moment he became the voice of one crying in the desert.

Immediately his mouth was opened and his tongue freed, and he began to speak, praising God. (Luke 1:64)

This verse confirms and supports what has been said: that *Zechariah speaks*. Zechariah, like John, was now in the order of grace and the interior. Zechariah's language was delayed until John's new name was given to mark that he is an apostolic person and that at this instant John was made an apostle who carried the Word. This is the secret of Zechariah's silence. He remained mute all the time that John was in his mother's womb to show that this was the time before John was admitted to the apostolate, to pass in silence the time in death and the sepulcher. The being of Elizabeth was like a sepulcher, a state of death, through which the soul must pass. John found life in the same place in which he had found the death of Adam. He became alive in the sepulcher, after a long time without knowledge of life and without use of this same life; now he entered into the day of perfect renewal and the day of his birth. His new name confirmed the day of his birth.

The *language* of Zechariah was *delayed* until the name was given. The soul lives immobile for a time in a life totally divine before entering into the apostolic state. When the soul is given a voice to carry the Word, Oh, then the language is free to speak. This is why all the mysteries are accomplished in Zechariah. But why does his mouth work and he begins to speak? It is to glorify and bless God.

> Fear came over all the neighbors, and all these things were talked about throughout the entire hill country of Judea. 66 All who heard them pondered them and said, "What then will this child become?" For, indeed, the hand of the Lord was with him. (Luke 1:65–66)

When such great things happen with prodigious occurrences among apostolic souls, *all these things were talked about throughout the entire hill country*. It is not only the hill country that benefits from this or listens to this. The voice of the eternal Word echoes in the hills and valleys. It is only in the valleys that these words are conserved. The mountains have the echoes but the valleys hear the word, that is to say, all simple and docile souls who use the light of their reason to listen to the word. All people who *listen* with docility, *preserve this in their heart,* guard it, and Christ is produced there. They then say, *What then will this child become,* the beginning of the seed of Jesus Christ in the soul? Because we experience this, the seed of life rests in us and gives it a particular protection. *The hand* of providence accompanies this child, that is to say, the highest grace.

Then the father Zechariah was filled with the Holy Spirit and spoke this prophecy:

> "Blessed be the Lord God of Israel, for he has looked favorably on his people and redeemed them." (Luke 1:67–68)

John secretly communicates to his father a portion of the Spirit that animates him. Zechariah has a part of the plenitude of the Holy Spirit and therefore is overwhelmed and in his prophecy about his son, he prophesies about Jesus Christ. He says, *Blessed be the Lord* whose goodness is infinite, for he has *looked favorably and redeemed* in his time *his people.* The visitation precedes John and will be done by John but Jesus Christ accomplishes the redemption for them. As soon as repentance appears we rejoice, because it is the sign of the approaching salvation, and soon Jesus Christ will follow. All depends on repentance and conversion; as soon as the time is perfect, Jesus Christ does not fail to come. To be perfect the change must not only be from sin to grace, but from exterior to interior, as it has been said many times. It is not from our own strength that we truly experience the Savior and our salvation.

> "He has raised up a mighty Savior for us in the house of his servant David, 70 as he spoke through the mouth of his holy prophets from of old." (Luke 1:69–70)

O God! You have given us a *mighty Savior*, given to us in your Son, you have communicated to us an abundant and infinite salvation. This is why the scripture reads, he has raised up a *horn of salvation*. He communicates to us a superabundance of salvation, an extremely high one, full of wonderful grace. This salvation is in the *house of his servant David*. O God! It seems that scripture says that the simplicity and abandon of David has attracted this salvation to his house and this salvation spreads with strength through souls. He has promised this in the *holy prophets from of old* and it is accomplished in this century. I will say, O Love! It seems that all the centuries past have done nothing but to predict what will happen in this century. They have spoken of interior states with shadows and valleys but you have lived this openly.

> "That we would be saved from our enemies and from the hand of all who hate us, That he has shown the mercy promised to our ancestors, and has remembered his holy covenant." (Luke 1:71–72)

God sends us a powerful Savior *to deliver us from our powerful and strong enemies*. Our Savior is an infinite and superabundant power, who surpasses the strength of our enemies. If our enemies are powerful and we are infinitely weak, as is true, how are we defended from our powerful enemies? It is impossible by ourselves. Therefore we have a powerful Savior who saves and delivers us from their hands. It is God who gives us Jesus Christ. But to enjoy the privilege and advantage of the Savior, we must let him act to fight and destroy our enemies. If we prevent him, he can do nothing and our salvation will not be useful, because we place obstacles before him by our revolt. This is most criminal. We also fight against him by our own will. Therefore let us abandon ourselves to him without reservation. He will defeat all our enemies without being wounded. God remembers the mercy he promised to our ancestors in the ancient law and accomplishes his promises through the merit and operations of Jesus Christ. All the holiness could not open the door into heaven without Jesus Christ. But the true *covenant* is for Christians and abandoned souls who participate in union with him. All others may participate in the mercy of salvation, but abandoned souls participate in the mercy of the covenant and union with salvation.

> "The oath that he swore to our ancestor Abraham, to grant us 74 that we, being rescued from the hands of our enemies, might serve him without fear, 75 in holiness and righteousness before him all our days." (Luke 1:73–75)

Scripture assures again of the promise *sworn to Abraham*, man of faith, that God would give grace to all who follow the way of faith and abandon. God promised we *being delivered* through his sovereign power *from the hands of our enemies, that we might serve him* and follow his will *without fear* and without concern for ourselves *in holiness*, that is the holiness that he has merited and communicates to us. The person does not make the holiness or destroy the enemies, but this is operated by God alone *in his righteousness*. He gives grace with his continual *presence*, in which the soul is confirmed *before him all our days in holiness and righteousness* without fear but in faith. Nothing is more clear than this. Nothing can be better expressed than the truth of the interior state with its firmness and stillness when there is only God.

> "To give knowledge of salvation to his people by the forgiveness of their sins." (Luke 1:77)

In the spiritual state of being like children, we are given the *knowledge of salvation*, different from everything we can imagine. Oh, the knowledge and experience of being as a child is like no other and more than all doctors of theology can imagine! And it is in this state of childhood that we receive *the forgiveness of our sins*. Children seem not familiar with their soul, yet in their powerlessness, they receive the happy state of salvation.

> "By the tender mercy of our God, the dawn from on high will break upon us." (Luke 1:78)

My God! How wonderfully this is expressed! *The tender mercy of our God*, that we alone consult for what God in his goodness and grace wants us to do. Without looking at our merits or demerits, God signals us that he sends *his divine Sun to rise* and dissipate the darkness of our ignorance and our sins, like the Sun of nature little by little dissipates the darkness of night. It is in this state of being that Jesus Christ rises upon us to communicate his life and light through grace, which can only come through the mercy of a Father full of goodness.

> "To give light to those who sit in darkness and in the shadow of death, to guide our feet into the way of peace." (Luke 1:79)

The divine Sun rises in the interior to *give light* to those *who sit* with him and repose in a total abandon in the state *of death* and in the deepest *darkness*. The soul is not in peace in this sepulcher and wants to be in the will of God. So the divine Sun, Jesus Christ, rises in this soul as light and *guides our feet in the way of peace*, exempt from all disorder and fear, walking entirely in freedom.

> The child grew and became strong in spirit, and he was in the wilderness until the day he appeared publicly to Israel. (Luke 1:80)

This verse contains all that he did from the time of his spiritual childhood until he entered the apostolic state. His interior *grew and became strong in spirit* as he believed. In the spirit he was raised and in his nature he was diminished. It was necessary that this child remain *in the wilderness* and in solitude, without which his interior state would not have grown and become strong. The soul must remain hidden until the time that it pleases God to draw him out of there to *appear publicly to Israel*. God calls this chosen soul destined to be interior out of his solitude to help his neighbor.

> In those days a decree went out from Emperor Augustus that all the world should be registered. 2 This was the first registration and was taken while Quirinius was governor of Syria 3 All went to their own towns to be registered. 4 Joseph also went from the town of Nazareth in Galilee to Judea, to the city of David called Bethlehem, because he was descended from the house and family of David. 5 He went to be registered with Mary, to whom he was engaged and who was expecting a child. 6 While they were there, the time came for her to deliver her child. (Luke 2:1–6)

It is not without mystery that God wills that this report contain all the circumstances that appear superfluous and that this history not be embellished. However, this simple narration contains two remarkable things. First, Jesus Christ at his birth and even before his birth practiced for himself and his parents what he taught, to render to Caesar the things that are Caesars and to God the things that are God. There is no state where we are not subject to the ruling authorities. There are some people who appear pious but yet believe that they have the right to shake off the yoke and take others away from their obedience. They believe they have the right to judge their own conduct and see what is just and right. Jesus Christ does not do this but he lives under the rule of the authorities. We must do the same unless it is directly opposed to divine law. The circumstances here are remarkable that the Savior Jesus Christ is born in Bethlehem to accomplish the prophecies; all this is done naturally and without anything extraordinary. What is more natural than that Mary comes to this place as it is ordained? This is the way God leads abandoned souls; he leads them in a manner all natural and without anything extraordinary, but it appears appropriate and admirable.

> And she gave birth to her firstborn son and wrapped him in bands of cloth, and laid him in a manger, because there was no place for them in the inn. (Luke 2:7)

Mary gives birth in a stable and puts the holy infant Jesus *in a manger because there was no place for him in the inn*. This is a coup of the divine hand, predicted throughout eternity, and announced by the prophets, but it appears all natural. O God! When you arrive, you arrive by eternal decree! Who then could not want all that you do and see that all things are in you? All things are held in you who are in a manger. The one who frees everyone is *swaddled and tied with bands of cloth*. O wonderful coup of the righteousness of the Most-High! The bands of cloth that Jesus Christ was enveloped at birth, marks how the soul in the spiritual birth must remain tied in his power and senses in a sweet captivity, to receive sweetness within, and to remain wrapped and captive as the infant Jesus Christ was in the manger. This is necessary that he be swaddled and rested in this strength. There is no state of being that Jesus Christ did not bear.

> In that region there were shepherds living in the fields, keeping watch over their flock by night. (Luke 2:8)

Shepherds must be particularly vigilant during the darkness and the *night* where death might happen. In the same way, the soul watches over things. She must be a vigilant pastor and take care because she is in a pitiable state where she cannot fully watch over herself or even look at God clearly. This is why scripture reads, that the shepherds kept *watch over their flock by night*. They guard vigilantly, like the soul must watch so that she does not make mistakes and become lost.

> Then an angel of the Lord stood before them, and the glory of the Lord shone around them, and they were terrified. 10 But the angel said to them, "Do not be afraid; for see—I am bringing you good news of great joy for all the people." (Luke 2:9–10)

When pastors are vigilant over their sheep with strength, this vigilance calls forth God who communicates with them with the illumination of his light, making them know truth within their souls. God shows them light on an impenetrable route, which only the divine light of *the glory of God* leads them to discover. All the light that show these states cause doubt and fear to spiritual directors who have not experienced this for themselves, but they are reassured by divine inspiration who speaks in the depths of the heart, *Do not be afraid*, for this is news of great joy. The state of this soul that appears new, far from afflicting us, fills us with joy.

> "To you is born this day in the city of David a Savior, who is the Messiah, the Lord." (Luke 2:11)

This brings great joy to pastors. In a state as dark as night, in a state they do not know, *in the city of David*, in the most profound center of the soul, *is born a Savior*, to save the soul by his own loss. The more the soul is lost, the more the soul finds its own salvation in the Savior, who is the Christ. Jesus Christ brings life to this soul to the measure that the soul is destroyed.

Before talking of these scriptures, it is good to reflect on the circumstances of the life of Jesus Christ.

First, to whom is announced the birth of Jesus Christ? To the doctors of the law, to the Pharisees, to princes, to kings? No, to poor and simple shepherds, to the simple without degrees, because these persons are the most appropriate to receive Jesus Christ, because they are not opposed to his simple spirit by their own sufficiency. They are already in the simplicity of his state and the character of his own spirit. If the angels had announced an infant king born in a manger to the doctors, they would have understood this as an illusion, as they do not have enlightenment and are far away from simplicity. They do not suffer. They want only grand things and extraordinary understandings. If the Pharisees had said this to Herod, they would have been persecuted. Instead, these simple shepherds, coarse and ignorant, receive the news of the birth of Jesus Christ. Oh, these simple souls by receiving the truth of Jesus Christ born in the depths of their souls are raised above the doctors! The doctors should announce to others the place where he lives, yet they ignore him and are ignorant of the experience of him!

> "This will be a sign for you: you will find a child wrapped in bands of cloth and lying in a manger." (Luke 2:12)

What signs are announced here of the grandeur and majesty of God? What! A Savior who cannot move and is lying, a King, a pastor, *lying in a manger*, in the place where beasts eat! A *child* God with all the weakness of infancy! O loving God! We see there the signs of your grandeur and your royalty! You come to reign, yet you are captive. You come to put us in freedom and you are *wrapped in bands of cloth*. You come to lead us and you are wrapped in bands of cloth without power and vigor. You come to provide for us and you are without power. O mystery! O secret of the interior! It is in weakness that we find your power. It is in captivity that we find your freedom. It is in the exterior of an infant that we find the hidden truth of God. There we may find the truth of the mystery and discover how Jesus Christ begins to be formed in the interior. We find an infant in simplicity, candor, and innocence where we may be formed in the will of God. Such a soul no longer has its own proper freedom and will but loses herself in this generous freedom because she may choose this divine will which holds her together and makes this happen. Finally, she too is lying in a manger. She is in an unvarying repose, in which nothing may trouble her. But as she appears to be in a manger, she finds nothing in herself except a stupid strangeness. This is the state that David experiences, when he said, *I was stupid and ignorant toward you; I was like a brute beast toward you. Nevertheless, I am continually with you; you hold my right hand* (Psalm 73:22–23). The soul resembles a beast, in entire powerlessness, but she is always attached to God in an unchanging repose.

> And suddenly there was with the angel a multitude of the heavenly host, praising God and saying, "Glory to God in the highest heaven, and on earth peace among those whom he favors!" (Luke 2:13–14)

One cannot express the joy in heaven than happens when Jesus Christ is born in a heart. At the time of the temporal birth of Jesus Christ, all the angels joyfully praised God. They do the same when Jesus Christ is born in hearts. O divine infant! You are born within hearts that do not oppose you! Come and be born in all our hearts. You came to be born in a stable in the fullness of time. In our hearts we also have the fullness of time. Therefore come be born in all hearts. If our hearts are like an empty stable and a waiting manger, Jesus Christ will not delay in coming. Jesus Christ was refused in all the houses in Bethlehem, and he was not born in them because they were all full and did not have a place for him. The same happens with our hearts if they are full. Jesus Christ will not be born there. There are only a few empty stables where he will be born and live, some annihilated souls who are like this poor stable, exposed to all contrary winds and persecution. But during this, he will be born in stables while the palaces are full and he will find no place for him. Oh, petite and annihilated souls are happy! You have a well-being that all the other souls refuse. They prefer their own fullness to the emptiness of poverty. This is why Jesus Christ is not born there.

The angels praise and glorify God, saying, "*Glory to God in the highest heaven!*" They say this because the glory of God is found in the highest place in the soul. It is the superior part of the souls that may fully glorify God. And according to the measure that it can glorify God, *peace* is made *on earth*, that is to say, the passions are calmed, so that nothing may trouble them. These double marvels operate in the souls of those of *good will* who is a soul who gives to God all her own will, which is the only thing that may make us good. Therefore she finds in herself the glory that God places in his saints in heaven that consists of perfect union with joined wills. And the perfect *peace* of those souls who belong to Jesus Christ in a special manner are possessed by him *on earth*.

> When the angels had left them and gone into heaven, the shepherds said to one another, "Let us now go to Bethlehem and see this thing that has taken place, which the Lord has made known to us." (Luke 2:15)

The angels announce the news of the place where Jesus Christ is born. Apostolic people also announce peace to souls of good will who search for Jesus Christ. These angels, though, are only the announcer. After this, they leave to show that it is Jesus Christ who does the rest. It is he who must be sought. If the angels had not left, good yet simple people would be arrested by the pleasures of the sight and sound of the angels, and not look for Jesus Christ. The Word that came from God carries souls so they do not stop at anything created, but they go directly to Jesus Christ to search in the manger, that is, the heart. It would make this experience little if after being told of the birth of Jesus Christ, these apostolic people did not want to taste and participate in this happy experience. This is why the shepherds, faithful to the grace that has been announced to them, say, "*Let us now go to Bethlehem*" which means enter into our heart *and see*, taste, experience, *this thing that has taken place*. O Word that has no beginning! O Word begotten through all eternity in the bosom of our Father! You have made an eternal Word wholly human in the womb of Mary, in the sacrament, and in the hearts of human beings. It is in our heart that we must seek, as in the stable, this Word that has been made. Go, go, my very dear brothers and sisters, taste this Word that is within you. Search for the divine Word, because God wants us to discover this way announced by the angels in the place where he inhabits. Oh, the great advantage to discover God within us! All happiness in life depends on this discovery alone. The great good announced by the angels is to discover God within us for it is the greatest grace to learn to know God within. If we search, God makes this known to us as an extraordinary gift.

> So they went with haste and found Mary and Joseph, and the child lying in the manger. 17 When they saw this, they made known what they had been told them about this child. (Luke 2:16–17)

The shepherds promptly go to look for that which had been told them, which shows the graces they had received. Like them, we must not delay when we seek Jesus Christ. When the shepherds went to find Jesus Christ, they *found Mary* and Jesus Christ, the mother and the child. We also discover the mystery of this holy family: like these innocent souls, we know them through our interior. It is there that we discover them. Nothing is said of the state of Mary and Joseph because the immense grandeur of their interior state does not permit us to speak. It is necessary to come to Jesus Christ to know and discern Mary and Joseph. It is the Son who gives intelligence about these profound states of these holy parents. The state of Mary and Joseph was an entirely interior state. O admirable uncreated Trinity! Who could ever speak of the sacred communion you had with the uncreated Trinity? These three holy people spent thirty years in a continual silence, in a communication that was entirely of the heart. There was a movement and response continually between them. Jesus Christ communicated continually with Mary, and Mary with Joseph. They gave to each other in the state of holy purity that they had received.

O the advantage of the interior life! There we discover the infant lying in the manger. That is to say, we discover in the interior this divine infant, who reposes in the foundation and center of the soul. He reposes so he can communicate his infant simplicity and his innocence. We can only comprehend this mystery by experience. Also, scripture tells us, that when *they saw this, they made known what they had been told them about this child*. As soon as the soul wants this experience, and she goes into her foundation to search for this, she proves the truth of what has been said, and tries to express the truth of this. O all of you who have difficulty believing this, experience this. You will discover Jesus Christ in your foundation and you will prove many times over what this scripture says.

> And all who heard were amazed at what the shepherds had told them. (Luke 2:18)

Nothing arouses so much admiration as seeing this discovery by simple people. We know and believe how the simple are susceptible to impressions of grace, as it is written in that God says, "*You who are simple, turn in here!*" (Proverbs 9:4). Simple people who are susceptible to the impressions of grace have a singular privilege and a gift to communicate to others that the wise do not have. In this experience, we are filled with admiration.

> But Mary treasured all these words and pondered them in her heart. (Luke 2:19)

Mary who is the realized model of the truly interior soul *pondered these words in her heart*. Scripture does not say that she thought these things in her mind, although the mind is the source of thought. We see that in her heart she discerned and distinguished these things, not by the reflections of the mind. She ponders these things in herself in a profound silence and understands much more than she expresses.

> The shepherds returned, glorifying and praising God for all they had heard and seen, as it had been told them. (Luke 2:20)

Souls who have experienced this know so clearly that everything they have been told will happen. This charms them and ravishes them with admiration.

> After eight days had passed, it was time to circumcise the child; and he was called Jesus, the name given by the angel before he was conceived in the womb. (Luke 2:21)

After Christ is born, he is circumcised. In a like manner, the soul enters into the first days of the spiritual life, days of tenderness and caresses, and then enters into circumcision. However, the soul experiences this passively and not in action. It is God himself who subtracts a small part of what he himself had given the soul. O God! You are a wonderful father who circumcises all his infants! This is why on the day of circumcision the name is given to Jesus Christ. We see that the adorable name of Jesus is the name of salvation, which happens only in circumcision and the taking away of death and corruption from all creatures. Salvation needs this circumcision taking away death and corruption. This circumcision is something that must be done to enter into interior life. This is taken away from the creature so that our Savior imprints his character of salvation in our soul.

> When the time came for their purification according to the law of Moses, they brought him up to Jerusalem to present him to the Lord 23 (as it is written in the law of the Lord, "Every firstborn male shall be designated as holy to the Lord"), 24 and they offered a sacrifice according to what is stated in the law of the Lord, "a pair of turtledoves or two young pigeons." (Luke 2:22–24)

After the circumcision is accomplished, purification is necessary. It is strange that to reach consummation through this purification, it is necessary that the soul offers again the sacrifice of this divine infant, that is to say, after the soul has taken pains to find in his foundation this divine presence and to possess this, she is obliged to lose what is sensible and perceptible, and to make a sacrifice to the Lord our God, like the rest. O God! Everything should be presented, abandoned, and sacrificed to your will because God does not withhold any of himself from us.

As it says in scripture, all *shall be designated as holy to the Lord*, means that the soul passes through the circumcision and purification, which are the first movements of going to the foundation, the source of grace, and the soul must follow. If she is faithful to follow the grace of the foundation, she will live perfectly within the will of God. All the instincts that come from the foundation of the soul, which are the first movements of the heart, are called *holy to the Lord* because they all belong to him. The passions no longer rule the soul because the purification cleanses the soul and the soul is no longer in war with itself. Now movements from the foundation of the soul (which are the motions from the Holy Spirit which are in us) make us holy to the Lord. These motions are from God. Anything contrary and opposed to God are only superficial reflections.

God still wants the *sacrifice* of *two turtledoves or two pigeons*, to show that these are agreeable to God, if they are done in simplicity. God loves this simplicity and only in simplicity are they agreeable.

> Now there was a man in Jerusalem whose name was Simeon; this man was righteous and devout, looking forward to the consolation of Israel, and the Holy Spirit rested on him. 26 It had been revealed to him by the Holy Spirit that he would not see death before he had seen the Lord's Messiah. (Luke 2:25–26)

When we *look forward to the consolation of Israel*, we never fail to receive consolation. This consolation is none other than Jesus Christ himself, who the soul desires to find. This is the consolation of interior souls, and they want only him. When a soul faithfully rests in a disposition of waiting, Jesus Christ never fails to manifest himself sooner or later.

The Holy Spirit rested on him. Simeon receives the revelation of Jesus Christ and says, "Now you are dismissing your servant in peace, according to your word, for my eyes have seen your salvation." The knowledge of the life of the Word is finally given to him in this place with full power.

It had been revealed to him by the Holy Spirit. Therefore he was filled with the knowledge *that he would not see death before he had seen the Lord's Messiah*. We may see Jesus Christ without death but one cannot possess this life of Jesus Christ without death. The scripture also promised that he would see the kingdom of Jesus Christ given and that of the demon destroyed and annihilated.

> Guided by the Spirit, Simeon came into the temple; and when the parents brought in the child Jesus, to do for him what was customary under the law. (Luke 2:27)

This passage proves the interior motion and how the true servants of God are faithful to follow *the impressions of the Holy Spirit*. It is certain that we must have a constant faithfulness to follow the divine motion and that the Holy Spirit never fails to move faithful souls. This is the spirit of the church that must let the Holy Spirit move it. But how do we know this motion? It is to know this as this holy man knew it. He discovered this because he was always looking forward and waiting. As he waited, he heard the movements that are subtle and delicate, that only people who wait in this disposition are able to discern. Furthermore, it was necessary that he had followed these movements up to this point. Without this, it would have been difficult to discover this moment because faithfulness to follow gives the experience. Waiting for the movement gives the discovery, because without this, we don't know the delicate impression. God is there, as when Elijah discerned this. Scripture reads: *Now there was a great wind, so strong that it was splitting mountains and breaking rocks in pieces before the Lord, the Lord was not in the wind.* Following this there was an *earthquake*, but *the Lord was not in the earthquake*. Next came a *fire but the Lord was not in the fire. After that came a still small voice and the Lord was there* (1 Kings 19:11–12). Therefore, we see that the Lord is not found in the strong and impetuous movements. These movements can always be discerned and we do not need to wait for them. But we must apply ourselves and wait to perceive a gentle breeze. This is why the motion of the Spirit of God, which is peaceful, sweet, and tranquil, cannot be distinguished easily unless we are accustomed to know it.

> Simeon took him in his arms and praised God, saying, 29 "Master, now you are dismissing your servant in peace, according to your word; 30 for my eyes have seen your salvation, 31 which you have prepared in the presence of all peoples." (Luke 2:28–31)

In this moment Simeon became a prophet and apostle. He *took the child* Jesus *in his arms*, to place him in hearts. We carry Jesus for a longtime in our heart, before we carry him in our arms: this is why the bridegroom says to his spouse, *Set me as a seal upon your heart*, because it begins there, and *as a seal upon your arm* (Song of Solomon 8:6). We have Jesus Christ in our hearts for ourselves; but we carry Jesus Christ in our arms for others. That is to say, we also receive him in our hands, that we may carry him to other hearts.

When this good servant of God in his strength receives the divine infant, he has in this moment fulfilled the duties of his apostolate. He speaks, *It is now, O Lord,* that I possess a peace so unchanging, that nothing in the world is capable of altering it. *I die in this peace*, because I hope that you accomplish in me this word of peace that you give in truth to this infant. I hope also that my life will be ended, *because my eyes have seen* in others and proven in myself, *the salvation that you have prepared* for all, like me, who watch and follow the movement of your Holy Spirit. There is nothing more for me on this earth since I have accomplished your holy will and I am happy at the sight of your salvation that you have given to all who trust in you and watch for you. You have brought me joy and you are destined to be the Savior and give salvation to us *in the presence of all people*. All the people may follow his example, to be formed by his life, to reflect on him, and to see in him all the states of this life.

> "A light for revelation to the Gentiles and for glory to your people Israel." (Luke 2:32)

The child Jesus Christ was *a light for revelation* for *all the nations*. Therefore, it was necessary that his light illuminate: he must shine light on the Gentile's darkness of ignorance and their sins of the night. He brings light for those who do not yet have light. He also brings *glory to your people Israel*, that is to say, interior souls, who do not yet have the glory of the divine Savior. He is their salvation with all the glory of salvation. Where he is, there is no darkness and confusion. O Love! There is only true glory in you; you are our only glory. This is why David said that God was his glory. Paul says he is glorified in God, as if he said, "There is nothing in me to glorify. I find in God all my glory."

> And the child's father and mother were amazed at what was being said about him. (Luke 2:33)

Why does the scripture say that Joseph and Mary *were amazed at what was being said about Jesus*? They had already been told many times that Jesus was God. Oh! It is as if they were in the most sublime prayer (that is in silence and a continual suspension, without anything extraordinary outside of them happening). When they heard Simeon speaking of this divine child, their continual state of amazement was awakened in them again with more force. They understood again and they comprehended more than they said.

> Then Simeon blessed them and said to his mother, Mary, "This child is destined for the falling and the rising of many in Israel, and to be a sign that will be opposed." (Luke 2:34)

Oh, the great words! These words said over the divine infant must be said throughout the centuries because they are fulfilled in all the centuries. This spiritual state of childhood, in which this divine infant dwelt and wants us to share with him, is *the falling and the rising of many in Israel*, that is to say, Israel who are the interior souls. The same interior souls *will be opposed* throughout the world. This opposition is the sign of the true interior. We must remember that faith says that the interior, spiritual life destroys all the sins of Adam within us and instead resurrects the life of Jesus Christ within. When Jesus Christ enters us as the *Way*, he destroys all the sins of Adam and establishes within its place the true way that leads to God. By reversing and ruining all human sins, he establishes many ways and practices to be in God, and witnesses to us of his love and faithfulness. When he comes as *Truth*, he dissipates all the darkness that lives in the soul and everything that appears to have been established by sin. His truth totally destroys and reduces sin to nothingness. We are placed in the true experience where we know our own nothingness and the All of God. Following this, he comes as *Word*, putting his life within us and fulfilling us, destroying sin so we may know the resurrection, which is our true life. There is no life except the life of Jesus Christ within us.

These are all the operations of Jesus Christ in the interior that Simeon discovered. In strength he assures us that destruction first happens so the resurrection may happen. Therefore, we are destroyed so we may be resurrected. Jesus Christ resurrects after he destroys.

Both of these two things, the falling and the rising, the destruction and the resurrection, are necessary for the perfection of Christians. As Paul says frequently in his Epistles, we are assured that if we *die* with Jesus Christ, we *rise* with Jesus Christ. We are a new creation in Jesus Christ, all the old has passed away, and all is renewed within us. Jesus Christ brings all of this, a state both grand and necessary, a state contrary and opposed to the world. Interior souls with Jesus Christ within them are a sign of contradiction to all the world. This is the true sign of God. I dare to say that one who knows these two things, the destruction and the resurrection, and have this true interior, are always opposed, blamed, condemned and censured. The Devil sees the great good they bring into the world, and puts all his efforts into destroying and hindering this way.

> "So that the inner thoughts of many will be revealed—and a sword will pierce your own soul." (Luke 2:35)

This passage expresses infinitely more than we can express. Mary gives birth to Jesus Christ, to all Christians, and all interior souls. With strength she must give birth. Therefore we know that God has spiritual mothers who give birth to souls for Jesus Christ and this birth gives them inconceivable pain. God has them carry all the unfaithfulness of their children. Mary who gives Jesus Christ to souls, feels all the unfaithfulness of her children, and she understands a large part of what will happen in the following centuries. Others must also bear what God gives them to help blind and ignorant humanity. Jesus has come to communicate his life of grace to those who are dead through sin, and he wants to put his life into them. Yet most put all of their efforts into living the life of nature, entirely contrary to the life of grace, and to prevent Jesus Christ from living within them because he wants the death of their self-will.

> There was also a prophet Anna, the daughter of Phanuel, of the tribe of Asher. She was of a great age, having lived with her husband seven years after her marriage, 37 then as a widow to the age of eighty-four. She never left the temple but worshiped there with fasting and prayer night and day. 38 At that moment she came, and began to praise God and speak about the child to all who were looking for the redemption of Jerusalem. (Luke 2:36–38)

It is not without mystery that holy scripture reports all of these mysteries. A woman who is a prophet and an apostle speaks so that we see that the Lord's hand is not too short to save (Isaiah 59:1). God communicates his Spirit to those who please him. He has nothing to do with those who call themselves wise among men and women. Instead, his people are the simple ones living in his hands, because they do not resist him. This woman is very pure. She is *advanced in age*, to show that she has made great progress. She lives in this state of being a prophet and apostle. How did she get here? *She never left the temple*, but was in a continual state of being with God. She lived in continual union with God and served him *night and day* with all her will. She was in continual *prayer*, having made a perpetual commitment in her youth that continued through her widowhood. She has the character appropriate to receive Jesus Christ and enter into the apostolic state.

Anna knew the way that the Lord leads all souls. She *came* into where they were naturally and through providence, yet in an ordinary manner. Discovering his grace and mercy, *she praised the Lord* and was put in the apostolic state. With strength she began to *speak* about Jesus Christ and the mystery of the interior *to all who were looking* and in a place to hear what she was saying. They could comprehend because they were already in a simple disposition of *waiting*. Scripture says that were *looking for the redemption of Israel*, that is to say, looking for deliverance for themselves from multiplicity by entering into an interior state as children of Israel. Those who are in the disposition of looking have a great advantage and a very appropriate disposition because they are prepared for an interior grace and the words that are spoken have an effect in the soul.

> When they had finished everything required by the law of the Lord, they returned to Galilee, to their own town of Nazareth.

> 40 The child grew and became strong, filled with wisdom; and the favor of God was upon him. (Luke 2:39–40)

Mary and Joseph *finished everything required by the law*, marking in this their submission to the law with the child who was the author of the law. This law was to be revoked, because Jesus Christ accomplished and consummated this by the one who removed it. This law was not one that always needed to exist. When Jesus Christ is born in a person's heart, he uses certain laws, methods, and practices with rigor and exactitude in order to destroy certain things but he only destroys things in order to perfect us. We must let him accomplish all these things in us and through us. But when he wants to destroy things, we must remain in him and not prevent this.

After the infant Jesus is born in a heart, *the child grows* and increases little by little, and insensibly *becomes strong*. But we must note that we do not know how the child grows and becomes strong but does this sweetly and imperceptibly. We do not perceive the progress of the interior or the growing life of Jesus Christ within the soul. This happens little by little. Scripture says he was strengthened in spirit; his strength was all spiritual and divine. *He is filled with wisdom*, and he is Wisdom. The soul in whom Jesus Christ lives and operates without possessing her own wisdom finds herself covered by true wisdom because Jesus Christ has in himself all *the grace of God*, in order to spread it to the faithful. He holds all the treasures of science and wisdom.

> Now every year his parents went to Jerusalem for the festival of the Passover. 42 And when he was twelve years old, they went up as usual for the festival. 43 When the festival was ended and they started to return, the boy Jesus stayed behind in Jerusalem, but his parents did not know it. 44 Assuming that he was in the group of travelers, they went a day's journey. Then they started to look for him among their relatives and friends. 45 When they did not find him, they returned to Jerusalem to search for him. (Luke 2:41–45)

We see here all the exactitude that Mary and Joseph used to accomplish all of the law because it was not for them to end the law, but to accomplish it perfectly. It was Jesus Christ who was to do this and this was not given to Mary or Joseph. They observed the law perfectly. Jesus Christ gave the work of ending the law to the apostles, because in Mary the ancient law was completed and in her was produced the new.

But isn't it a wonderful thing that Mary and Joseph who were so united with Jesus Christ, lost him and *lost him without perceiving it?* This loss of Jesus Christ is extremely mysterious and very consoling to good souls who often find they have lost the perceptible presence of Jesus Christ. They lose this presence without perceiving it because this loss happens without the soul's knowledge and they do not distinguish this until after it happens. They search for some time for Jesus Christ. They believe that he is only gone for some moments but when they do not find him, they search with great diligence. O Mary! How did you search for Jesus Christ *among the people and your parents and relatives?* He would not be found there. Jesus Christ is absent and he was not with them. He left and was with the ancient law, to give birth to the new. He left Mary for some days, because the Synagogue, who was like the mother of Jesus Christ, was deprived of Jesus Christ and needed him. Jesus Christ should not be separated from the Synagogue. Mary was not able to find him who is the new church except in the temple. It is in this sense that Mary's search took place. Mary would not search under her own strength because this is an imperfection that Mary is incapable of. This search is the accomplishment of the mystery within her. For this reason her son remained in Jerusalem and she returned for him. Because when one has lost Jesus Christ, it is not necessary to retrace our steps, but must wait for him to return. Mary knew this well but she knew how the Jews, who know about the Messiah from the scriptures, retrace their steps and look for the Messiah in the law, among themselves, and in their nation and ceremonies. They will find the Messiah only in the temple and in the church, where Mary finds him after three days.

> After three days they found him in the temple, sitting among the teachers, listening to them and asking them questions. 47 And all who heard him were amazed at his understanding and his answers. (Luke 2:46–47)

Jesus Christ is found *sitting among the teachers*, who were the doctors. He shows by this the true apostolic state and how often we have the dispositions of the apostolic state without entering into it. The true apostle remains always in the repose of God, even when he appears to others to be externally engaged. Jesus Christ wanted to do the actions of an apostle a long time before he exercised his apostolate. As we have seen, the soul is placed for a long time in the practice that she will do one day. But she is first only placed in a passing manner, after which she rests for very long time in this hidden life, with her zeal and desire to help others. She remains in repose and perfect quiet until it pleases God to draw her out of this state. There is not a state that is not in Jesus Christ and that he does not want to bear for us. If there were a state not in Jesus, it would not be true. I know that Jesus is not subject to the state of miseries into which we fall but he carries all our miseries without wounding his holiness and purity. All who hear Jesus Christ when he speaks as an apostolic souls, are *amazed at his understanding and his answers* because such a soul confounds all the doctors. Furthermore, his words are full of astounding wisdom, which his adversaries can neither resist nor contradict.

> When his parents saw him they were astonished; and his mother said to him, "Child, why have you treated us like this? Look, your father and I have been searching for you in great anxiety." 49 He said to them, "Why were you searching for me? Did you not know that I must be in my Father's house?" (Luke 2:48–49)

It seems that Mary was astonished because she was ignorant of the ways of her son. This was a manifestation for her that caused her astonishment to see Jesus Christ already in the apostolic state and doing the external work of his Father. They do not doubt him that he has work when he says the following well-known response, "Did you not know that I must be in my Father's house?" The words, "Did you not know?" are words they could not ignore.

The soul who has lost the sensible presence and perception of Jesus Christ, searches for him. He says to them, "Why were you searching for me?" It seems that you love me for yourself. Because if you love me for me, you will know that it is necessary to be strong in the faith, so that I may do my Father's desire. As if he were saying, when I deprive the soul of my perceptible presence, I have the disposition of the apostolic state. It is not necessary to search for Jesus as we do with deep desolation, and not appropriate love. To the contrary, we should be content when he leaves, so that he may work for the glory of his Father. Mary searched for her dear child, but as she was taught by this separation, that she must not search more, as he worked in the apostolate.

> But they did not understand what he said to them. 51 Then he went down with them and came to Nazareth, and was obedient to them. His mother treasured all these things in her heart. (Luke 2:50–51)

Scripture tells us that the parents of Jesus Christ *did not understand what he said to them* yet Mary *treasured all these things in her heart*. We may experience some of the taste and intelligence of Jesus Christ's words without having perfect intelligence. The words of Jesus Christ are hidden from our senses, because only God can conceive the profundity of his mystery. Intelligence about the Word is always necessary but God gives this to only a very few people. But we need the taste of the word that is received and treasured in the heart, like Mary did. Scripture tells us that the Word is experienced in the heart and that is where the Word is and not only in the mind and in intelligence. Let us do like Mary and experience the Word in the foundation of our heart. We do this both to live in and understand the Word.

From the moment that Jesus Christ appeared in the temple at Jerusalem until the time he entered the apostolic state was eighteen years. Nothing was said of him during this time except that he *was obedient to them*. Jesus Christ passed all of his life in a hidden manner, in absolute dependence, full of divine motion inside of him, but externally doing the will of his parents. He had nothing spoken of him since his birth during this time because all he had was obedience. Jesus Christ reveals to all Christians the example of what they must do. He was given to us as a model upon which we ought to mold ourselves and try to live with the same characteristics. Jesus Christ lived his whole life hidden and unknown, in entire solitude, without working for the conversion of anyone, although he lived for this. This was because his hour had not come. He had only passed a moment of time in his apostolate. We must do the same and love to be hidden and unknown. We must do the same and never leave our retreat except by a particular order of providence. Leaving our solitude is what causes so little fruit in our souls and from our actions. We put our faith in ourselves and leave before we are grounded. It is necessary to be grounded in our retreat before we give to others. Unless we do that, we have only the necessities and run out of what we need.

But what did Jesus Christ do during those thirty years of retreat, in which he was forged as a light? In the temple as a child, he showed a beautiful brilliance who appeared for only a few minutes and like the Sun is then covered by a cloud and was buried away with strength. He was obedient internally to the Divine and led and moved by God's will without resisting in any way. He was obedient externally to the will of his parents, who had God's infallible orders for him. Oh, that we also were obedient! Let's become like Jesus Christ!

Without carrying superfluous cares, let us understand that we only have two things to do. First, we should be obedient to God internally, following the movements of his Spirit. We are to be subject to the events of his providence, understanding that all we must do is to arrive moment to moment in God's will for us. Secondly, we are to be obedient in the exterior to our superiors. We must follow the example of Jesus Christ in all the rest.

> And Jesus increased in wisdom and in years, and in divine and human favor. (Luke 2:52)

How is Jesus Christ able to *increase in wisdom and grace*, when he has the fullness of God at the moment of his incarnation? He is the wisdom of the Father, and there is no moment when he has less wisdom than God the Father. Yet he increases in wisdom which has no beginning or end. As a human being, he grows and increases in merit. As both God and man, he always merited infinitely and there was no moment when he did not merit salvation for a million worlds. That is to say, when we arrive in God, one continues to advance, because we see that Jesus Christ who has the fullness of God, continues to advance. We do not advance by human means, but we advance in God, where we lose ourselves in God and continue to grow.

> In the fifteenth reign of Emperor Tiberius, when Pontius Pilate was governor of Judea, and Herod was ruler of Galilee, and his brother Philip ruler of the region of Ituraea and Trachonitis, and Lysanias ruler of Abilene, 2 during the high priesthood of Annas and Caiaphas, the word of God came to John son of Zechariah in the wilderness. 3 He went into all the region around the Jordan, proclaiming a baptism of repentance for the forgiveness of sins. (Luke 3:1–3)

All of these circumstances that appear unnecessary actually are quite needed. The evangelist notes the historical time of John the Baptist that happened when he became a preacher. The events precede the time and work of Jesus Christ. Then we see that repentance prepares the way before Jesus Christ comes himself. There are priests and kings but however *the Word* is not produced in them but in John, who was destined to be in the apostolate. We must understand that all priests are not apostles. As Paul says, it is necessary to have a different disposition to be an apostle than a priest. As scripture says, that *the word of God came to John*, that is to say, that he was placed in the permanent state of an apostle. This is only done then Jesus Christ, the eternal Word, is formed in the soul. *He went into all the region around the Jordan* so he could prepare all the people to pass through the Jordan, to enter into the source of calm and tranquil which is Jesus Christ. John preached the *baptism of repentance*, which is absolutely necessary after sin. Because in sin we have turned away from God and it is necessary to return to God through repentance.

> As it is written in the book of the words of the prophet Isaiah, "The voice of one crying out in the wilderness: 'Prepare the way of the Lord, make his paths straight. Every valley shall be filled, and every mountain and hill shall be made low, and the crooked shall be made straight, and the rough ways made smooth.'" (Luke 3:4–5)

It is written, that he must *prepare the way of the Lord*. The *voice of one crying out in the desert*, he may cry no other message than to prepare the way of the Lord. We let him enter so that he may become our way. We want him to lead us on his path. *Make his paths straight*. This means to turn away from things that warp us and prevent the divine Sun from sending his ray fully upon our soul to be attracted to him. We look only at God and through doing this, we experience the strong virtues that draw the soul to faith, as the Sun attracts a mist that is exposed, and in attracting it, the mist becomes subtle and pure.

Next, the scripture adds that *all valleys shall be filled*. To be filled, we must first have emptiness. The more profound our emptiness, the more plenitude we will have. But we must note, that John does not say, Come to me and you will be filled. As John says, repentance is always an active operation of the creature aided and helped by grace. The emptiness and void, though, can never be operated on by the creature and neither can the fullness. The soul is operated on in a passive state. This is why John says, that all valleys will be filled because only God can fill the void. Next is added, *every mountain and hill shall be made low, and the crooked* and crude *shall be made straight, and the rough ways made smooth* united and easy. We shall find no more pain in what appears to us as difficult. Because all that is tortuous and warped will be made right through a righteous and simple way. That is, the soul is in a place of perfect righteousness and simplicity so that nothing is in it that is warped; oh, then there is nothing to do that is difficult. This is why the prophet-king said, *I have run the way of thy commandments, when thou didst enlarge my heart* (Psalm 118:32). When what is raised is brought down and when what is empty is filled, then all injustices are removed. God makes a united path, very large and spacious, that enlarges the soul, which makes it run without any fear of falling.

> And all flesh shall see the salvation of God. (Luke 3:6)

Jesus Christ is the *salvation* and the benefit that *all flesh shall see*. It is he only who can heal this flesh of all its infirmities and weakness. O flesh! You are agitated by the revolt of the passions brought about by self-domination. Jesus Christ brings this salvation to you. If you abandon yourself to God, you will see the salvation of God. Salvation may never come through any other way. O poor souls to suffer strange temptations for so long, trust in God and give yourself to him who will support you in your affliction, provided that you are faithful and do not withdraw your abandonment. Believe that you will see the salvation of God and Jesus Christ himself will save you!

> And the crowds asked him. "What then should we do?" 11 In reply he said to them, "Whoever has two coats must share with anyone who was none; and whoever has food must do likewise." (Luke 3:10–11)

John next tells them about the acts of mercy that go along with repentance. By abstaining from evil, it is necessary to do good. He teaches them that their first change is to leave behind superfluous things. Here all the servants of God can do their part but for other changes, it is necessary that God work in them.

> Even tax collectors came to be baptized, and they asked him, "Teacher, what should we do?" He said to them, "Collect no more than the amount prescribed for you." (Luke 3:12–13)

There is never a state where we can save ourselves. God is not contrary to himself and when he calls us to a state, he faithfully gives us all that is necessary to be saved in that state. If there is a job contrary to salvation, that must be the tax collectors. However, John does not tell them to leave this job, but only tells them to do their duties in this job. How otherwise would they support the peace of the kingdom? The imposition of taxes is not an injustice. It is bearable if tax collectors only *collected the amount* prescribed for them. But alas! The vexations and stealing that overwhelm and ruin people, enrich the collectors who against the wishes of the king ignored the rights of the people. The king ignored the tax collectors' thievery. If the tax collectors and servants of the king who unlawfully received these collections were content with justice, the poor would be consoled and not overwhelmed.

> Soldiers also asked him, "And we, what should we do?" He said to them, "Do not extort money from anyone by threats and false accusation, and be satisfied with your wages." (Luke 3:14)

John does not tell the soldiers to quit the army. It is true that all persons in any condition may be saved. But they must *not extort money* from their neighbor. If they are guardians of justice, they must do their duty to their neighbor, and never do injustice. We owe this to ourselves to content ourselves with what we are and by doing this render honor to God. We give our brothers what we owe them and we do not extort and take anything from them. We must give our brothers and sisters love, charity, support, and assistance. We must do no harm, either directly or indirectly. We must not demand what is not due to us. In confusion we must not show contempt. In all the disorders of life, we must do our duty and not take for ourselves what is not due.

> As the people were filled with expectation, and all were questioning in their hearts concerning John, whether he might be the Messiah, 16 John answered them by saying, "I baptize you with water; but one who is more powerful than I is coming; I am not worthy to untie the thong of his sandals. He will baptize you with the Holy Spirit and fire." (Luke 3:15–16)

As it has been said many times, John was a figure of repentance who prepared the way for Jesus Christ. We must do the same today. All repentance prepares us for the way of Jesus Christ and for Jesus Christ himself. Any false persuasion that all Christians are the most virtuous stops us from going on Christ's way and meeting Jesus Christ himself. Repentance introduces us to Jesus Christ and nothing else will let us find Jesus Christ in himself, unless the soul is still perfectly innocent. This door of repentance is necessary and useful, if only we enter it. This advances us on the way and so we pass out of repentance. John knew the sentiments of people and if people stopped with him, they would not go on to Jesus Christ, the true way. Therefore, John was only the door, as repentance is the entrance. He warns and says to them, Do not stop with me because I only *baptize with water*, that is to say, I only wash the outside. But it is Jesus Christ who *comes after me* and does the true purification inside. Let him do this. *He will baptize you with fire* separating and radically purifying all that is most intimate. He will *baptize you with his Spirit* removing and consuming with his fire the selfish life. As it is written, *When you send forth your Spirit, they are created; and you renew the face of the ground* (Psalm 103:30). Not only the interior is purified by his operation, but *the face of the ground is renewed*, that is to say, the exterior.

> Now when all the people were baptized, and when Jesus also had been baptized and was praying, the heaven was opened, 22 and the Holy Spirit descended upon him in bodily form like a dove. And a voice came from heaven, "You are my Son, the Beloved; with you I am well pleased." (Luke 3:21–22)

Jesus Christ who is a model for all humanity into whom all must be shaped shows us each necessary stage for our salvation and perfection. It is needed that we go through these stages for two reasons. First, we see that Jesus is there and we join with him in this stage. Secondly, we see that he sanctifies all states, and for us to understand that he has gone through every stage and he makes these states holy. His presence and value works for our salvation. We live only through the merit and value in Jesus Christ and for Jesus Christ.

The heaven was opened shows the admiration about this action of Jesus Christ and to give us the knowledge that Jesus Christ is the Savior. The heavens opened to show the graces in repentance and baptism. The heavens had been closed until Jesus Christ, although there were many holy penitents in the ancient law but all their great actions were not able to open the heavens. Only Jesus Christ could do this. O divine Savior! What good we have if we only go to you! We must go to you. The heaven, that is the bosom of our Father, opens to us. You alone are able to open this to us. We abide in the Father with you. It is necessary to go first to Jesus Christ, that he may lead us to the Father. He assures us that no one can go to the Father except through him.

The Holy Spirit descended upon him in bodily form like a dove. This shows us the simplicity we will find in Jesus Christ. It is he who will place true simplicity within us. God delights to shape us so we resemble Jesus Christ *with whom he is well-pleased.* The soul who abandons herself to him and is carried by Jesus Christ becomes strong. Jesus Christ carries and forms the soul who never displeases God.

> Jesus was about thirty years old when he began his work. (Luke 3:23)

Before this time, his life was entirely hidden in the interior. He who came to save the world through his word was hidden his whole life and kept in silence. Oh! His silence did as much for humanity as his word! As the grace of the interior life is most sublime and essential, Jesus Christ spent *thirty years* to establish and merit this in souls. He only works three years in the exterior in the care of others. Jesus Christ is not content just to preach to us in his words but he shows us that the interior life is uniquely necessary. We see in his example the practice of the interior life himself as he makes this the center of his life.

> Then Jesus, filled with the power of the Spirit, returned to Galilee, and a report about him spread through all the surrounding country. 15 He began to teach in their synagogues and was praised by everyone. (Luke 4:14–15)

Here we see we need to be led in our interior by the divine motion. Jesus Christ who was filled with power went where the interior Spirit led him. When the soul is placed in this apostolic state, she must follow the divine motion in all external matters. Paul also used this strength. It is not the same in the less advanced states, where one must be conducted by obedience in external matters. Jesus Christ uses this interior strength. Earlier he had obeyed with a full submission his parents but on the inside he was in the apostolic life. He fully obeyed his parents in the exterior, but in the interior he followed the divine motion. This is why when he began his mission with the first mission at Galilee, he said to his mother Mary who thought to avail herself of the right she had formerly of ordering him, "*Woman, what concern is that to you and to me?*" (John 2:4). All these words are mysterious, and Jesus and Mary say this only for our instructions. This is why Mary added, "Do whatever he tells you." For Jesus Christ was no longer in the state of obedience to her on the outside, but now followed the motions of the Spirit alone.

His reputation was heard everywhere, and everyone praised him. It is always this way at the beginning of the apostolic state, but the great acclaim of the people is the infallible sign that this will end in the cross, shame, and ignominy.

When he came to Nazareth, where he had been brought up, he went to the synagogue on the Sabbath day, as was his custom. He stood up to read, 17 and the scroll of the prophet Isaiah was given to him. He unrolled the scroll and found the place where it was written:

> "The Spirit of the Lord is upon me, because he has anointed me to bring good news to the poor. He has sent me to proclaim release to the captives and recovery of sight to the blind, to let the oppressed go free." (Luke 4:16–18)

O God! What appears to be by chance is actually a great work of your providence! All that is greatest in the spiritual life is done quite naturally. If there is a great conquest to make, it appears to be by chance. Yet the words and action are most divine, and are done without premeditation. It appears that Jesus Christ opens the book by chance. However, he finds the passage that is about him and was written about the apostolic life in the prophet Isaiah.

This place in scripture expresses well the true qualities of a apostle, as Jesus Christ showed us on when he was on earth. *The Spirit of the Lord is upon me* because God found his repose in Jesus Christ who follows all God's movements and never resists him in anything. The apostles also repose in God in a perfect immobility and the Spirit of God rests upon them, because they do not resist him. God moves them as he likes. The Holy Spirit finds a repose in them and *anoints them*. This is the apostolic fruit of the anointing because by the measure it is spoken, it passes inside and spread throughout the soul. This is why it is necessary that the soul is full of this unction before it may help others because without the divine unction, the word is a clanging gong and nothing remains of it (1 Corinthians 13:1).

After this, the Holy Spirit reposes in apostolic persons, so that it may conceive the child Jesus in hearts, who prepares the divine anointing for the great mystery. He sends them to *preach the gospel* to two sorts of people. First, to those who are already *in poverty* and simplicity and need to advance. Secondly, he sends them to those who have a *broken heart*, that is to say, to those who are destroyed to make a new heart within them. God takes away the heart of stone, and gives them one of flesh, so that he can give them a state in which to receive the impressions of the Word.

> "He has sent me to proclaim release to the captives and recovery of sight to the blind, to let the oppressed go free 19 To proclaim the year of the Lord's favor." (Luke 4:18b–19)

There are two types of *captives* that Jesus Christ comes to deliver, and to *proclaim release*. The first are those who are held captive under sins and engagements with creatures. They want to turn away from sins and turn toward Jesus Christ, who presents grace to them. Jesus Christ wants himself to deliver them and their deliverance is certain. The other captives, for whom their captivity is very dangerous are not comparable to those in sin. These are those who after being given to God and walking in his way have a present desire to unite with him but they are hindered because they are again captive to themselves. Their captivity is insupportable, because they know what consists in true liberty, yet they separate from him. They cannot shake off the yoke and that which keeps them in subjection. It is only you, O Jesus who can free them! You will do this undoubtedly to those who abandon themselves to your adorable way. Jesus Christ preaches this deliverance to those he chooses.

He comes to give *sight* to people who are blind in their sins and to those who are in darkness and obscurity. He puts them in the full day of divine light.

This is a time of the *year of the Lord's favor* and mercy, a great gift to enjoy. When God sends an apostolic person in a place and in a country, there are a thousand graces attached to this time. If we benefit from his words, treasures of graces are found there and all people of good faith who receive this word will experience these effects. Yet people who are only curious and insincere will not benefit. But O simple souls, these will receive in abundance! God *gives to each according to his merit*. The same sun melts the ice and breaks the mud. Also, the same words are those who melt the well-disposed heart. We see in the same time that the simple are touched and won by the actions and words of Jesus Christ, while the Pharisees are indignant and look for ways to end his life.

> And he rolled up the scroll, gave it back to the attendant, and sat down. The eyes of all in the synagogue were fixed on him. 21 Then he began to say to them, "Today this scripture has been fulfilled in your hearing." (Luke 4:20–21)

O Love! When you begin your apostolic life, you also begin your consummation and fulfillment. When the soul enters into the apostolic life, Jesus Christ is fulfilled within her. Therefore, all that is written in the prophet Isaiah is fulfilled.

Jesus Christ had *the eyes of all in the synagogue*, that is to say, had their attention. If we have the eyes of our soul turned toward Jesus Christ in our interior, and if we have all of our attention turned toward him only, we have the benefit of hearing his words in our foundation, where what is written in the *scriptures* in our interior *will be fulfilled*.

> All spoke well of him and were amazed at the gracious words that came from his mouth. They said, "Is not this Joseph's son?" 23 He said to them, "Doubtless you will quote to me this proverb, 'Doctor, cure yourself!' And you will say, 'Do here also in your hometown the things that we have heard you did at Capernaum.'" 24 And he said, "Truly I tell you, no prophet is accepted in the prophet's hometown." (Luke 4:22–24)

Most human beings are attached to appearances, instead of sticking to truth and reality. We look at the outside and we do not see the interior. These people had seen the birth of Jesus Christ and his relatives and yet did not have faith in his words. He spoke *words of wisdom* and all the world was *amazed* and in admiration. Because they looked only at outside appearances, they removed all the fruit from his word. Most Christian do the same thing: they listen to the word of God. They hear the word of God: they receive this word with pleasure, and reflect on the exterior of the person and what he is, instead of looking at God, whom they reject. There was nothing remarkable in the exterior of Jesus Christ, and he told them what is said of most people who help others, *Doctor, cure yourself!* That is to say, Correct your defects, and then you will be in a state to help others. If we see faults in the appearance of an apostolic person, we see this as a mountain when actually it is a very little thing, and we take this opportunity to condemn his doctrine. Jesus Christ assures us, *No one is well-received in the place where he is known,* because of the censure of people who only stop at the outside appearance. Also, when God puts a soul in the apostolic state, he draws her from her country, for most people do not bear fruit in the place of their birth.

> "I assure you that there were many widows in Israel in Elijah's time, when the sky was shut for three and a half years and there was a severe famine throughout the land. 26 Yet Elijah was not sent to any of them, but to a widow in Zarephath in the region of Sidon. 27 And there were many in Israel with leprosy in the time of Elisha the prophet, yet not one of them was cleansed—only Naaman the Syrian." (Luke 4:25–27)

Jesus Christ confirms here what has been said earlier, and how apostolic people are nothing in their own home country. This is not without mystery. This is to show us that no true apostle or prophet is in his true country, that is to say, in himself. It is necessary that she leave herself absolutely to be a true apostle and to have the fruits of the apostolate. To show how God operates in a person, she must only take what God does in her and through her. When a soul is in herself, she is always proprietary and self-interested. She takes away from God without will or thought. This is why it is a great necessity that an apostle leaves herself and be exempt from propriety. Without doing this, God allows that she will bear very little fruit, because God is jealous of his proper glory.

> When they heard this, all in the synagogue were filled with rage. 29 They got up, drove him out of the town, and led him to the brow of the hill on which their town was built, so that they might hurl him off the cliff. 30 But he passed through the midst of them and went on his way. (Luke 4:28–30)

Because of the inconstancy of creatures, we must be able to distance ourselves from their applause and their condemnation. If they approve at one time, they will condemn at another. Within an hour, they were filled with admiration of Jesus Christ, and then they tried to kill him. Those who speak general truths have admirers but when faithful people speak particular truths they are condemned because some are offended. Former supporters turn against them. We must scorn both the esteem and the blame of human beings and look only to God in all things. Usually, though, we only consider the creature in all that we do and this is what afflicts and ruins our success. We see in Jesus Christ, that those who admire him and are astonished at the profundity of his doctrine are those who immediately want to throw him off of the precipice. Also, those who six days before the Passion cry, *Blessed is he who comes in the name of the Lord*, are those who cry, *Crucify*.

> But Jesus said to them, "I must proclaim the good news of the kingdom of God to the other cities also; for I was sent for this purpose." (Luke 4:43)

O Love! You cannot *preach* anything but the *good news of the kingdom of God*. That is what you want to preach everywhere for you were *sent for this purpose*. You are the King who reigns and you came to the world to teach and show us that you reign. This wisdom is enough for us. Let God rule and command his kingship in his. What is deplorable is that we oppose him in letting his reign be established in us.

> When he had finished speaking, he said to Simon, "Put out into deep water, and let down the nets for a catch." 5 Simon answered, "Master, we've worked hard all night and haven't caught anything. But because you say so, I will let down the nets." 6 When

they had done so, they caught such a large number of fish that their nets began to break. (Luke 5:4–6)

Jesus Christ is already beginning to instruct Peter about the apostolate, so Peter can gradually enter into the disposition of the apostolate, before he enters in the state of an apostle. Jesus commands him, *"Put out into deep water and let down the nets for a catch."* That way the mission is not restricted so that Peter may bear great fruit. But when is he to fish and to enter into the apostolic state? When he has *worked hard all night and hasn't caught anything*, that is to say, when he passed through the obscure and naked night of faith before seeing the futility of his own self-centered experience and work. He then despairs absolutely in what he alone can do. This describes Peter when he says to his Master that he has worked in futility all the night. *Working hard all night* is when the soul sees itself as useless with a strange obscurity and nudity, searching through its work to find something. Seeing herself as useless, she wants to work outside in some work of charity. She would like to do something for God but her work remains unfruitful because it is not done in the order of God. The soul therefore sees its uselessness and understands that she should stop trusting in work. She no longer wants to do anything but repose in her abandonment. When suddenly, the Master commands her to stop her repose and to work externally. She at first defends herself, defending her powerlessness. However, through a submission of her self-centered spirit, and through an entire loss of her will, a light is then given her that tells her that her work has little success because she works for herself, and that she is not submitted to God. She then surrenders herself to him again, saying, *I will throw the net in on your Word.* I no longer act for myself alone but for you. The Word that you give is not sterile and ineffective but your Word is always powerful and efficacious. Peter mirrors the astonishment we feel at the profundity of the spirit, through which everything is done and without which nothing is done. Oh, all my heart wants to throw my net into your Word. I throw in the net and you will catch it. I will receive the word but it is you who make the Word, which you place in the heart, and which produces all the effects you intend. In this way you make the apostolic person. When we do things by our own power, we can do nothing. But when we stop operating out of ourselves, then we stop being a weak instrument. Oh, then we see marvels! Also the scriptures tell us, *When they had done so, they caught such a large number of fish that their nets began to break.* O divine Fisher! It is only you that can make such catches and we know that you act powerfully in apostolic people.

> So they signaled their partners in the other boat to come and help them, and they came and filled both boats so full that they began to sink. (Luke 5:7)

Fishing is sometimes so intense that one needs other workers. Peter is the prince and premier of the apostles. This is why it is necessary that he is the first fisher who captures the word of his Master. The large quantity of fish shows already the great number of souls who will enter the church through the preaching of Peter and the apostles. There are two boats which show the uniqueness of the church, to show the exterior and the interior. Many souls enter into the exterior of the church, submit to the faith, practice the ceremonies but are not in the spirit. Instead, the interior needs to be entirely submitted to the divine motion, leaving the actions to God, to be moved by God's Spirit and follow God. These two boats plainly signify that when the church spreads everywhere and is reunited in the boat of Peter, it will have his same spirit, that is an interior spirit and united in sentiment. Because they will be confirmed in perfect charity, that is the consummation of union.

> Luke 5:8 But when Simon Peter saw it, he fell down at Jesus' knees, saying, "Go away from me, Lord, for I am a sinful man!"

There is no way to the apostolic state except through the passage of a simple disposition. The person who does not yet know the secrets of the apostolic life sees the marvels that God does by him and wants to serve by his humility. With such a sublime state, the person still feels the effects of the corruption of Adam, which is not destroyed in him in a fundamental way. Not being able to reconcile this high state with his weaknesses, he cries, *O Lord! Leave me, because* I feel that *I am a man full of sin.* So, *leave me,* because I cannot suffer uniting this wonderful holiness with this strange corruption. Or, heal me of this corruption so I stop being a sinner, if you want to use me to do such great marvels. O Peter, you misunderstand. It is the experience of your misery that will enable you to work these miracles, because it prevents you from attributing these miracles to yourself but only to God.

Peter's words show us the state of his soul, as we have just said. Beginning souls support and flatter themselves because God does great things through them. They have certain joy and secret vigor. Although they do not want to attribute this to themselves, they believe in their own goodness. It is not the same for advanced souls who experience their corruption. The grand things that God does through them annihilate them. It seems that there is a new light that helps them discern and they understand their baseness. The favors God gives them are more insupportable than any chastisement. The more time that the soul spends in an insensible perfection, God acts through her. In the first state the soul lives in the graces of God. In the second state the soul in annihilated. But in the third state, the annihilated soul, which no longer exists alone, enters and is established in the apostolate and God is in us and ministers through us. The first state would make us proprietors and owners of what God does in us and through us. The second state prevents us from acting in full liberty by the sight of our own baseness. But in the third state, the soul, not ceasing to deny what it is or what it is not, executes with a full freedom of Spirit the will of God.

> For he and all who were with him were amazed at the catch of fish that they had taken. (Luke 5:9)

Why where the apostles who had seen so many miracles so astonished at this? It was because they were more sensitive because God had increased their capacity. We admire some extraordinary things when they are really nothing. But miracles of providence make us more aware because they increase our capacity for receiving the grace of God.

> When they had brought their boats to shore, they left everything and followed him. (Luke 5:11)

According to the testimony of Matthew, Jesus Christ passed by and called them, and they left everything and followed him. They followed his call with faithfulness which is the first vocation. They had already given up their nets and the ordinary way they served through fishing. But to abandon the fish when one has the great advantage of having received them is a second degree of abandonment that is a second vocation. This call is higher with a greater grace. When Matthew and Mark speak of the first call, they say they left their nets to follow Jesus Christ. But in the second, Luke says, they *left everything*, without exception, without holding anything back of the world. They enter this entirely second vocation destitute.

> One day, while he was teaching, Pharisees and teachers of the law were sitting nearby (they had come from every village of

> Galilee and Judea and from Jerusalem); and the power of the
> Lord was with him to heal (Luke 5:17).

In this place in scripture we see that although Jesus Christ was always powerful and in a state of *healing the sick*, he did not always do this. He governed this miraculous *power*. At times, he spread his power and souls were blessed by his miracles. The soul moved with the power of this secret virtue is clearly seen, because the soul is blessed by both actions and words. When the soul is not ready, nothing will happen. The soul must be ready to perform miracles. We see that the instinct to perform miracles is dependent on the unction of grace that is ready to spread them on the soul readied to receive them. Grace gives movement to the soul to receive them. But this grace of miracles is at no point in the will of human beings and does not depend on our will, but in the preparation and rapport of grace. We also notice two things. First, that Jesus Christ was *seated for teaching*. On God's side, all grace comes from God's repose and tranquility who acts only in strength. On the side of the creature, we must receive this manner of action from our Creator.

> Then he looked up at his disciples and said: "Blessed are you
> who are poor, for yours is the kingdom of God." (Luke 6:20)

Jesus Christ assures his disciples that they are *blessed because they are poor*. It is certain that the greatest happiness in this life consists in the poverty of all things, which enlarges and relieves us. St. Catherine of Genoa writes in her autobiography, chapter 31, "*The love of poverty is a kingdom of tranquility.*" Nothing is so happy as losing the will to possess and being in poverty in all things. Because then she desires nothing and does not fear losing anything, she possesses an inconceivable happiness. *The kingdom of God is for the* truly *poor* because God reigns perfectly in him. Because nothing dominates her, she acts with God as king and he is above everything and is not subjected to anyone.

> "Blessed are you that hunger now, for you shall be filled. Blessed
> are you that weep now, for you shall laugh." (Luke 6:21)

The soul who is *famished* for God is *happy* because she will be soon perfectly satisfied in her possession of the object of her hunger. We hunger for the way needed to support our being, life, and needs. God is the sovereign being, and the only one who is sovereign, from whom all other supports are derived. God is the essential and true life, who protects and supports all lives. The soul has a strong and secret tendency to hunger for God who can support her being and maintain her life. This hunger brings the soul to unite with God at its end. The soul has this quality different than the body. Because the soul is spiritual and not material, she has no use for anything material. In ordinary life we usually follow the material. When the soul follows this desire of spiritual hunger, the soul slowly approaches until she find herself united to what caused the hunger and the soul finds at the same time fulfillment. The power that makes the hunger causes the perfect satisfaction. *Laughter follows tears* because joy succeeds sorrow. This hunger so great and strong causes tears and pain but once the hunger is satisfied, sorrow is converted to joy, and tears to laughter.

> "Blessed are you when people hate you, and when they exclude you, revile you, and defame you on account of the Son of Man. 23 Rejoice in that day and leap for joy, for surely your reward is great in heaven; for that is what their ancestors did to the prophets." (Luke 6:22)

The beatitude that Jesus Christ speaks here is very different from that which all people imagine. We think that we will be happy when people approve and respect us, especially when all the learned people and those in authority approve of us. We believe a person is lost when she is condemned by people because we believe that the salvation or loss of persons is only judged by human beings. This is actually very different from the judgment of God, as Jesus Christ says here: *I do not judge things as human beings judge them*. It is as if Jesus Christ says, "Humans judge only by the appearance and I judge the bottom of the heart." People do this injustice, because they judge based on the judgment of other human beings and not on the truth of the judgment of God. When they see a person criticized and persecuted, they take the occasion to condemn her, yet Jesus Christ's own mouth canonizes her who assures us that in all times his servants are treated in this way. These servants are *separated* as if they were infamous. These servants are *rejected* and the people of the world applaud this. They separate and withdraw from a person and suspect their conduct and life. They have no difficulty excluding a person whose life is very holy and innocent, and yet the world condemns and rejects them because she is not approved. The servants of Jesus Christ are condemned because they are not understood. Deceitful people describe the righteous as wicked and ungodly. Yet the righteous remains in *joy* in the middle of all their afflictions because *their reward* will be measured on all their work. Because their work is great, their reward will be perfect because God only gives himself according to the measure of afflictions suffered for him. If Jesus Christ was condemned, why should we be surprised that we are also condemned? St. Paul assures us that he *dies every day for the love of God* (1 Corinthians 15:31) by all the things he must suffer, but far from afflicting him he is in joy. I would not measure the respect I have for any person based on the condemnation of creatures. The more we bear the states of Jesus Christ, the more we will be treated like Jesus Christ.

> "But woe to you who are rich, for you have received your consolation. 25 Woe to you who are full now, for you will be hungry. Woe to you who are laughing now, for you will mourn and weep. 26 Woe to you when all speak well of you, for that is what their ancestors did to the false prophets." (Luke 6:24–26)

The world takes pleasure in contradicting the words and sentiments of Jesus Christ. The world calls unfortunate those whom Jesus Christ calls blessed. The world regards those as very happy whom Jesus Christ assures us are unfortunate. When a person is condemned, other people heap on more condemnation without mercy. The world feels free to condemn these holy people because the world does not approve of them. But, O divine Jesus! If I enter into your principles and sentiments, I find joy and pleasure in my condemnation, and pain in my approval. Many people leave the way of God, hesitate and stagger, because people condemn them. This condemnation, though, is what ought to most strengthen them and yet shakes them the most. David, who was well-instructed in the ways that God holds his faithful servants, assures us that *seeing the prosperity of the wicked, my feet had almost stumbled* (Psalm 73:2–3). We see the just condemned and those that love themselves approved, while those who love God with purity are rejected in all the world. *But*, adds this holy and afflicted prophet, *If I had stayed in this sentiment, I would have betrayed all of your children* (Psalm 73:15). But the children who are treated in this way are the most dear. According to the testimony of Jesus Christ, the true prophets are those who are condemned by humanity. The *false* prophets are those who are approved.

Jesus Christ assures us more, by saying that those who are hungry, will be satisfied and that those who are satisfied now will be hungry. The people of the world do not experience the hunger of God. They do not know it. Because they do not turn toward God, they do not know the hunger or the vehement desire to have God. To the contrary, the just souls separate themselves from outside things, and have a continual desire for God as their end. Those who are self-focused and fill themselves will have an extreme hunger for God throughout eternity and therefore they will never be satisfied. They enter into this most strange hope that they will be satisfied with goods, honors, and pleasures. Instead, they will be eternally hungry for the Sovereign Good, without there being anything for them. Those who are in God are now in tears and persecutions. The others are in pleasures and laughter. But the afflicted will laugh last, when the others are in immortal tears.

> "But love your enemies, do good, and lend, expecting nothing in return. Your reward will be great, and you will be children of the Most High; for he is kind to the ungrateful and the wicked. 36 Be merciful, just as your Father is merciful." (Luke 6:35–36)

The soul that has only God in view in all she does and who has banished her own self-interests finds this commandment the easiest in the world. When only God's interest leads and governs us, we have no enemies and we treat them as God treats them. According to what Jesus Christ says, our greatest enemies are also our greatest friends; the persecutions that they give us procure for us the greatest good. Our Lord recommends that we have no self-interest in what we do for our neighbor: we desire no recompense. But O God! Where do we find these persons who serve you without their own interests? All look to their own interests and none look for the interests of Jesus Christ. Yet Jesus Christ assures us, those who do these things without their self-interest are the *children of the most high*. We can discern the children of the mercenary who serve the Father out of their self-interest and receive pleasure for their self-interest. The mercenary only acts for his reward. God does so much good for us, wherever we are. Why then do we not have the same regard for our brothers and sisters? We must learn from God to have mercy, and to leave justice and vengeance to him. Also, we learn from scripture, that vengeance is *reserved* only for God.

> "For each tree is known by its own fruit. Figs are not gathered from thorns, nor are grapes picked from a bramble bush. 45 The good person out of the good treasure of the heart produces good, and the evil person out of evil treasure produces evil; for it is out of the abundance of the heart that the mouth speaks." (Luke 6:44–45)

People may only judge another person by the *fruit* that she makes. If they see that the fruits are not good, they may interpret this as interior corruption. If we do justice to the truth, we will see that if the interior is corrupted, the fruits will not be pure and abundant. Only a good heart can produce external *good fruits*. A heart that is full of God can speak only of God. When we speak of God, we give generously and superabundantly with ease.

> "I will show you what someone is like who comes to me, hears my words, and acts on them. 48 That one is like a man building a house, who dug deeply and laid the foundation on rock; when a flood arose, the river burst against that house but could not shake it, because it had been well built." (Luke 6:47–48)

These words alone should convince us of what has been said about the interior. Jesus Christ teaches us *who is like the one who comes to him*. Come to Jesus Christ—this is the first step in the interior conversion. We should be converted from within and seek Jesus Christ, to give ourselves and to abandon ourselves to him without reserve. When we come to Jesus Christ, we have made the first step when we turn inside. There it is necessary to *hear his words* because he wants only to speak to the heart of Jerusalem, and he only goes to Jerusalem to speak. It is necessary therefore to go to Jesus Christ, to listen in the bottom of the heart, and then *practice the words* in the external life. It is necessary to be attentive to our interior and listen to the will of our Master and then be active externally, putting his words into practice. His children and servants listen attentively to the words of their master, to understand his will. But as soon as they learn his will, they must undertake to do his will. She begins in interior unity and simplicity. Then passive reception inside must be followed by action outside; the external action outside must support the passivity of the interior. The perfection of the way mixes this interior reception and external action into one and then it multiplies.

Whoever lives this way is *like a man building a house*, which is his spiritual edifice. To *begin by digging deep* is nothing other than annihilation. The first annihilation is that of against the self-focused operations. Once the annihilation ends, God comes into the place left by the annihilation. We can discern that this is God, because it is God's constant operations and we stop gradually the operations of the creature. The second annihilation is that of our moral being, of all that we are and all that we subsist in. The foundations were only earth which filled the place which through annihilation will be made empty, so as to enable it to lay the foundation. Also, the annihilation and the foundation in the interior is only done by omitting what we have of our own self-will and propriety. As soon as this done, we find the living *rock* Jesus Christ, for which all the edifice is built, and which is only built on Jesus Christ. Everything not of Jesus Christ is to be destroyed within us.

When this is the case, the edifice can no longer fear anything. All the floods and the *rising streams*, the strongest temptations, the worst persecutions, *cannot shake these souls there* because they are not founded on the moving earth of our self operations, neither on self concern, but on the unshakeable rock, Jesus Christ. These souls far from fearing, the more everything comes upon them with impetuosity, the more they have assurance. What shakes them, strengthens them. If Jesus Christ himself had not said this, it would be difficult to believe it.

> "But the one who hears and does not act is like a man who built a house on the ground without a foundation. When the river burst against it, immediately it fell, and great was the ruin of that house." (Luke 6:49)

There are a great number of people who are this type, *who hear*, listen when they are told what God wants of them, and appear well-disposed when they speak of the interior, but who do not wish *to put this in practice*. Instead of working underground, they stop at the surface. Their house is all exterior, but what happens? At the first temptation, when they are persecuted, this *edifice*, which appear beautiful and grand, *overturns* and is destroyed, and its *ruin was great*, that which had appeared elevated.

> Soon afterward he went to a town called Nain, and his disciples and a large crowd went with him. 12 As he approached the gate of the town, a man who had died was being carried out. He was his mother's only son, and she was a widow; and with her was a large crowd from the town. 13 When the Lord saw her, he had compassion for her and said to her, "Do not weep." 14 Then he came forward and touched the bier, and the bearers stood still. And he said, "Young man, I say to you, rise!" 15 The dead man sat up and began to speak, and Jesus gave him to his mother. (Luke 7:11–15)

Death is the figure for sinners newly dead through their sins. Jesus Christ paid dearly through his resurrection for sinners.

This death represents also in the mystical sense, the soul who is dead to its own actions and therefore is aware and sensitive. This is an *only son*. This soul is very dear yet desolate until she attracts the compassion of Jesus Christ who restores her and makes her pure.

Jesus Christ resurrects us from three different types of spiritual deaths. God alone chooses which deaths a soul may pass through. Some God is content with just one. In others, God has them pass them through the first and the second. Very few are tested in the third death. The death is quickly followed by a resurrection.

The first spiritual death in the soul is almost no death. It is a change and the privation of a life that appears sweet and superficial. It is like the daughter of the prince of the Synagogue in Matthew 9:18 with the deprivation of graces, gifts and extraordinary lights, that which truly marked the daughter of a prince. All this belongs to the prince but after she has deprived of these for a while, she receives a considerable advantage. As she passes through this death, which is usually accompanied by circumstances which do not support her, she believes that she has passed through all death but this is far from the truth.

The second death is more bitter and intimate. The soul dies to her own operations that are intimate and essential. This is an only son, which we love tenderly and appears absolutely necessary. She becomes a desolate widow, who has already lost, or seems to have lost, her spouse, the one who had worked and produced in her very dear operations. This soul perceives nothing good within her. All is lost to her. The death of her Spouse puts her in a state of helplessness and in despair of ever having any other. Jesus sees the weakness of this creature, and her incredible pain, and has compassion, resurrects the only son with new advantages. This death is more profound than the first. She is already in the circumstances of a true death. This is not a sleep. The dead is laying in a coffin but is not corrupted and buried, like the last. This is the death of things that appear essential and necessary. The first death does not the same character, but is a death of powers that are not essential, like lights, tastes, knowledge, favors, the gifts of all that is seen in God.

The third death the soul passes through is infinitely stranger than the others. This sound and radical death is the death of all self-justification and propriety. This is accompanied by very rough and different circumstances. It suffices to say, that this death's circumstances are different than the others, like the difference between sleep and death. The son of this widow will be resurrected. God restores to the soul the facility of operating the good that she had lost. God restores this soul in a way very advantageous and exempts her of a thousand faults that she had the first time.

> Fear seized all of them; and they glorified God, saying, "A great prophet has risen among us!" and "God has looked favorably on his people!" 17 This word about him spread throughout Judea and all the surrounding country. (Luke 7:16–17)

The souls that pass through these first deaths let themselves become workers of grace, and they attract the astonishment and admiration of people. God only lets them use these gifts for others, and *the report* of miracles that God does in them and for them, *spreads everywhere*. These people go through crosses and infamies, like the last death, and their apostolic life will end gloriously because their life will end like the life of Jesus Christ. After they shouted in his favor, *Blessed is he who comes in the name of the Lord !* they cry, *Take him and crucify him!*

> (And all the people who heard this, including the tax collectors, acknowledged the justice of God, because they had been baptized with John's baptism. 30 But by refusing to be baptized by him, the Pharisees and the lawyers rejected God's purpose for themselves.) (Luke 7:29–30)

It is necessary in this passage to note two great circumstances. First, those who have been *baptized by John* go to Jesus Christ. We know it is necessary to pass through the tears of repentance before we are introduced to the interior. No one can enter without this. The other circumstance is the opposition of the *doctors* and people of highly regulated lives who do not wish to yield to God. They have even more trouble than the biggest of sinners. They deride and mock others who give themselves to God. They think themselves above all others, as scripture says, as they *oppose God's plan* to sanctify them. They invent excuses so they can abuse others and are offended by everything and accuse it of error. Heatedly they support the letter of the law instead of the spirit of the law. Yet the sinners and simple ones submit very willingly to God. They suffer the first purgation, which is that of baptism. They are introduced to Jesus Christ. The doctors and others, though, are filled with self-love and independent life. They remain attached to themselves, to their own light and fight against the light of truth.

> "For John the Baptist has come eating no bread and drinking no wine, and you say, 'He has a demon'; 34 the Son of Man has come eating and drinking, and you say, 'Look, a glutton and a drunkard, a friend of tax collectors and sinners!'" (Luke 7:33–34)

Jesus Christ here contrasts the penitent and purgative life with his common life. Jesus Christ wanted to live a life that everyone could practice. He is the exemplar and model for us all. We must follow the example of his life and not base it on the saints. Most see the beautiful virtues in the lives of the Saints and would like to do as they do. They sometimes imitate one and then the other, and because of this they never have a unified conduct. There are an infinite ways to imitate Jesus Christ, each Saint has her own particular way to imitate him. But it is not the saints in particular that we must imitate in action. For which saint have we been told to follow as the model? Which saint was shown us on the mountain? If we are told to imitate the saint, it is to look at their faithfulness to move with the grace of God, to fulfill their vocation, and to be led on the path that God wants for them. But we should not work to follow each action of the saints because our vocation is different. Jesus Christ allowed the saints to do things that cannot be imitated, to teach us that we should not be imitating the saints. Instead, we must faithfully follow the movements of the Spirit of God. Jesus Christ himself led a life we cannot imitate. We must allow him to mold us and to express his character within us according to our vocation and the designs of God. This life led by Jesus Christ is easy, common, holy, and admirable, and yet is condemned by sinners and those who appear as just. The false leaders also condemn the way of John that was extraordinary and miraculous. People even judged the exterior of John the Baptist, so austere, reformed, and extraordinary. They also judged the external life of Jesus Christ who led a common and gracious life, but they reproached him saying he was friends with *tax collectors and sinners*. Oh, the goodness of God who graciously suffered these sinners and even called them his friends!

If the sinner is disposed to convert, and he wants to listen well to Jesus Christ, he becomes his friend and because he does not oppose Jesus Christ, he receives his Spirit. Oh, how blind humans are in their judgment! Who would be able to satisfy these superb Pharisees and the doctors who were entangled in their own knowledge, since Jesus Christ the man-God could not satisfy them?[2]

---

2. Jeanne Guyon writes the following in a footnote: Gregory, Bede, Bernard, and

"Nevertheless, wisdom is vindicated by all her children." (Luke 7:35)

It is only the children of wisdom who are justified by wisdom. Their simplicity, candor, and their innocence are the mark of the wisdom of God, not of science. The learned fight against it, and the children defend it and support it. O childlike simplicity! You are more glorious to God than all the false wisdom of all the sages of the world. This is why Jesus Christ says, *I thank you, Father, Lord of heaven and earth, because you have hidden these things from the wise and the intelligent and have revealed them to infants* (Matthew 11:25). Yes, it is the small infants who know and test the impenetrable roads of Wisdom.

> One of the Pharisees asked Jesus to eat with him, and he went into the Pharisee's house and took his place at the table. 37 And a woman in the city, who was a sinner, having learned that he was eating in the Pharisee's house, brought an alabaster jar of ointment. (Luke 7:36–37)

How is it that this woman Magdalene has an alabaster jar of ointment and she is a sinner? The alabaster vase means the whiteness of her soul, her soul was full of scented balm, that is to say, her soul was full of the unction of grace. Oh! It is because this woman was no longer a sinner. She no longer deserved this name. She was a sinner before Jesus Christ looked at her with favor and gave her grace. His love penetrated her. After he regards us favorably, our dirty earthen vessel, as hers was, becomes an alabaster vase, ready to hold the most excellent perfume of grace. But, generous lover, your apprenticeship are the blows of the master. What is the transport and the generosity of your love! Your transport carries us out of all the considerations of reason and pride, to go into public places where you are not invited, to give the signs of your love. The generosity of this same love brings your soul back to Christ with all the graces that he has given it, in order to sacrifice to him. You give him back what he has given you. Learning not to be proprietary, you give him back what he has given you. O loving woman, wonderful master of the interior! You were first a master of abandon: neither reflection nor reason was the most

---

many other ancient fathers and philosophers hold the opinion that is the most common, which is that Magdalene and Mary, the sister of Martha and Lazarus are one and the same. We follow this assumption. The essential thing about the dispositions of the soul is that God agrees and rewards infinitely when they are animated by pure love and the strong effects are seen. Anything else is a critique of personalities.

valuable part of you, but instead pure love was. Your abandonment was very blind, since you followed the instincts of your heart. You come in extravagance, because what could be said to you, except that you were impassioned and crazy? You had a bad reputation. Were you not afraid of doing wrong to Jesus and diminishing his own reputation? No, no, my Magdalene says, I am not capable of these thoughts. I love. And I am abandoned to following the movements of my love. I have a heart that is only for loving. I loved a hundred different things that shared my infinitely vast heart without being able to satisfy or fill my heart. But now all these one hundred loves are found together in one love. My heart is entirely collected in one love. I feel another torment about my pain and my pleasure, that is, my heart so large and spacious that it can be filled with many different loves that I occupy it with, is too small for only one love, which fills her with so much abundance, that she has grief that in her smallness she cannot contain so immense a love, that it fills her with pain and sorrow that she was always empty, because she had filled it with other loves, and they were not sufficient to fill even a small part of her heart. O hearts that are so great and that you share in many different places! Are you like Magdalene? Collect yourself in your love for Jesus, who will fill you with superabundance. O doctors, who says that it takes years before abandoning oneself to love. Magdalene did not wait to love absolutely. She has chosen the better part; she chooses love first. Why leave a good that we can have now? Magdalene's purity of love prompted her, so that she moved instantly, leaving her sins behind, and she loved. Jesus Christ looked at her. And like a sunflower, she faithfully followed the movement of the Sun, and she turned toward his look. O look so penetrating and powerful! His look melts the hardest ice. Oh, if we turn toward his divine look! In an instant we can be changed from demons to angels. If Magdalene had not followed her sister's advice to go and talk to Jesus, she would not be the model of interior souls.

Magdalene had to do only two things to enter into this sublime state. First, she approached Jesus Christ, exposing herself to his divine look that darted like a ray and merged with her heart. Secondly, she listened. She exposed herself and listened. Here is the preparation that Magdalene made for this state so sublime. Because she had listened, she could say with the bride, *I arose to open to my Beloved* (Song of Songs 5:6). She melted and liquefied and because of this, her fire burned ardently and it turned Magdalene into a strong operation of love. This fortunate lover showed vehemence and ardor. If she had not been supported by an extraordinary grace, her love would have died in an instant, but the same fire that burned within her gives her a new birth. Magdalene burned brightly and was consumed. She was reduced to a cinder but in the same instant, these cinders turned into another Magdalene. The same movement that caused her death then gave her a new life. She was a Phoenix that is burned and consumed in an instant by the fire of the divine Sun. This same moment of her consummation of love was also the new life of love.

Magdalene in her conversion went through a first death followed by the first life. Jesus Christ on Calvary experienced his last death and last life. O two deaths all entirely different! Oh the sweetness, fire, and presence of the love in the first death! Oh death! Oh life! Who can comprehend you? The fire of love gives the first death and the first life. The cold gives the second death and the second life. But the cold changes into fire and makes a wonderful unity between lover and love. Magdalene died. Jesus Christ died. There was then a wonderful metamorphosis, leading to a complete mélange, that Magdalene was dead in Jesus Christ and Jesus Christ passed into Magdalene. It was no longer Magdalene; it was Jesus. Where are you, my Beloved? And I will look for you. You looked well because you no longer looked within the tomb, when you looked. You became the sepulchre where he lived, when you looked for your Beloved. You became a sepulcher but a sepulcher glorious and triumphant. This is why he said, *Do not touch me*. In other words, do not stop and caress my humanity. I am in you and you are in me. And as I have not yet ascended to my Father, I have the time to teach you the new secret of our new love. Oh, that we may have the freedom of Magdalene with Jesus, and the bonding they have between them! O Lover! You tell us more about this by your conduct, then all the possible knowledge expressed in words.

> She stood behind him at his feet, weeping, and began to bathe his feet with her tears and to dry them with her hair. Then she continued kissing his feet and anointing them with the ointment. (Luke 7:38)

She was *standing behind* Jesus Christ; her humility would not permit her to do otherwise. But, although her humility was strong, this did not prevent her from approaching Jesus, to kiss him and touch him, to wash his feet and to wipe them with her hair. Oh, this does not express the real pain that comes from love! Love banishes all fear, but it does not banish all pain. The love of Magdalene was like a furnace, which burning in her heart purified her eyes. She weeps with love and pain. The power of love draws tears of joy that tell of the happiness she possesses. She dies of grief at having loved so late such a friendly beauty. She says nothing. She keeps a profound silence because she knows only love. She has nothing to speak. Oh, when the heart loves fully, language cannot express this! She has the true marks of love! The heart gives proof of love in an infinite number of ways. She has a heart that loves with strength, and a sorrow but a strong love and a violent grief forbids all speech. *She kissed the feet of her Master* and spread her heart like a perfume in the presence of her God. All love at the beginning is for the sacred humanity of Jesus Christ. They think only of loving, listening, and imitating him. Oh, the soul that listens is well-instructed by Jesus Christ in all that she must do. She only has to hold on to be united with him.

> Now when the Pharisee who had invited him saw it, he said to himself, "If this man were a prophet, he would have known who and what kind of woman this is who is touching him—that she is a sinner." (Luke 7:39)

It is not only today that the actions of simple and interior souls are condemned, but also at the time of Jesus Christ. We often take saints for sinners, and sinners for saints. A moment makes a big change in souls. They were astonished that Jesus Christ suffered the approach of Mary Magdalene, and she was friendlier to Jesus Christ than many others who appeared to be righteous. They rejected the sinners who were with Jesus Christ and were scandalized that he allowed them to approach. Oh! If they would be willing to convert to Jesus Christ with all their heart, they would cease to be sinners.

> Jesus spoke up and said to him, "Simon, I have something to say to you." "Teacher," he replied, "speak." 41 "A certain creditor had two debtors; one owed five hundred denarii, and the other fifty. 42 When they could not pay, he canceled the debts for both of them. Now which of them will love him more?" 43 Simon answered, "I suppose the one for whom he canceled the greater debt." And Jesus said to him, "You have judged rightly." (Luke 7:40–43)

We are all debtors to God throughout infinity. Every day we contract a new debt, yet there are those who owe him infinitely more than others. Some have communal debts common to all people, but others have particular debts for crimes, the great sinners, the sinning Magdalenes of the city. O God! You give more to these souls that have larger debts because where sin abounds grace abounds more. Where God has forgiven sins is where love abounds more. O God! You save criminal hearts by sending an ardent and brilliant fire that consumes both the sin and the sinner in a moment. O the love of a sinning soul after conversion, you are strong! You reduce the soul to a state! She dies of triple love and a triple pain. She has the pain of previously having hated him without knowledge. She experiences the pain of having passed time without loving him, and not to have loved him as much as you want. These triple pains cause a triple love, which grows in vehemence. Pain augments the love, and love seems to irritate the pain. But this is not a troubling pain or a worried love. It is a tranquil and peaceful pain; a painful love and a loving pain. The more profound the wound she has, the more the pain, plus the more sweetness. The soul is only strong with both pain and love. It is both sweetness and pain. There is not one without the other. O God! She says, I was and I still am a criminal. If I told you all my disorders in detail, you would not believe them. However, every time I dive into the mud of my sins, I cannot but discover that my heart can only love you, and that it finds you only kind. If your hearts do not love him, we will not love anything. She discovers love through her disorders, the purest and strongest love.

Magdalene is consumed by his love, so that she does not think about what is said against her or for her. Far from thinking of defending herself, she lets them say what they will. One thought only occupies her and that is love of God. She cannot envision anything except this love. She does not even think about asking for forgiveness. Nor does she ask if she will be forgiven. She forgets first of all everything that concerns her. She has no interest of her own, because she does not own her heart or soul. Her heart is abandoned, and is not her heart. Magdalene's heart is abandoned and is no longer only her heart. Her heart is in Jesus. He does not need to search for the heart of Magdalene in Magdalene. Jesus searches for her heart in him. So she finds in him an advocate, a defender, a doctor, and a lover. Jesus does all these services for Magdalene, and he does this for all souls who forget themselves for him. Jesus defends all who do not defend themselves. Jesus shows care to all who surrender themselves to him. Jesus heals all those who wounded by divine love, and who do not think about other wounds. He is the lover of those who love him. These souls who love God and forget themselves can no longer be concerned about their perfection or salvation. It is appropriate that passionate love transports some with such force that it is impossible for them to think about anything but this love. They can only think of ways to please their lover. Magdalene is so transported that she comes in a strange disorder. She behaves with extravagance. She takes her hair and, with tears coming out of her eyes, wipes the feet of Jesus Christ. Impatient love cannot wait for release. If we do not allow this impetuous love, it becomes even more fiery. A mediocre love is hidden easily, but a passionate love can never be hidden.

> Then turning toward the woman, he said to Simon, "Do you see this woman? I entered your house; you gave me no water for my feet, but she has bathed my feet with her tears and dried them with her hair." (Luke 7:44)

Jesus *turns toward Magdalene*, because Magdalene had approached Jesus. O happy turn! This was a turning for union, the agreement of love. Jesus was blessing Magdalene with love and Magdalene was also blessing Jesus. She *bathed his feet with her tears and dried them with her hair*. She kept Jesus in her continual sight without looking at herself. Wiping the feet of Jesus Christ, she thought only of him, and he fully occupied her thoughts with delight. O Lover, you were pleased to receive the tears of Magdalene! You speak well the language of the heart while she wiped your feet, and she gives you signs of her love! Your heart was given to Magdalene to the measure that she gave you her heart. To some it might appear that Magdalene is not filled with humility. She does not stop to see if Jesus agrees to her approach. She thinks only of expressing her love and ardor with her tears. Yet, instead of diminishing her love, her tears give more ardor to her fire, and her fire augments her tears. This is wonderful because this distills her fire. The water increases the fire and the fire augments the water. The fire does not put out the water, but to the contrary, it becomes more ardent. The fire does not dry up the tears. They become more abundant! O wonderful conflagration! The tears and heart of Magdalene made sacred fire hidden in the well of her heart which was previously muddy. It is not exposed to the Sun that ignites and consumes it. It is fire, and it is mud. It seems like mud at Magdalene's home and it appears criminal. But as soon as the water touches the feet of Jesus Christ, it becomes fire of the most pure love. O sinners! Sinners who are only mud! Come, approach the divine Sun, and you will become fire that consumes all things. Jesus Christ looks at Magdalene. He turns toward her to speak, as if to say, "I give myself to you, O fortunate lover! Because you have given yourself to me." Jesus is content to place the debts of Magdalene in the secrecy of his heart, before making known to the whole world that he has forgiven these sins. He wants to make others know what he has done for Magdalene. O generous love of Jesus toward Magdalene! And toward all the souls abandoned to him! It seems that he forgets that we are indebted to him who is infinite, for we have done only a few small things for him and that he holds within himself.

Jesus after having declared the remission of Magdalene's debts declares himself the debtor of Magdalene. O divine Jesus! Tell us, I implore you, what you owe to Magdalene. I owe her my heart, in return for mine, because whoever gives me her heart, I commit myself to give mine to her. That is what I owe to Magdalene and this is the debt I will pay her. Our hearts are changed. I take her heart and give her mine. O Love! You do this admirable exchange and do it for all who love you. That is why in dying you open the place of your heart, to make known to all people that it is up to them to do this wonderful exchange. O human beings! Put your heart in this place and draw from that same place the heart of Jesus. This is the advantage given to all human beings by Jesus Christ that as they give him their heart and all their love, having no heart, no love, they live and love only through Jesus. Because the heart is the source of life and love, the one who has the heart of Jesus needs no other love or life except the life and love of Jesus Christ. He also has another advantage, which is, our heart is changed into his heart. We receive the heart of Jesus. He converts all of our hearts into his, like the Philosopher's Stone converts the basest metals into gold.

> "You gave me no kiss, but from the time I came in she has not stopped kissing my feet. 46 You did not anoint my head with oil, but she has anointed my feet with ointment. 47 Therefore, I tell you, her sins, which were many, have been forgiven; hence she has shown great love. But the one to whom little is forgiven, loves little." (Luke 7:45–47)

Jesus continues to enumerate everything Magdalene did in her favor. O Love! You are eloquent in favor of Magdalene. You are her panegyrist and not her judge. You do not speak of her sins and you hardly remember her offenses. If you speak of them, it is to make her see that her sins yield to his love burned and consumed her sins. Magdalene was from that moment in the union of powers, represented by her kissing his feet. She would have gladly told him, *Let him kiss me with the kisses of his mouth* (Song of Solomon 1:2) but she waited on him. She was content to *kiss his feet*, remaining in the union of powers until she was attracted and raised to this union, which will be granted after this first connection. Then Magdalene runs with all her strength to this spiritual fragrance and spreads her perfume on his feet. As if to she said to Jesus, "All the fragrances and attractions are united in you. That is why I am consecrated to you and give you everything at your feet, to show that I give all to you and I do not want grace or fragrance of my own. My heart lives and empties into your heart. If I had any fragrance of my own, I would stop there and not run to your fragrance. I always want to run after you until you hide me with you in your Father's bosom."

Jesus then assures that he *forgives many sins, because she loves much.* Love covers a multitude of sins. Not only does love cover sins, but it consumes and annihilates sins. Ah! If we only love a little, in a moment all the sins will be consumed! If we place the greatness of our sins next to the greatness of our love, we measure the greatness of love over the number of sins. Then the soul experiences the mercy that God has given her and feels warmed by the mercy. It is strange to see that it seems the more she has offended God, the more God does good things for her. God's benefits increase the soul's desire to never offend such a kind God.

> Then he said to her, "Your sins are forgiven." 49 But those who were at the table with him began to say among themselves, "Who is this who even forgives sins?" 50 And he said to the woman, "Your faith has saved you; go in peace." (Luke 7:48–50)

Jesus Christ is not only content to tell others that Magdalene's sins are consumed in his love. He also assures her directly, *Your sins are forgiven*. He wants her to hear this. Other people condemn Jesus Christ because vain and arrogant people condemn all that is of God. They overtly blame his conduct, but they do not dare to attack God directly, so they attack him indirectly, attacking his Spirit and his particular conduct with souls.

Following this Jesus assures Magdalene, *Your faith has saved you.* Ah! If we knew the advantages of faith, and how good it is to trust God! We would only hold firmly and with strength to this single practice and by that we have all the rest. The measure of our faith is the measure of our love. When we love God very much, we trust him a lot. Nothing signifies love as much as trust. This is why Jesus Christ declares in all places the benefits of our faith. After he gives peace to Magdalene, he says, *Go in peace.* The words of Jesus Christ are always efficacious and when he says to a soul, *Go in peace*, she enters into an inconceivable and unalterable peace, immense and immutable peace. Jesus Christ gains the soul and offers himself substantially so that this soul becomes all peace and tranquility. She tastes and perceives only peace.

> Soon afterwards he went on through cities and villages, proclaiming and bringing the good news of the kingdom of God. The twelve were with him. (Luke 8:1)

Jesus went everywhere preaching the kingdom of God because this was the main goal of his incarnation. He was to establish the kingdom of God in souls, telling everyone that the reign of the God is within. God must be allowed to be sovereign. All of the sermons of Jesus Christ make known the truth of God and his sovereignty. He came to establish the truth of God because it was necessary that we know the true God and that we are to yield to his kingdom, to let him reign within them. All of spirituality has this as its goal: to know the fullness of God and the nothingness of the creature, and that the creature submits to the kingdom of God. Any spirituality not doing this is not true.

We need to know that God is everything and the creature nothing, and that God remains sovereign over the creature. The creature so filled with weakness cannot do any good, and retains nothing without grace. The soul can, however, commit evil and prevent God from sowing within herself the good God wants to do. The creature stops God, like a small fish stops a very large ship. The human does not have the power in himself to prevent God, because God is able to do anything in the human that he pleases. But God has created the human in freedom and God respects the freedom he has placed in the human. But the human is so unhappy that he wastes and abuses his freedom. His misuse of freedom makes him criminal and the human chooses to be a slave. Instead of the bad use we make of our freedom, we should instead give our freedom to God and he uses this as sovereign and we have assurance. This is the safety and confidence of those who abandon themselves to God, that we no longer use our freedom for evil, but entirely gives herself to God. God takes the soul and she finds within herself the happy necessities to do the will of God, to which she submits with pleasure. Isn't it better for us to be captive under the will of God?

> As well as some women who had been cured of evil spirits and infirmities: Mary, called Magdalene, from whom seven demons had gone out, and Joanna, the wife of Herod's steward Chuza,

and Susanna, and many others, who provided for them out of their resources (Luke 8:2–3).

Scriptures tell us that we have seen the graces that our Lord had made in Magdalene, to have delivered her from her misery. The seven demons that had possessed her are the seven mortal sins that accompany all who are in vain glory. When a woman is beautiful and she pleases others by her beauty, she falls easily into all sorts of sins. The desire to please others and to give love brings sin within her. This sin brings along with it other sins. Jesus Christ was not ashamed of these women who followed him wherever he went and these woman had the advantage of providing for his needs.

> He said, "To you it has been given to know the secrets of the kingdom of God." (Luke 8:10)

It is a great advantage to know the mystery of the kingdom of God because once we have known this, we know through faith that God reigns absolutely. Oh, the great mystery! Happy are those who are enlightened with this knowledge and receive this generous gift! *It has been given* to some to know this mystery only for themselves, but others receive the mystery and the gift to teach it to others. Those who teach the kingdom of God have the greater advantage because God gives them both knowledge and faith.

> The man from whom the demons had gone begged that he might be with him; but Jesus sent him away, saying, 39 "Return to your home, and declare how much God has done for you." So he went away, proclaiming throughout the city how much God had done for him. (Luke 8:38–39)

Jesus Chris calls some to follow him and refuses others. He forbids some to speak of the miracles he has done for them and tells others to speak openly. Oh, this is wonderful! When God tells us to let this remain unknown, we must be obedient. When we are told to speak about the glories of God, we must speak out for God requires this. We speak for ourselves out of self-love to give ourselves glory. When we give God the glory, we speak out of justice to help others know and love God. This witness is not done out of propriety. The virtue of humility does not consist in silencing the graces of God, but in all things giving God the glory. A sinner will confess the mercy that God has had for him, to invite other sinners to give themselves to God, and to go look for others. An interior soul will tell the graces the God has given him in the interior way to encourage others to follow. Silence is necessary when it is only about ourselves, but silence is offensive to God and prejudicial to our neighbors when it hides the glory of God and hopes for salvation from others.

> Now when Jesus returned, the crowd welcomed him, for they were all waiting for him. (Luke 8:40)

God takes pleasure in hiding so that we desire him more. If he were not absent, we would not feel the happiness of his presence. But if he is absent, we must wait. Following the wisdom of the sage of Proverbs, who urges us to bear this state of absence from the God and wait with patience, our life grows and is renewed. There are some souls who retreat when Jesus Christ is absent: this saps their strength. It is necessary to wait his return. He never fails to come back to his people and he fills the soul with joy at his happy return. What pleasure do we receive? We forget all the sorrows of his absence and all the tears that we have shed. We make loving reproaches about how he has abandoned our heart during this time, but at the same time we discover that he returns to us full of new charms. With his return, God does not bring pain but delicious pleasure. O those who have tested his absences and his returns who can testify to this! All the faith that we have in his absence appears sorrowful, but when he comes back, his presence always brings new sweetness, and fills the soul with abundance. We may say like the Spouse, *Who is that coming up from the wilderness, leaning upon her beloved?* (Song of Solomon 8:5). The text reads *with an affluence of delicacies*. That is to say, the beloved pours upon us water filled with pleasures and delicacies, a river of pleasures which encourages growth and flowing fruit with abundance. O souls who suffer the absences of fugitive love, wait and never stop waiting! O you will find this good! You will find this amazing which is why the tested soul knows that the waiting will be a thousand times worth the advantages of the absence of the Bridegroom and he will bring new good with him at his return. Yet she could not help crying during his absence and thinks he will never return. When he returns, she feels like he will never leave.

> On their return the apostles told Jesus all they had done. He took them with him and withdrew privately to a city called Bethsaida. When the crowds found out about it, they followed him; and he welcomed them, and spoke to them about the kingdom of God, and healed those who needed to be cured. (Luke 9:10–11)

Jesus Christ retreats to a deserted place to have the pleasures of the spiritual search, but when he sees the faithful people following him when he is absent and show no signs of leaving him, he was ravished and charmed. He received them with all his heart. It seems, O amiable Savior, that you have pleasure is seeing your people coming after you to find you! You receive them in a way that says you have pleasure in the sight. The little time you have had for retreat has caused you fatigue. When a loving person has been without the sight of his beloved even for a short time, he is happy to see the beloved. O wonderful communion of love! What does Jesus speak about to his people who are his beloved? *The kingdom of God.* He teaches them to let God reign within them. He teaches this both to those who already have the kingdom within them and to those who still need conversion and to be *healed*.

> Jesus said, "The Son of Man must undergo great suffering, and be rejected by the elders, chief priests, and scribes, and be killed, and on the third day be raised." Then he said to them all, "If any want to become my followers, let them deny themselves and take up their cross daily and follow me." (Luke 9:22–23)

Jesus Christ begins to prepare his apostles and all souls by telling them the story of his *suffering*. He wants to suffer first before we must suffer. He presents the cross to us before we engage with it. He does not say, "Carry your cross and I will go by a different way. I will leave you alone with this." Instead, he goes through the suffering first. He says to us that he must suffer and that we cannot be saved without his suffering. He must pass through what we will pass through. Who is the soldier who will follow a captain who leaves him with all the dangers? But if we have participated in his cross and death, we have the consolation that we will participate in his *resurrection*. It is good that the Gospel explains to us the circumstances that will cause us difficulty. He says this to all the world without exception: this is not a point of counsel to only a few of us. My brothers and sisters, whoever you are, young or old, rich or poor, Jesus Christ speaks to all of us: *"If any want to become my followers, let them deny themselves."* It is necessary that we leave ourselves. By approaching God, we leave ourselves. The more we move away from ourselves, the closer we approach God.

We must *take up our cross*, our own cross that providence chooses for us, and that we must carry *all our days*. All the Gospels report this and Luke says this in two places. But what happens to the soul who carries his cross with strength? She will *follow* Jesus Christ. It is impossible to follow him in any other way.

> "For those who want to save their life will lose it, and those who lose their life for my sake will save it." (Luke 9:24)

Jesus Christ repeats again the benefits in this scripture. All of the gospels report the necessity of this crucial message. Jesus repeats this because of its necessity. The one who wants to be saved by his own care will be lost, but the one who abandons herself to God without reservation, losing herself admirably, will be saved. O God! The more salvation is desperately needed by ourselves, the grander it is in you! If we want to save our soul, we should lose ourselves in God with a total abandon and then we are unmistakably saved.

> "What does it profit them if they gain the whole world, but lose or forfeit themselves?" (Luke 9:25)

We hear two things here. First, if we lose our soul in God, we will save it with the loss of all the rest. If we give our soul to God, we must not give it to any other created thing. Secondly, in ministering to others, we must not lose ourselves in vain complacency. Paul feared this and writes in 1 Corinthians 9:27, "But I punish my body and enslave it, so that after proclaiming to others I myself should not be disqualified."

> Then from the cloud came a voice that said, "This is my Son, my Chosen; listen to him!" (Luke 9:35)

We need to listen to Jesus Christ as Word. Even with all the testimonies we have in the Old Testament and in the words that Jesus Christ says, God wants to teach us from heaven. Listen to this divine word because it is the source of life.

Jesus did not have to take Peter and James and John to this transfiguration. They had the words of Moses and they have his words, and yet he wants to present them to the Father. When Jesus Christ approaches our soul, we become pure and clean and all brand new. We become his child. Yet the glory of heaven overwhelms us and we fall on our faces. With a touch of his hand we stand again. Let me stand! Let me approach you only, Lord Christ and your Father! Let me have your Word and live in your Word and dance in your Word and be ravished by your Word. I want your Word only. Your Word only is life. What is the Father inside? Jesus Christ is the only way to the Father. We find there depths of meaning and wonder; splendors of truth; rational being; the way to the Source. We must return to the Source of All Life and that is what this scripture is about. We find the Tree of Life. Let me be one, Father, with you in your glory. Let me see you in your transfiguration. Jesus Christ approaches us like a child and says, "Come and meet my Father!"

> When the days drew near for him to be taken up, he set his face to go to Jerusalem. (Luke 9:51)

O Jesus! You give strength and assurance to souls who suffer; would you have no lack of assurance? Jesus Christ *set his face to go to Jerusalem*, which marked the contentment of his soul and the desire that he had to suffer for humanity. O God! You only come to the world because you are destined to die.

> And he sent messengers ahead of him. On their way they entered a village of the Samaritans to make ready for him; 53 but they did not receive him, because his face was set toward Jerusalem. 54 When his disciples James and John saw it, they said, "Lord, do you want us to command fire to come down from heaven and consume them?" 55 But he turned and rebuked them. (Luke 9:52–55)

Indiscreet zeal does not please God: true charity is always patient. She suffers everything, believes everything, and hopes everything. We often believe that our passion glorifies God. True zeal is sweet and patient. Who refuses the Spirit of Jesus Christ in one time, receives him in another. Patience and a long wait bring sinners back.

> "For the Son of Man has not come to destroy the lives of human beings but to save them." Then they went on to another village. (Luke 9:56)

To take souls away from Jesus Christ is to take them away from salvation. Yet what most people fear actually becomes the height of happiness. It takes many extraordinary things to go to Jesus Christ. To see the way most people act, it seems that God, who has come with so much goodness only *to save* people, has instead come to lose them. Some say that it is dangerous to abandon yourself to God; they think that to abandon one's self is only for strong and advanced souls. Yet it is the weak and sinful souls who must abandon themselves to God. These are the ones who have so often tested their weakness and powerlessness. They no longer expect anything from themselves but sin. This is why they allow themselves to be led to God, and give God their liberty, so they no longer abuse their liberty, as they once did.

> As they were going along the road, someone said to him, "I will follow you wherever you go." 58 And Jesus said to him, "Foxes have holes, and birds of the air have nests; but the Son of Man has nowhere to lay his head." (Luke 9:57–58)

The extreme poverty of Jesus Christ calls all Christians to enter into and bear the dispositions of poverty. Yet where do we find a person without support and without retreat? Or without consolation, friends, refuge, support both interior and exterior? Or where do we find one who wants to lose everything for God and will remain in this loss? The state most difficult to bear is the deprivation of all interior and exterior support. Where will we find one who will pass through this state long? Some will enter into the first deprivation, where he finds there is no support and there are always new losses, which we did not know. We discover the new losses only because we experience the loss. There is always some hiding place but those willing to experience the total loss and deprivation is rare.

> Another said, "I will follow you, sir, but first let me go and say goodbye to my people at home." Jesus said to him, "Once the hand is laid on the plough, no one who looks back is fit for the kingdom of God." (Luke 9:61–62)

This passage tells us that the only necessity is to reflect on faith. Oh, a person who goes without looking at himself, will live, and will take surprising steps! A traveller does not stop for little because it would delay him. If he stops constantly, he will never advance. But if he does not look at himself, even through reflection, he will never stop. Therefore, reflecting on ourselves is an impediment to perfection: We do not regard what we are passing through, nor what happens, but we only look at the end. We must always walk without stopping. If we do not do this, we are not *fit for the kingdom of God*. When we have undertaken the work of our perfection, we must follow him without stopping at anything. Scripture supports this when Paul says, *I am racing toward the finishing point to win the prize of God's heavenly call in Christ Jesus* (Philippians 3:14). When we took the way back to God, all we need to do is that which advances us toward God.

"Whoever listens to you listens to me, and whoever rejects you rejects me, and whoever rejects me rejects the one who sent me." (Luke 10:16)

Nothing displeases God more than contempt for his word. Some mock God's word and try to convince others to do the same. They taunt and rail against Jesus Christ. He says in another place what these people do to him will be done to one of Christ's little ones. Often they ridicule devotion and they cry out against those who trust and establish devotion. These people try to stop the fruit of devotion. What will these people do? They attack Jesus Christ himself, yet they think they only attack particular persons. They can understand this if they listen to these words and understand the truth of them: *Whoever rejects you rejects me*. It is Jesus Christ himself whom they reject, and he holds them accountable for how they treat his servants.

> The seventy returned with joy, saying, "Lord, in your name even the demons submit to us!" He said to them, "I watched Satan fall from heaven like a flash of lightning. See, I have given you authority to tread on snakes and scorpions, and over all the power of the enemy; and nothing will hurt you. Nevertheless, do not rejoice at this, that the spirits submit to you, but rejoice that your names are written in heaven." (Luke 10:17–18)

It is certain that one only enters into the care of souls and into the apostolic state by the order of God. It seems that *demons submit* to these people and that they have extraordinary power over them. Jesus Christ assures them that he *saw Satan fall like a flash of lightning*. The Word of God in these souls has an amazing effect. It makes Satan fall from the soul who wants to listen to the Word of God, with as much speed as a lightning flash coming out of the sky.

> "I have given you authority to trample on snakes and scorpions and to overcome all the power of the enemy; nothing will harm you. 20 However, do not rejoice that the spirits submit to you, but rejoice that your names are written in heaven." (Luke 10:19–20)

We have been given a very considerable advantage *to trample our enemy underfoot,* and to breakdown his strength, which is no other than sin, because our elevation is the surest mark of our vocation to the apostolic state. The advantage of the soul within God (after being free from subjection to the spirits) makes her sovereign over evil spirits and sinners.

But this should not be that which makes us *rejoice*, but that our *name is written in heaven*. Our names are written in heaven when we carry the states of Jesus Christ and the character of the divine Son because we are formed and molded on the excellent original. We find ourselves with him and our names are written in him. He is the great book written inside and outside of us, which contains all that is expressed. His character marks and seals us among the number of the predestined.

> At that same hour Jesus rejoiced in the Holy Spirit and said, "I thank you, Father, Lord of heaven and earth, because you have hidden these things from the wise and the intelligent and have revealed them to infants; yes, Father, for such was your gracious will." (Luke 10:21)

This is a wonderful situation in this passage. Jesus *rejoiced* and was filled with *joy* before he declares these admirable words that he tells us to hear. These words are infinitely glorious because Jesus Christ speaks to the Eternal Father. No one anticipates the power and righteousness of Jesus Christ. This is why he was transported in joy by the strength of the Holy Spirit. But why, O my divine Savior, did you have such a powerful transport of joy? Oh! It says in the scripture that he was filled with joy. "My transport and my ravishment," responds my adorable Master of simple souls. This comes from your Father that he has *hidden these things from the wise and the intelligent* who depend so heavily on their own wisdom, prudence, and industry. Instead, God the Father *reveals them to infants* who depend only on him. These infants know they are weak. They do not want to make one step without God. They regard their own self-inspired wisdom as folly and their prudence as bewilderment as well as an obstacle to the way of God's providence. *Yes, Father, I give you thanks* that you have hidden these things from the wise and prudent, and from those who do not want to depend on your Spirit, who attribute all things to their own wise conduct and to their measure of prudence. Instead, you have *revealed them to infants* who attribute nothing to themselves and give you glory in all things. *Yes, my Father, you did it this way because you chose it* that you should be glorified in all things and that you will be glorified in me in all things. This is why everything was made through you and without you nothing was made. You, Father, are only pleased by Jesus Christ and what is done by him, as you testify yourself from heaven, when you speak with your voice, "This is my Son, the Beloved, who pleases me uniquely, with whom I am well-pleased." Oh! If we know the advantage of being small and how our own prudence and wisdom is opposed to the spirit of Jesus Christ, we aspire to simplicity as this very great good.

> "All things have been handed over to me by my Father; and no one knows who the Son is except the Father, or who the Father is except the Son and anyone to whom the Son chooses to reveal him." (Luke 10:22)

Jesus Christ confirms what he has said and explains clearly about his joy and ravishment, assuring us that *his Father has handed all things over to him* and that he has sovereign power over all. The Father reveals his secret mysteries to Jesus Christ and this brings joy to the simple and small ones who do not resist him. These small ones do not oppose the kingdom of God and the motion of the Holy Spirit by their own false wisdom. This is why scripture says he was filled with the Holy Spirit before he said these things because all that Jesus Christ desires is to find hearts open to the divine movement. Only the little ones allow themselves to be led without resistance by the movements of the Holy Spirit. The Father has given all things to his Son, and we prevent this adorable Son from using his rights, and we usurp his rights because we want to lead ourselves, instead of letting him lead us to himself. *No one knows the Father except the Son.* We ought therefore not hope to know the divine Word through the efforts of our own reason. Therefore, it is not knowledge that leads us in the search, but love, that we will find the secrets hidden in the bosom of the Father and that will lead us to the Father. We will be given all the knowledge that we may hope for in this life and in the other because the Father may only be discovered through the Son who perfectly and entirely expresses the image of God. The Son is perfect because he is in no way different than the original and represents the Father in enter perfection. There is no trait in the Son that is not in the Father and nothing in the Father that is not perfectly expressed in the Son.

> Then turning to the disciples, Jesus said to them privately, "Blessed are the eyes that see what you see! 24 For I tell you that many prophets and kings desired to see what you see, but did not see it, and to hear what you hear, but did not hear it." (Luke 10:23–24)

Then turning to the disciples to show them how to understand the truth of the expression of the Father within him, *Blessed are*, he said, *the eyes that see what you see!* Because you see me, you also see the Father who is only expressed in me. Blessed are the souls who discover who I am, and to whom I manifest myself! Many saints and *prophets*, who were pleasing to God, *desired to see what you see*, that is to say, to have knowledge of the Father within the Son and the Son in my Father. *But they have not heard what you hear.* They have not heard the Word that is the Word of God: our passion must be to be entirely and continually attentive to the divine Word, which is the counsel of God: *This is my beloved Son; Listen to him.* O God! This is all we need to do.

> Just then a lawyer stood up to test Jesus. "Teacher," he said, "what must I do to inherit eternal life?" 26 He said to him, "What is written in the law? What do you read there?" 27 He answered, "You shall love the Lord your God with all your heart, and with all your soul, and with all your strength, and with all your mind; and your neighbor as yourself." 28 And he said to him, "You have given the right answer; do this, and you will live." (Luke 10:25–28)

These words are beautiful and bear repeating, as I have a number of times. *Love God with all your heart* without reservation. This is a great good to use all your heart and all your strength and the vigor of the soul to love. This is true life. O a loving life! Without love, our lives are living death. But where are these fortunate lovers who love everything? In whom all their energy is used to love? They are very rare!

O God! You are loving and the strongest of all love. As much as we can love you, we will find love everywhere. O the pure love of God, you are the life and the vigor of the soul. This love makes our soul vigorous. We must love to have life. Death with love is a wonderful life and life without love is truly death.

> But he, willing to justify himself, said unto Jesus, "And who is my neighbor?" (Luke 10:29)

Self-love is extremely clever and cunning. There are a thousand ways to say things indirectly that we would not say openly. We practice cunning like this in order to attract praise to ourselves. We pretend to ignore something to be clever. This lawyer interrogates Jesus and wants to test him and prove Jesus ignorant while justifying himself.

> Jesus replied, "A man was going down from Jerusalem to Jericho, and fell into the hands of robbers, who stripped him, beat him, and went away, leaving him half dead." (Luke 10:30)

This man who descends from Jerusalem to Jericho is the figure of a soul who turns away from his God, leaving behind his foundation, which is Jerusalem. He has been pleased to leave, to descend into outside objects, in the multiplicity of creatures, which is like Jericho. He falls into the hands of demons, which are like robbers ready to plunder and take the prey, as he passes by where they live. It is dangerous to leave our foundation without falling into the hands of these dangerous enemies. They cause many wounds, very frequently fatal, and always very dangerous, along with falling into a thousand sins.

> Now by chance a priest was going down that road; and when he saw him, he passed by on the other side. 32 So likewise a Levite, when he came to the place and saw him, passed by on the other side. (Luke 10:31–32)

Next came the priests who did not walk in the way of the Spirit, but instead walked in the way of many imperfections and full of faults. They did not perceive the danger they are in as they walk this way. Seeing all the wounds does not move them to the point of compassion. They do not want to get close to this dangerous state, where they would help these souls. This is not their ministry. However, these priests, who are not interior, are unaware of the damages caused to the souls who leave Jerusalem to go to Jericho.

> But a Samaritan while traveling came near him; and when he saw him, he was moved with pity. 34 He went to him and bandaged his wounds, having poured oil and wine on them. Then he put him on his own animal, brought him to an inn, and took care of him. 35 The next day he took out two denarii, gave them to the innkeeper, and said, "Take care of him; and when I come back, I will repay you whatever more you spend." (Luke 10:33–35)

Here Jesus Christ describes the character of some people, who God gives to minister to their neighbor, because they are serving in the will of God. God supplies the state and ordinary mission. God is not a respecter of persons. People who live in the world of creatures are like poor, wounded people, full of foibles, inconstancy and infidelity. They become damaged. Yet others live for charity and, because of God, they nourish their neighbor. There are many, many ways to do good. God uses the charitable Samaritan, as we see. God frequently gives to secular people the spirit of the priest because the priests do not use it as they should in their ministry. They refuse the spirit of Jesus Christ, which is a spirit of tenderness and love. Thus God gives their spirit to others and they are deprived.

Putting oil and wine on the wounds is another way to use the strength and tenderness of love with the unction of the Word to help this person return to the path that he had left. The Samaritan has a great compassion for this soul and bandages his wounds, which is like hiding them, so to speak, to let them heal. Without this, he will not advance forward out of the nothingness. If these wounds are not addressed, they will lead to death. Some of the biggest sinners need to be intimidated. But some souls who have fallen easily see their faults but see them as larger than they are. They believe them to be without remedy. Some out of scruples and out of a false humility abandon the way, and do not return to Jerusalem. They lack the energy for the return journey. They persuade themselves that being in Jerusalem actually caused these problems. They need to consider that this evil fell upon them because they left this way.

> "Which of these three, do you think, was a neighbor to the man who fell into the hands of the robbers?" 37 He said, "The one who showed him mercy." Jesus said to him, "Go and do likewise." (Luke 10:36–37)

This is the true Shepherd of the soul who helps the needy and nourishes them with true food, support, and relief. The ones who had been called to this refused to help. Jesus Christ teaches this lawyer through this comparison what he must do and how he must engage in ministry.

> Now as they went on their way, he entered a village; and a woman named Martha received him into her house. 39 And he had a sister called Mary, who sat at the Lord's feet and listened to his teaching. (Luke 10:38–39)

Martha *receives Jesus into her house* of living the active life. But Mary, who signifies the contemplative life, was seated. Being seated marks the repose of contemplation, where she was. In this sacred repose, she is engaged with her dear Master, who teaches, nourishes and invigorates with his word. O Mary! She was happy to hear his peace, tranquility, and silence: to leave the multiplicity of life and trouble of action and to be in the repose of contemplation. You placed her in a state of teaching. Mary listened and reposed in the silence and in the peace, without which it is impossible to hear the Word that speaks in the silence of the heart.

This is where she will bear fruit. It is why she was made and the Word appears to her in the night, because this is the time of profound silence of our nature. O Word that speaks incessantly! It is never interrupted while teaching the soul and puts her in a disposition to listen because this Word is very profound and sweet, and teaches us in peace and tranquility.

> But Martha was distracted with much serving; and she went to him and said, "Lord, do you not care that my sister has left me to serve alone? Tell her then to help me." But the Lord answered her, "Martha, Martha, you are anxious and troubled about many things; the one thing is needful. Mary has chosen the good portion, which shall not be taken away from her." (Luke 10:40–42)

Ah! My brothers and sisters, if we fight against the interior way, or do not want to enter into it, shouldn't this one passage convince us of its necessity and advantage? All that has been said in the Old and New Testament is almost all contained in these words: leave multiplicity, care, worry, and distractions, and enter into simplicity, unity, abandon, surrender, peace, tranquility, and silence. Leave the multiplicity and trouble of action, to enter into the repose of contemplation. After this we may practice a mixed life; that is, to be outside in action without leaving the repose of contemplation. All evil comes from our desire to have two states different and separate, the two states that should be united within. Action is not bad in itself but there is stress in action. Or an action might not be distracted but it is still not a simple and surrendered action. The action must come out of the contemplation of the good, because that is how we imitate God. That is why Jesus Christ says to us, *Be perfect as your heavenly Father is perfect* (Matthew 5:48). God is one and many: he must be for the union of the interior and the multiplicity of the exterior in the will of God, but this exterior multiplicity must only engage with God as we unite with him. Jesus Christ, the perfect model that we follow, had to spend thirty years hidden before he was given an exterior life. Like him, we must be entirely established in the interior, before we are given an exterior. All the many cares and concerns under good pretexts are very useless and superfluous, according to the testimony of the truth, and we are assured, *only one thing is necessary* and that is *needful* that Mary has chosen. What did you choose, Mary? To listen to God and to repose in him. It is needful to be attentive to God: it is *the better part* that we must choose. But inconceivable happiness! When we make this choice, the advantage will *not be taken away from us*. Nothing can take this great good from a human that possesses this. Because once this great good is given to us, nothing can snatch this away. It is the foundation and support for the Word of Jesus Christ. Paul also says, *We are assured that neither death, nor life, nor angels, nor principalities, nor powers, nor height, nor depth, nor anything else in all creation, will be able to separate us from the love of God in Christ Jesus our Lord* (Romans 8:37). This is founded and established in God and not on any merit within us.

> He was praying in a certain place, and after he had finished, one of his disciples said to him, "Lord, teach us to pray, as John taught his disciples." (Luke 11:1)

The prayer that Jesus Christ taught his disciples was very different than the one that John taught his disciples. However, we must always pray, and many do not believe they pray unless that distinguish and know an active prayer. Jesus Christ condescends to their weakness and teaches them a prayer of this type.

> He said to them, "When you pray, say "Father, hallowed be your name. Your kingdom come, 3 Give us each day our daily bread 4 And forgive us our sins, for we ourselves forgive everyone indebted to us. And do not bring us to the time of trial." (Luke 11:2–4)

Here is this short and good prayer. Jesus Christ would teach us nothing else because it keeps us in the unity and simplicity of the prayer. He is content with only a few words of the mouth because this prayer must be continual and comes from the heart. We must *pray without ceasing* as Paul says in 1 Thessalonians 5:17 in the prayer from the heart. We can do this prayer continually because Jesus Christ did not overload us with vocal prayers. Some vocal prayers are good but most are not. There is little to say, unless they are obligatory. Interior people can only say the ones that are from the heart. These prayers of faith are the ones that satisfy the most because they express more.

> And he said to them, "Suppose one of you has a friend, and you go to him at midnight and say to him, 'Friend, lend me three loaves of bread; 6 for a friend of mine has arrived, and I have nothing to set before him.' 7 And he answers from within, 'Do not bother me; the door has already been locked, and my children are with me in bed; I cannot get up and give you anything.' 8 I tell you, even though he will not get up and give him anything because he is his friend, at least because of his persistence he will get up and give him whatever he needs." (Luke 11:5–8)

Under this story, Jesus Christ tells us how needed perseverance is in prayer because we may obtain nothing without this perseverance. Through perseverance we obtain all that we need and desire when the demands are just. Jesus Christ speaks here of a *friend* praying in grace. He compares himself to the one who sees this as an inconvenience and refuses to help his friend. Yet the person continues to knock at the door and gets what he needs. In a like way, the sinner perseveres to ask God for his conversion and gets this sooner or later. The just who ask for things they need for their soul and for the glory of God do so with faith. God has us wait for a long time at the door. The person asks for entry with much intensity. We want him to open to us as soon as we knock. Most refuse and leave if he does not answer immediately. However, we advance by the way of perseverance. It is necessary to *knock at the door* so that finally God may give us entry and we may rest there with him.

The *three loaves of bread* represent the three theological virtues that the soul needs to makes its voyage. She may understand nothing without love, faith, and hope in God. Pure love sustains, animates, and vivifies the believer. Faith is the door through which abandon and trust in the hands of God. Hope animates her courage to pursue what she wants, without being discouraged by the obstacles that she encounters. To the contrary, hope redoubles all the more when there is less reason to hope.

> "So I say to you, Ask, and it will be given you; search, and you will find; knock, and the door will be opened for you." (Luke 11:9)

Therefore it is necessary to *ask* for the things that are needed and they will be given. When they are given, we enter into them with abandonment and faith into the hands of God. When the soul obtains what she asks, she feels a certain powerlessness to ask again but this is a sign that she has obtained what she desired. She must remain in total abandon and openness to God. When we look for God within the heart, we never fail to find God. If we do not find God, it is because we are not searching as is needed. O God! You who are truth, you assure us, *search and you will find*. However, many people complain that they search for God without finding him. This is because they do not search where he will be found, that is, at the bottom of their heart, the place of his abode. Or they do not seek him in the time that he can be found. It is the same way with knocking: it is necessary to knock on our heart until he opens, which he will not fail to do. But when he opens the door, we receive a facility and knowledge to remain in repose. Then we must stop knocking and enter into God's heart when the door is opened.

> "If you then, who are evil, know how to give good gifts to your children, how much more will the heavenly Father give the Holy Spirit to those who ask him!" (Luke 11:13)

It is true that we render less justice to God than we give to a father on the earth. We would not believe that a father on the earth would give us what is harmful and would refuse us what is necessary. However, we desire the infinite goodness of God. He never refuses *the Holy Spirit*, which is an interior spirit of prayer, which we ask from him.

> "When a strong man, fully armed, guards his castle, his property is safe. 22 But when one stronger than he attacks him and overpowers him, he takes away his armor in which he trusted and divides his plunder." (Luke 11:21–22)

The soul armed and sustained by grace is like *a strong man* guarding his castle. She appears that she has *peace* and *possesses everything with tranquility*. Yet God comes with divine strength a thousand times stronger than the soul. God overpowers and destroys this first strength. But God only surmounts so that he afflicts the soul, takes away her armor, and distributes the plunder. My God! You have such mysteries! This is the way God holds souls. God first gives weapons and power to defend against her enemies. She is like a strong fort, employed to guard her castle. But when God wishes to come himself—Oh!—it is a power and a strength that tears apart all that he has given. God seems to be troubling the soul: God afflicts and disarms. The soul is without defense and power but she does not understand that God has made all this ravage to deprive her of all defenses. She is in a state of becoming and she can be attacked without any power to resist. O soul! What will you be? Her ways of resisting God have been taken away so she will not have the sin of resistance. Others might see this soul as one having misfortune which is less painful if it is shared and there are companions in this disaster. But alas! To the contrary, far from seeing this faith as misfortune, we see that others divide up the spoils and seem to be enriched by her loss. As naturally described in this passage, those who have experienced this will understand it clearly.

> "Whoever is not with me is against me, and whoever does not gather with me scatters." (Luke 11:23)

Our excellent Master, our sovereign doctor, instructs us as to what happens in these interior states and shows us how to conduct ourselves. *Whoever is not with me,* says Jesus Christ, *is against me.* That is to say, "Whoever does not enter into my interests against his own is against me." So instead of grieving the afflictions or defending ourselves against the losses, we are content that everything should be removed and taken away so that we enter into God's interests. We let this happen and abandon ourselves to God's will. Those who do not do this are not with him in his operations, resist him, and are against him. *Whoever does not gather with me* is the one who does not let God take everything and does not restore it to God. This person is not gathering with Jesus Christ and for Jesus Christ. Instead, she gathers things for herself and *scatters.*

> "When the unclean spirit has gone out of a person, it wanders through waterless regions looking for a resting place, but not finding any, it says, 'I will return to my house from which I came.' 25 When it comes, it finds it swept and put in order. 26 Then it goes and brings seven other spirits more evil than itself, and they enter and live there; and the last state of that person is worse than the first." (Luke 11:24–26)

Here we hear of the sinner who after having been delivered of sin does not take precautions for the future, and so his end is worse than his beginning.

In this passage about the interior life, we have a proprietary soul with his gifts, graces, and favors. So that this soul does not become arrogant over grand graces and sublime revelations, God lets an angel cast out an unclean spirit who leaves the person. This proprietary soul though feeling itself purified, yet still rejects truth, humiliation, and annihilation, and is not delivered through this state of testing. Instead, she returns to her first propriety and even stronger than the first. This soul sustains itself in these things. Therefore, the soul finds itself adorned, and rests and satisfies itself in her own beauty. What does this spirit do that had been ordered to torment this soul? He goes with seven worse spirits to torment the soul. Now these spirits bring mortal sin that gives the soul violent shocks, so that the last state is infinitely worse than the first. She is constrained to give up everything and leave, or she will suffer intolerable pain until death. All the sorrows of souls come from this: they resist and refuse to abandon themselves to God and so they remain corrupt and destroyed.

> While he was saying this, a woman in the crowd raised her voice and said to him, "Blessed is the womb that bore you and the breasts that nursed you!" 28 But he said, "Blessed rather are those who hear the word of God and obey it!" (Luke 11:27–28)

Jesus Christ shows here that the sovereign *happiness* consists in *hearing God*, which is a great advantage. Yet to have opened the door and be nourished by hearing God is not the greatest advantage. Instead, to *hear the Word of God* and *guard his Word* in the bottom of the heart is more than anything else. Mary had this special privilege, to hear and guard the Word as scripture says in many places: *Mary pondered these things in her heart*. This attention to God, and not expelling what is received from God, is the thing most needed.

> "Your eye is the lamp of your body. When your eye is healthy, your whole body is full of light, but when it is bad, your body is full of darkness. 35 Therefore be careful lest the light in you be darkness." (Luke 11:34–35)

The eye is intention and attention: the simplicity of intention and attention must be grounded in righteousness. If the intention is all in God and attention all for God, she receives righteousness. Therefore, if my attention and my sight are always fixed on God, without turning toward the reflection of created things, then *my eye is simple*; my intention is always right; and my *exterior*, my actions, which are signified by *the body*, are always *full of light*. These simple and righteous actions, which participate in interior purity and light, give true light to actions. Our divine Master also adds, *Therefore, be careful lest the light in you be darkness* because everything depends on the light of the foundation. If the foundation is in truth, it is in light. This truth consists in being in the light of all of God and nothing of the creature. To be enlightened by God, we remain penetrated by his light and his divine clarity, which often blinds us. We are defeated if we use our own lights.

> "If then your whole body is full of light, having no part dark, it will be wholly bright, as when a lamp with its rays gives you light." (Luke 11:36)

Your whole body is full of light through the divine light, which is a strong and brilliant light within. All actions are penetrated by this simple light, and in all things and you will be *full of light*.

> While he was speaking, a Pharisee invited him to dine with him; so he went in and took his place at the table. 38 The Pharisee was amazed to see that he did not first wash before dinner. 39 Then the Lord said to him, "Now you Pharisees clean the outside of the cup and of the dish, but inside you are full of greed and wickedness." (Luke 11:37–39)

People attached to many exterior ceremonies are not attached to the essentials of religion. They were astounded and scandalized by Jesus. These ceremonies are only a good and praiseworthy custom. Instead, interior people are occupied with God within and they think on other things, and not all the small exterior things that are not absolutely necessary and serve only as a distraction. The Pharisees complained to Jesus Christ, who made them understand that they were attached only to the bark and not to the foundation. It is necessary that the foundation is pure and all for God. Without this, all that we have on the outside is little. It is necessary that the interior be purified. But if we are attached to the exterior and the exterior rules us, while the interior is full of propriety, (signified by *greed* and *wickedness*), we are claiming for ourselves the righteousness of God. To not attribute to God justice in all things is propriety.

> "You fools! Did not the one who made the outside make the inside also? 41 So give for alms those things that are within; and see, everything will be clean for you." (Luke 11:40–41)

It is truly a strange thing that when most people speak of becoming interior and of interior work, they speak of this as an extravagance. They take this as a new law that is only invented out of caprice. As if *the one who made the outside* did not *make the inside also* where he wants to prepare a place for himself. This happens by abandoning one's self to God's way. Jesus Christ himself has commanded that we *give for alms those things that are within* and of those things that belong to us. This is the way *everything will be clean* and pure for us. Through these alms of that which is within, we will obtain a pure interior and see purity of faith in the alms. It is not that alms-giving creates the purity. As St. Paul says, *If I give away all my possessions, and if I hand over my body so that I may boast, but do not have love, I gain nothing* (1 Corinthians 13:1). But it is that almsgiving attracts the grace of the pure interior.

> "But woe to you Pharisees! For you tithe mint and rue and herbs of all kinds, and neglect justice and the love of God; it is these you ought to have practiced, without neglecting the others."

Jesus Christ condemns all people who are only attached to the bark and not to what is essential, which is the *love of God*, perfect love, and truth of religion. As John 4:16 says, "Those who abide in love, abide in God." We must not, therefore, neglect our interior, which is solid, and stop at small and petty things. We must make our focus the love of God and the justice we owe to him. These small accessories only have value if they are connected to the living principle of perfect love. This is so true that the best actions, if not made in charity, are dead works. Therefore, it is charity that gives life to all our actions. The more love there is, the more life there is, and the more the actions are good, perfect and agreeable to God. It is therefore necessary to have this life-giving principle within our heart (Luke 11:42).

> "Therefore also the Wisdom of God said, 'I will send them prophets and apostles, some of whom they will kill and persecute,' 50 so that this generation may be charged with the blood of all the prophets shed since the foundation of the world, 51 from the blood of Abel to the blood of Zechariah, who perished between the altar and the sanctuary. Yes, I tell you, it will be charged against this generation." (Luke 11:49–51)

Not only the apostles and the prophets were persecuted but today the Word of God is still persecuted. If they had not announced the Word of God, they would have remained like other people. Therefore, it is only the Word of truth that they persecute. The Word of God was already there at the beginning of the world and will remain always.

The bloodiest wars are ones waged against interior people. The greatest enemies would not push things more rigorously. Because the interior light is the light of truth, we discover errors and lies with this truth. Some people are like owls living in the dark who cannot suffer this light. The light irritates them and causes them to be against the light. These people provoke persecutions against the faithful people.

> "Woe to you lawyers! For you have taken away the key of knowledge; you did not enter yourselves, and you hindered those who were entering." (Luke 11:52)

It is a strange thing that wise men who have *the key of knowledge* are the most opposed to the interior. They will not let their own light and self-centered propriety be taken away. This is why they do not enter into life because the door is narrow and they have to be small to enter. Because they are full of their own self-sufficient notions, they cannot enter. This is why *they did not enter themselves* and *in sin hindered others from entering* who were attracted to knowledge. They turn them away with all their might. This is a terrible misfortune.

> "Are not five sparrows sold for two pennies? Yet not one of them is forgotten in God's sight. 7 But even the hairs of your head are all counted. Do not be afraid; you are of more value than many sparrows." (Luke 12:6–7)

Jesus Christ gives us this assurance that we have the care of providence, so because of this shouldn't we abandon ourselves without reservation into the hands of God? We may entirely forget ourselves. What do we have to fear? God does not forget us for a moment; God cares for us greatly. There is not one thought we have that he does not care about; God counts and governs our thoughts. Why therefore do we fear and not abandon ourselves to him without reservation? We should give ourselves to him and allow his hands to guide us. God will act for us.

> "When they bring you before the synagogues, the rulers, and the authorities, do not worry about how you are to defend yourselves or what you are to say; 12 for the Holy Spirit will teach you at that very hour what you ought to say." (Luke 12:11–12)

My God! You are good to those who abandon themselves in all things to you! You miss us and you desire that we abandon ourselves to you with strength and you show us with particular care how to abandon ourselves to you. It seems that you take pleasure in preventing our difficulties and solving them when they happen. You assure us that in every situation we are not to be afraid. Jesus Christ tells us that we must not be worried about tomorrow. He tells us again that he will show us what to do in particular situations. Do not think of defending yourself when it comes to your honor, life, and even the interests of God. Worldly-wise people consider his wisdom folly and tempt God by planning their responses. Jesus Christ himself warns us not to premeditate our responses and not to plan what we are to say. Oh, if all the preachers did not premeditate what they were saying, but instead give themselves with all their heart to the interior, and they abandoned themselves to the movement of the Spirit of God, oh, what good they would do! The apostles preached with strength but they were led by the movement of God's spirit. When we preach by moving with the Spirit of God, we have many conversions. When we want to preach and pray by our own efforts, we do not advance and we do not have any fruit. Jesus Christ assures us that *The Holy Spirit will teach you at that very hour what you ought to say.* Why not let us be instructed by the Holy Spirit? If the Spirit tells us not to premeditate anything, it is certain that premeditations stop the Spirit of God from instructing us.

> Someone in the crowd said to him, "Teacher, tell my brother to divide the family inheritance with me." 14 But he said to him, "Friend, who set me to be a judge or arbitrator over you?" 15 And he said to them, "Take care! Be on your guard against all kinds of greed; for one's life does not consist in the abundance of possession." (Luke 12:13–15)

Jesus Christ here does not speak only of temporal riches, which can do so little and cannot do what a well-disposed heart can do. Those that value riches have a very small heart because they fill it with very little. On the other hand, a noble heart raised above the common by the virtue of the Son must not stop. O the heart that amuses itself with riches, which flatters itself with possessions, who makes this all their pleasure! What amuses you? You hate yourself by submitting to things vile and reprehensible, to which you give your esteem. *One's life does not consist* in riches. There are poor people who live very well and rich people who live poorly.

Jesus Christ here also gives advice about spiritual riches. They are not necessary in order to enter the life of grace and their abundance does not bring certainty that we are more agreeable to God. We should not be attached to these things, because they are not essential. We need to be attached to God alone, and we let God decide all the rest. When we have difficulty losing either our spiritual or temporal wealth, it is a sign that we are attached to something.

> Then he told them a parable: "The land of a rich man produced abundantly. 17 And he thought to himself, 'What should I do, for I have no place to store my crops?' 18 Then he said, 'I will do this: I will pull down my barns and build larger ones, and there I will store all my grain and my goods. 19 And I will say to my soul, Soul, you have ample goods laid up for many years; relax, eat, drink, be merry.' 20 But God said to him, 'You fool! This very night your life is being demanded of you. And the things you have prepared, whose will they be?'" (Luke 12:16–20)

This parable serves to show us the state of a soul who reposes in the gifts, graces, and favors that she has received from God. She *amassed* gifts on gifts, riches on riches, graces on graces. She is filled with all virtue and full of all good. She has so much it cannot be contained. She says then, everything is done; everything is accomplished. Now she should *repose* in these same goods, be nourished and filled with this. She has the strength of many virtues. She says to her soul, "It is now, my soul, that you enjoy the accomplishments of your work. You have acquired all these goods through your penances and by your own practices." It is a pity that she is so full of herself and believes that she has all the virtues. These gifts were given to her to lead her to God but instead she has attached to the things.

But what does God say to this soul who has all these things? God says, *You fool!* You believe you have arrived at the end, and there is nothing to do but repose in my gifts. You regard these gifts as acquired riches that belong to you and make you proprietary. I am going to make you enter in *the night*, in obscurity and loss. It is there that I *demand* not only the gifts, graces, favors, and virtues that I have given you and which have made you proprietary, but I also demand your own *soul* because it is not enough to lose all your riches. You will still have to lose your soul because without this loss you will always be proprietary. When you have lost your soul, *all these assets* that you have amassed for yourself, *what will they serve you*? What is the use of your propriety? This scripture confirms what has been said.

> "So it is with those who store up treasures for themselves but are not rich toward God." (Luke 12:21)

Oh, these grand words! Therefore all the good, gifts, graces, and virtues become proprietary when we amass them for ourselves. We want the best and we work only for ourselves. But all these amassed riches will be undermined even in their foundation. They are not riches amassed in God, so they will be lost.

The riches we amass in God are exempt from propriety. The soul takes nothing and, because of this, reposes and remains always faithful. These riches are found only in God, by an entire surrender of self.

> Jesus said to his disciples, "Therefore I tell you, do not worry about your life, what you will eat, or about your body, what you will wear. 23 For your life is more than food, and the body more than clothing." (Luke 12:22–23)

Jesus Christ exhorts his disciples, "Do not worry, even about your soul." We must abandon it to him and let it remain with him.

"Do not be afraid, little flock, for it is your Father's good pleasure to give you the kingdom." (Luke 12:32)

Jesus Christ does not only say this to his apostles but to all abandoned souls who are the little flock of Jesus Christ. This is way he talks about entirely abandoning ourselves to him, to the hands of God, and he instructs us not to be anxious. After this he says, "Do not be afraid, little flock." I have chosen you to be entirely devoted to me in a particular manner. Do not be afraid, poor little flock, afflicted, persecuted, and abandoned, for it is the pleasure of your heavenly Father, because of his goodness, and not because of your merits, to give you the kingdom. You have been given and practiced the laws that have disciplined you and brought you to the kingdom. You will reign with him. But sadly, this our little flock is attacked on all sides by wolves, and we have no power or vigor to defend ourselves. Jesus Christ will guard and defend us. We may graze on the herbs without fear, even in the midst of wolf attacks, because in the divine pasture there will be neither damage nor injuries because we are chosen in a particular manner.

> "Sell your possession, and give alms. Make purses for yourself that do not wear out, an unfailing treasure in heaven, where no thief comes near and no moth destroys. For where your treasure is, there your heart will be also." (Luke 12:33–34)

Only in God do we have an incorruptible treasure. If our heart is in God, our treasure will also be in God. Therefore, it is good to remove our heart from all the things of this world and to sink into and attach our heart to God. When we pray from the heart, we amass an interior treasure that is hidden from attack from humans. All exterior powers may not attack and steal this treasure. It is inaccessible from them. The worm of sin and the germ of corruption may not attack because our heart is in God. Where your heart is, there is your treasure also. If our heart is in God, our treasure is in God. And if our treasure is in God, our heart is inevitably in God. We look to God only.

> "Be dressed for action and have your lamps lit." (Luke 12:35)

Having your loins girded is to be disciplined from all pleasures. We must be ready to leave anything that diverts us from God and be ready to be collected at home. Mortification that accompanies prayer is a good thing but mortification without the interior spirit is nothing. We say again that our lamps must be lit which means that our heart must be filled with the fire of charity and pure love. We must have ardor in our heart and deprived of external pleasures. We burn with love for God within. Our heart must always be aflame with love that longs for union with the will of God. Our lamp must be in the hands of God so that all exterior actions and virtues participate in the life-giving principle and animated by charity. All the charity also must also be accompanied by the practice of virtues. Our lamp in the hands of God reveals righteousness and simplicity that we must have. When our heart is in his hands, we say what we think when we think it. Our actions are guided according to the interior spirit. This makes us true and right in our words and actions.

> "Be like those who are waiting for their master to return from the wedding banquet, so that they may open the door for him as soon as he comes and knocks." (Luke 12:36)

Jesus Christ tells us again the disposition that he asks of us is to wait. We must wait in repose. A person should wait in repose for the Bridegroom to come, but not to become idle or dissipated. Wait with the prayer of silence and simple words. And be ready to open the door to the Bridegroom. Oh, that we wait attentively with our heart to open when the Bridegroom appears. With justice and simplicity, we will have no resistance when he knocks on the door of our heart. But in what way do we wait? We must have our lamp always illuminated, our heart full of ardor, love, and holy unction. Our love and attention ask us to be silent and watchful in repose, so that we may not be surprised. Oh, if we know the happiness of this watching! Because the Bridegroom will never be late. When he enters the soul, he will call us his lover and caress us with the nuptial kiss.

> "Blessed are those slaves whom the master finds alert when he comes; truly I tell you, he will fasten his belt and have them sit down to eat, and he will come and serve them." (Luke 12:37)

O what an inconceivable happiness to watch God and to repose attentively in his presence! God puts the souls at his table and serves them himself. O incomparable advantage!

> "If he comes during the middle of the night, or near dawn, and finds them so, blessed are those slaves. 39 but know this: if the owner of the house had known at what hour the thief was coming, he would not have let his house be broken into. 40 You also must be ready, for the Son of Man is coming at an unexpected

hour." 41 Peter said, "Lord, are you telling this parable for us or for everyone?" And the Lord said, "Who then is the faithful and prudent manager whom his master will put in charge of his slaves, to give them their allowance of food at the proper time? 43 Blessed is that slave whom his master will find at work when he arrives. 44 Truly I tell you, he will put that one in charge of all his possessions." (Luke 12:38–44)

This is a confirmation of the advantage of watching and waiting on God. Peter asks if these words are meant for them only or if they are spoken for the whole world. But the answer makes it clear that no one is excluded from this advantage. Whoever listens well, will participate in this happiness.

"I come to bring fire to the earth, and how I wish it were already kindled!" (Luke 12:49)

Jesus Christ came to the earth to bring the fire of love: he wants this to be aflame in us. We must aspire to this. Oh, that he desires us to be on fire with love on both earth and heaven! But we do not give the place to our divine Master to light the fire of sacred love within us! O Love! Let us love you so that you may consume our hearts! This sacred love will burn away anything that opposes you. Then the sacred fire continues burning. Oh, that he consumes all of us! This fire burns, consumes, and destroys in its burning. By this, he produces infinity within us. His love is within us. This same love purifies, consumes, destroys, and annihilates our heart with his burning power.

"I have a baptism with which to be baptized, and what stress I am under until it is completed." (Luke 12:50)

The baptism with which Jesus Christ must be baptized is suffering and the cross where he will shed his blood. All Christians are baptized with him in the effusion of his blood. This is the first thing he imprints in the heart: the burning of his fire and the love of suffering. Then we too wish to suffer, like Christ who was satiated with the suffering of reproach!

"Do you think that I have come to bring peace to the earth? No, I tell you, but rather division." (Luke 12:51)

The work of Jesus Christ is to divide. When he comes into the soul, he first divides away the senses from outside objects; then he divides away the spirit away from the senses. Then he divides the superior from the inferior; then he even divides the soul out from its foundation. He divides everything so that he can make use of it.

> At that very time there were some present who told him about the Galileans whose blood Pilate had mingled with their sacrifices. 2 He asked them, "Do you think that because these Galileans suffered in this way they were worse sinners than all other Galileans? 3 No, I tell you; but unless you repent, you will all perish as they did." (Luke 13:1–3)

These scriptures tell us that the cross, torments, persecutions, and calumnies are not the marks of crime. There are innocent people persecuted. However, some criminals live and are applauded. O God! Your judgments are very different from people. Those who pass for innocent among humans are very guilty in your eyes, while others regarded as criminals are your delights! We should never judge ourselves or others based on the estimation or condemnation from people. We should never judge people but let God alone judge. We excuse everyone and condemn no one. When disasters do arrive, we are penitent.

> Then he told this parable: "A man had a fig tree planted in his vineyard; and he came looking for fruit on it and found none. 7 So he said to the gardener, 'See here! For three years I have come looking for fruit on this fig tree, and still I find none. Cut it down! Why should it be wasting the soil?' 8 He replied, 'Sir, let it alone for one more year, until I dig around it and put manure on it. 9 If it bears fruit next year, well and good; but if not, you can cut it down.'" (Luke 13:6–9)

Here we see that the days of sinners are shortened by the misuse they make of their life. God sometimes makes known to holy souls the loss of sinners, so they see what happens to those who abuse the time that is given them as a gift. God hopes that these good souls will be concerned about the salvation of sinners and oppose the loss of them. How great is the desire of God to save humanity! God gives his friends graces which the sinner cannot receive. Usually when God makes known to his servants that a soul is in danger, God also inspires the desire to work for the sinner's conversion and then gives him success with this.

Dig around the foot of the tree means that the person enters the work of penitence. Then through putting manure on the tree, the person acquires life-giving heat, which makes him feel his faults and their stench. If I take this care for the sinner, says the holy soul, this does not oblige him to bear fruit, and he may be cut down if he does not. I am not opposed to God's justice. We see there the consequences of how we use moments of graces that are presented to us and ideas we are given for our conversion. Because if we do not use these through our own negligence, we risk losing our salvation.

> 10 Now he was teaching in one of the synagogues on the Sabbath. 11 And just then there appeared a woman with a spirit that had crippled her for eighteen years. She was bent over and was quite unable to stand up straight. (Luke 13:10–11)

The most dangerous evil is when we look only at ourselves and things on the earth and do not consider God. The devil tells us only to reflect on ourselves and the material world. Instead, we must return to the God's side and look at Jesus. He guards us from the demon and heals us of this malady, the most dangerous of all, because it is the source of all other evils.

> When Jesus saw her, he called her over and said, "Woman, you are set free from your ailment." (Luke 13:12)

O the goodness of my God! You never fail to *call* over this bent soul, so that she returns to you! If she is faithful to hear your voice and to follow it, then in this moment she is *delivered from her infirmity*. But if she resists, she will perish in her misery. Oh, if we hear the voice of Jesus who calls us inside, then we will be healed of our miseries! But if we do not listen, we will not hear that adorable voice within. Then we will not follow and we will not go to Jesus to be delivered from our miseries. Let us go to him, all of us who are afflicted with pain, or carry a heavy burden, and he will relieve us.

> When he laid his hands on her, immediately she stood up straight and began praising God. (Luke 13:13)

The scripture says that Jesus called to her saying, *You are delivered*. In Jesus Christ to say is to do. Therefore, she is delivered in that moment. However, it also says here that Jesus Christ *laid his hands on her, immediately she stood up straight*. This is very mysterious. There was time between her deliverance and her righteousness yet a time that was not long. We note that we must be delivered from things that hold us captive. Here is the healing. Then it is necessary to take a posture entirely different. It is necessary that the soul stand up straight to the things of the earth, straighten and turn toward God. This is the operation of Jesus Christ when he laid his hands on her. First, he calls her. Then he delivers the soul from the ties and ropes that attached her to things of the earth and to herself, that kept her bent over and turned away from God. Following this, he lays his hands on her which is an application of power and she turns toward him, taking a posture entirely different that the one she had. This great good only comes to this soul because she is exposed and open before God.

> But the leader of the synagogue, indignant because Jesus had cured on the sabbath, kept saying to the crowd, "There are six days on which work ought to be done; come on those days and be cured, and not on the sabbath day." (Luke 13:14)

All the people who are attached scrupulously to the letter of the law usually have only a little of the spirit of the law. A law that commits us to do a good does not forbid us from doing a greater good. To the contrary, the law commits us by this mediocre good to a greater good. As the law is for us, it contains things common things to be done or avoided so that no one can be exempted from the law or say it is too difficult. This does not prevent the law from being perfectly fulfilled by those who do things that the spirit of the law contains and which are of a greater perfection. However, those who are obstinately attached to the letter of the law and only want to practice what it says are scandalized and offended by those people who our Lord asks for perfection and do not stop at the letter of the law and instead do what the Spirit contains. These people condemn with power those following the law with perfection. They abuse those following the spirit of the law. For example, the church makes an absolute commandment of taking communion, yet they do not condemn the faithful taking communion more frequently. The church would like all to take frequent communion so they live in perfection in this great good, but because of human weakness and malice, the church cannot command this. However, good souls who take communion daily accomplish the perfection of this commandment!

> But the Lord answered him and said, "You hypocrites! Does not each of you on the sabbath untie his ox or his donkey from the manger, and lead it away to give it water? 16 And ought not this woman, a daughter of Abraham whom Satan bound for eighteen long years, be set free from this bondage on the sabbath day?" 17 When he said this, all his opponents were put to shame;

and the entire crowd was rejoicing at all the wonderful things that he was doing. (Luke 13:15–17)

It is certain that some people condemn with bitterness certain omissions of little consequence and do not practice actions that have great perfection. Yet these people act frequently out of self-interest. They condemn actions done out of charity and of the will of God. Jesus Christ tells these people that they are wrong. He throws them into confusion, while he fills those with joy who seek his greatest glory.

> At that very hour some Pharisees came and said to him, "Get away from here, for Herod wants to kill you." 32 He said to them, "Go and tell that fox for me 'Listen, I am casting out demons and performing cures today and tomorrow, and on the third day I finish my work. 33 Yet today, tomorrow, and the next day I must be on my way, because it is impossible for a prophet to be killed outside of Jerusalem.'" (Luke 13:31–33)

Jesus Christ is not astonished by the threats made to him. He continues his ministry. The true apostle will accomplish his ministry until the day when he is *consumed*. There are people like Herod who combine a pretense with cruelty. This is why Jesus Christ calls him a *fox*. They cover themselves with pretext only in order to persecute and are so skillful that they seem to have grace by killing. But all the threats and menaces do not hinder a true apostolic soul from doing all the good God has willed for them to do in a place, until everything is consumed, that is to say, all the good that God has willed to do through this person in this place is consumed, when all his life and sufferings end his actions. Jesus Christ assures us that *it is impossible for a prophet to be killed outside of Jerusalem*. This means that a prophet and apostle must not die outside of the exercise of his ministry and must die by the persecution of those from whom he has done the most.

> "Jerusalem, Jerusalem, the city that kills the prophets and stones those who are sent to it! How often have I desired to gather your children together as a hen gathers her brood under her wings, and you were not willing!" (Luke 13:34)

In all times those who have been sent by God to destroy vices and to practice virtues are persecuted. All those who have been sent by God to make him known, loved, and adored and to bring God's Spirit are those who are condemned and persecuted as guilty. What is most distressing is that the ones who ought to maintain and support the good prevent it.

We see again the goodness of God and his desire he has to save us, yet how the creature does not return this. God truly wants our salvation, yet will not violently end our human freedom. Jesus Christ assures us that he wants to *gather your children*, that is to say, reunite all your powers of the soul in him. But some rebel and criminally *were not willing*.

> "See, your house is left to you. And I tell you, you will not see me until the time comes when you say, 'Blessed is the one who comes in the name of the Lord.'" (Luke 13:35)

When our Lord sees that all his pursuits serve no purpose and that he calls without being answered, then he chastises the rebel and unfaithful soul by his absence. He omits some support that ordinary grace gives. The soul finds herself in a frightful *desert* without anything from God. Then she neither sees nor perceives until she repents of her faults and desires that he comes. Therefore, she knows that she abused God's graces. Then she says with a good heart, *Blessed is the one who comes in the name of the Lord!* Oh, that I might again experience your goodness! Oh, that I might not rebel against your grace! Oh, that the Lord might be welcome! As soon as the soul remains in these dispositions, the Lord appears and comes with an infinite goodness to bring salvation which this soul has refused with so much injustice.

> On one occasion when Jesus was going to the house of a leader of the Pharisees to eat a meal on the sabbath, they were watching him closely. (Luke 14:1)

Worldly-wise and proper people examine continually simple and sincere souls who give everything to God without reserve. They examine *all their actions* and all their movements to have occasion to surprise them in some fault, in order to decry and condemn. Frequently they do not find anything criminal to condemn in justice, they regard and examine the best actions and change them through venom, like a poisonous snake, and they spoil and corrupt the best things. They resemble spiders who tend their nets so they can catch flies. If they watch those following a simple path, they frequently are caught and embarrassed in the traps they set for them.

> Just then, in front of him, there was a man who had dropsy.
> 3 And Jesus asked the lawyers and Pharisees, "Is it lawful to cure

> people on the sabbath, or not?" 4 But they were silent. So Jesus took him and healed him, and sent him away. 5 Then he said to them, "If one of you has a child or an ox that has fallen into a well, will you not immediately pull it out on a sabbath day?" 6 And they could not reply to this. (Luke 14:2–6)

Jesus Christ confounds these doctors and lawyers by an action that they could not condemn because it was accompanied by a miracle. It seems that our Lord takes pleasure in healing on the Sabbath day so that the doctors do not stop at the letter of the law, but have the spirit of the law. He innocently violates this law on the Sabbath for a great good. So we understand that we can violate the letter of the law without forfeiting the spirit or the will of the Law-Giver. Then we understand how to obey in a manner more perfect. The doctors were scrupulous in this trivia but not in the essentials. They lived, ate, and feasted on the Sabbath day and they did not see anything to complain about. Yet they understood a charitable action as a crime on that day. If someone walked around entertaining themselves on Sunday, they found nothing to complain about. Yet if someone served his neighbor or did something that God asked of him, all the world murmured and complained.

> When he noticed how the guests chose the places of honor, he told them a parable. 8 "When you are invited by someone to a wedding banquet, do not sit down at the place of honor, in case someone more distinguished than you has been invited by your host; 9 and the host who invited both of you may come and say to you, 'Give this person your place,' and then in disgrace you would start to take the lowest place. 10 But when you are invited, go and sit down at the lowest place, so that when your host comes, he may say to you, 'Friend, move up higher'; then you will be honored in the presence of all who sit at the table with you." (Luke 14:7–10)

We place importance on our own honor because of our excessive pride and vanity. Out of vanity we seek the first places. Or out of a pretend humility, we say we want the last so that we can get the first places. Doing this, we strongly abuse the counsel of Jesus Christ and have turned his wisdom into venom.

Some say that we should not be practicing the prayer of the heart and affection and that we should remain in our place until we are told, *Friend, come higher*. This needs to be clarified. First, it is false that the prayer of affection and of the heart, and to remain in a respectful silence before God, is of elevated degree. This is not a raised state but it is rather resting in annihilation and in a lowered state to rest before God in simplicity, humility, and in a movement of the heart. The operations of the Spirit are things that raise us and we ought not to do these things our self unless the master does this to us. Instead, we rest in our lowness and baseness. This is the place that is appropriate for us. We must hold on to this place. We must never undertake for our self the things of the Spirit of light, sublime knowledge, gifts, graces, and favors. This is a state to which we must never aspire, but we remain in a state of smallness and annihilation, to remain in our baseness. We are content to express to God our love and respect in a simple, naïve, and efficacious manner. This is not an elevated state. However, we reverse the order if we think that the practice of this smallness with the humble and small way of faith is elevation. The way of reasoning is contrary to this state of annihilation and humility. Humility does not consist in being filled with a spirit of light but to remain annihilated before God in a small and low state, content to be nothing in her own eyes, as well as the eyes of God and people. Jesus Christ himself adds:

> "For all who exalt themselves will be humbled, and those who humble themselves will be exalted." (Luke 14:11)

Those who hold on to their annihilation and baseness are very frequently *exalted* because God unites with them. However, those *who exalt themselves* by their own lights and knowledge are *humbled* by their increasing ignorance.

> He said also to the one who had invited him, "When you give a luncheon or a dinner, do not invite your friends or your brothers or your relatives or rich neighbors, in case they may invite you in return, and you would be repaid. 13 But when you give a banquet, invite the poor, the crippled, the lame, and the blind. 14 And you will be blessed, because they cannot repay you, for you will be repaid at the resurrection of the righteous." (Luke 14:12–14)

Jesus Christ tells us here to act without self-interest. Almost all of our actions have a motive of interest as we expect a return from the action. Yet will there be someone who will serve God freely without self-interest and will love God for who God is? Oh, this is very rare! Some mercenary and self-interested souls consider only the reward and want to pass their love off as perfect. They criticize and condemn those who consider God in all things. They even say because their motivation is self-interest that this is the only way people are. Yet those who act without self-interest receive the best reward. He who acts only in proportion to being rewarded is not worthy of being rewarded. We should serve and love God for God alone and to love the neighbor for God. These are the infallible rules of charity.

> One of the dinner guests, on hearing this, said to him, "Blessed is anyone who will eat bread in the kingdom of God!" (Luke 14:15)

Eat bread in the kingdom of God is understood in two ways. First, in church is the manifestation of the kingdom of God. *Blessed are those who eat* and eat often! This is a prophecy that says people are blessed who are in the church of God.

Secondly, to *eat bread in the kingdom of God* is also the way of the life of the Word which nourishes the soul. The Spirit flows and moves into our soul to the measure that our propriety has left. In heaven will be the nourishment of the blessed. The One who is the bread and nourishment of the angels will also be the bread of human beings. O the Love of God! O the Word of the Father! Some have said that the intimate union with you is not for this life but only for the other. This is a dangerous abuse to say this and a persuasion that the devil puts in our spirit, so that we do not aspire for this union. Oh! The bread of angels is also the bread of humans! Yes, the Word nourishes the angels and Saints with himself in this life and unites and fills the soul with himself. Oh, happy are those who eat this bread in the kingdom of God in our interior where God lives forever! O true nourishment, supersubstantial bread, daily bread that is always the bread for today! Those who taste and eat this bread are blessed! You pass into them. But those who could taste this so easily but do not are to be pitied! They deprive themselves of this the greatest good and they deny God and grace, so they can preserve a little pleasure.

> Then Jesus said to him, "Someone gave a great dinner and invited many. 17 At the time for the dinner he sent his slave to say to those who had been invited, 'Come; for everything is ready now.' 18 But they all alike began to make excuses. The first said to him, 'I have bought a piece of land, and I must go out and see it; please accept my regrets.'" (Luke 14:16–18)

We are all *invited to a great* and admirable *dinner* but some are invited in a way stronger than others. Those to whom Jesus Christ gives this honor of expressly inviting, an invitation that brings a thousand goods, are these who show an appalling ingratitude by defending themselves against this invitation. A small temporal interest stops them from this honor and pleasure. A *dinner* is the manifestation of Jesus Christ who is the evening's dinner and sacrifice. It is participation in his sufferings and the reception of himself. It is the dinner, because all of this happens in the evening of this mortal life and under the darkness of faith. We should be passionately excited about these great advantages but they are refused because we occupy ourselves with petty bagatelles. This is a strange thing that those who were called more to enjoy this state, refuse and defend themselves against this great good.

> "So the slave returned and reported this to his master. Then the owner of the house became angry and said to his slave, 'Go out at once into the streets and lanes of the town and bring in the poor, the crippled, the blind, and the lame.'" (Luke 14:21)

At the same time that those who are invited to the dinner are exempted, those who were not invited and who are the least in appearance are admitted. Oh, the wonderful way of providence! Amazing for those living by their own ideas of wisdom and justice but consoling for the afflicted poor, who appear to be banished from all hope because they are destitute of all merit. Come, *poor* who are empty. You will be admitted to the feast and Jesus Christ himself will be your plenitude. Come, you *crippled* who appear unable to act for the good. Come to the feast! Jesus Christ sends his ministers to invite you. Jesus Christ himself is your action. Come, you *blind* who seem to be overwhelmed by the darkness. Jesus Christ himself is your light. He is the essential truth who enlightens you. Come, you *lame* who have only crooked paths and have no strength to support yourself. Jesus Christ himself is your strength, support, and righteousness.

These four types of people are opposed and excluded by those who refuse to come to the feast. First, the *poor* are welcomed. Yet, the rich, those taken with their own propriety, will be banished from the feast. The *crippled* are welcomed. Yet, those walking under their own power and refusing to give a place to Jesus Christ within are banished from the feast. This is why they will be deprived of the interior feast. The *blind* are welcomed. Yet, those who are full of their own light and their own reason are banished. They will not yield their own light to that of Jesus Christ's light which is eternal truth. This is why they will be deprived through their own fault of this great goodness. The *lame* are welcomed. Yet, those who rely on their own strength and do not want to allow Jesus Christ to lead them as the Way are banished. They are deprived of the feast, which is to possess Jesus Christ as life and nourishment.

Rapport with Jesus Christ brings justice because there is nothing more. Yet there are three forms of excuses why they do not commune more. Some say they cannot come to the feast because they are embarrassed and attached to things they cannot stop. Others say they cannot come to the feast and pray because it is incompatible with their grand occupation. This is wrong because no occupation should prevent the taste for the admirable interior life, which is an enduring taste. Others excuse themselves from the feast because of their love and enjoyment of pleasures.

> "'Sir,' the servant said, 'what you ordered has been done, but there is still room.' 23 Then the master told his servant, 'Go out to the roads and country lanes and compel them to come in, so that my house will be full. 24 I tell you, not one of those who were invited will get a taste of my banquet.'" (Luke 14:22–24)

Jesus Christ addresses this to pastors, apostles, and priests. It is not enough that they invite sinners and those who have gone astray to come to the banquet but they must have them enter. We must not be discouraged in the pursuit of sinners, because sooner or later they will come to their end, but we must have much gentleness and patience. We see that we must not only pray for the sinners, but we must invite them to come. Far from keeping them out of communion, we must invite and draw them into communion with the kindest disposition. We must ask all the world to enter into this triple feast, but some are contrary enough to keep them away and tell them they cannot take communion. Instead of this, we should help them understand the advantage of going to communion and the necessity of this banquet. We should help them understand that this is both grand and necessary and give them desire to take communion. After they have been given this desire, we must gently help them understand the great price of communion, we are in the position to benefit from this. But without this, one does not take the trouble to acquire it and remains indifferent to its possession. We should only deprive souls of this great good if they are not ready for it and do not understand the grandeur of this and there is no way to help them become ready. This is when they are separated from prayer and communion, without desiring to hope to be introduced to this. They think that this is fine that they are not prepared for communion. Help them enter, O you who have charge of souls and help inspire the appropriate dispositions necessary for them to want to do this. Show them the way to enter, which is the easiest and most comfortable path in the world. We frighten people from this path. We do not teach them how to do this. Instead, we act like this way is practically impossible. Those who have the key do not enter and do not let others in.

But this becomes a terrible place because *those who were invited* to the interior banquet, and who have a special invitation, do not want to enter and make all sorts of excuses. They will never taste of this great good. Not one of them *will get a taste of the banquet* that only taste and experience can make known. *Oh, taste and see that the Lord* is good (Psalm 34:8).

> Now large crowds were traveling with him; and he turned and said to them, 26 "Whoever comes to me and does not hate father and mother, wife and children, brothers and sisters, yes, and even life itself, cannot be my disciple." (Luke 14:25–26)

Oh, that this wisdom be heard! How do we understand the profundity of this? To be a disciple of Jesus Christ, we need to have these dispositions. Jesus Christ proposes two dispositions that hold many others and will in the end bring us to consummation. He does not only say to soften our attachments but to end all that attach us to this world, however just and necessary that they appear. This is a complete and absolute separation of that we hold most dear outside of ourselves, so that nothing can prevent us from following Jesus Christ to all the places that he wants us to go, and on all the paths that he wants to lead us. This is absolutely necessary to be his disciple, but it not necessary for those who do not wish to be his disciple. But again, where do we find people generous enough to leave all the things in the world because of their love of God? For *the proper and self-interested soul* this is impossible. However, this is what must be done and is the consummation of perfection. This hatred carries us to God where we lose ourselves in him and find salvation, as Jesus Christ himself assures us. Oh, this Word brings great things and those who have tested it listen to this wisdom! Without the experience, it is difficult to understand the point of what he is saying.

> "Whoever does not carry the cross and follow me cannot be my disciple." (Luke 14:27)

We need to *carry the cross and follow Jesus Christ*. He is our example. He carried a cross himself, and we should also carry one. We are only pretending to follow Jesus Christ, if we do not suffer as he did. Jesus Christ carried all his states so that we can follow him. This is why he is a unique model so that we can be molded by him. There are some who imitate Jesus Christ and do wonderful things yet cannot imitate him in all things. The lives of the saints are very helpful when we can see how they imitate Jesus Christ. The example of Jesus Christ is the model for all saints and for us to be molded in the same way. As it says in this passage, *And see that you make them according to the pattern for them, which is being shown you on the mountain* (Exodus 25:40). We would have thought this has nothing to do with us because we say, he is God and we are weak creatures. Yet we do what God commands us to do. We deprive ourselves of a great good when we do not look to the examples of the saints, who animate our courage.

> "For which of you, intending to build a tower, does not first sit down and estimate the cost, to see whether he has enough to complete it? 29 Otherwise, when he has laid a foundation and is not able to finish, all who see it will begin to ridicule him, 30 saying, 'This fellow began to build and was not able to finish.'" (Luke 14:28–30)

Jesus Christ tells us this parable to show us that we must take his way to arrive at a successful end. We must first *sit*, that is to enter into the repose of prayer and there in repose we must pray if we have enough to succeed. All the problems of the spiritual life come when we do not take these measures. We think about the temporal and we do not think of the things of God. Then we have marvelous beginnings, fall suddenly, and become the subject of people's ridicule. Some attack devotion and say it is dangerous yet because of this, we have little success. Without devotion, we lose our work and fail. We would build an edifice perfectly, yet one without a foundation. The ardor passes away, the taste dies, and we stop the devotion.

To *build* a solid building, we must *sit down* in the repose of prayer, and examine our strengths and what we are. Unless we want to deceive ourselves, we will soon see our poverty, weakness, and powerlessness. Then far from making a building that will fail, we engage and give it to a powerful and strong man who wants to build a building, provided that it will always be his property. Here is true wisdom. Give your soul to God, so that your soul is always his. He builds a spiritual edifice but a superb one, full of magnificence and dignified for a grand King. He lets us have the use, pleasure, and profit from it while we are content to let him be the owner. O you who want to be saved, accept God's strength!

> "Or what king, going out to wage war against another king, will not sit down first and consider whether he is able with ten thousand to oppose the one who comes against him with twenty thousand? 32 If he cannot, then, while the other is still far away, he sends a delegation and asks for the terms of peace." (Luke 14:31–32)

It is the same with combat against our enemies. All of the spiritual life has only two things: building the spiritual edifice and combatting our enemies who oppose our building. This is why Jesus Christ gives us these two comparisons so appropriate and fair. We have to *oppose* a powerful enemy, who is the Prince of this World: our forces are very weak. If we are not able to overcome the enemy, we must try to *make peace* with him that would only be to our *injury* and *defeat*. What will happen in such a pressure-filled situation? The enemy is already in campaign and coming against us. Against this enemy, there is no assurance of success. He will take away everything we possess. In war against the enemy, we have no power and defense. He is powerful. Our principal soldiers, who are our senses, are half-won by the enemy. When we least expect it, they will turn against us and we will be defeated. What shall we do then? We must commit ourselves to a strong, powerful, and generous Prince, who will defend our kingdom, provided we recognize and acknowledge him as sovereign and principal King. He fights for us, supports us, and destroys our enemies. It will be then that our enemies will not dare attack us, seeing that they do not fight against a weak person but All-Mighty God. Jesus Christ has come into the world to *destroy the Prince of the World*, and he assures that he has *overcome the world* (John 16:33).

> "So therefore, none of you can become my disciple if you do not give up all your possessions." (Luke 14:33)

Jesus Christ makes these two comparisons so beautiful and pure. He assures us that *if we give up all our possessions*, or ourselves, giving him all things in us and for us, we *can become his disciple* because he wants as his disciple people without propriety. O happiness of renunciation! We renounce ourselves so that God possesses us. We give up everything we possess, so God may possess everything. Those who want to be the disciple of Jesus Christ, and still retain the rights over themselves are mistaken.

> "Salt is good; but if salt has lost its taste, how can its saltiness be restored? 35 It is fit neither for the soil nor for the manure pile; they throw it away. Let anyone with ears to hear listen!" (Luke 14:34–35)

Salt is wisdom. This wisdom only has a taste if it comes from divine wisdom and not from human wisdom. If it is not from eternal wisdom, it has *lost its taste* and it is *good for nothing*. It is not even good for the world, that is to say, it cannot even help worldly people. It is not fit *for the manure pile*, or to preserve things from corruption, or to serve to help germinate the earth and make it fruitful. This is why our wisdom, prudence and providence, which we esteem and feel is important, is actually a very little thing. All human measures are frequently used up in a moment. Our wisdom and prudence are found to be without power and efficacy. This passage is support for what we talked about with building and war. All the words of Jesus Christ are for us to know our own uselessness and the advantage we have when we reign with him and remain with him as master of all things. We need only *ears* to understand this truth, and we need to pay attention to God. He will teach us the ear of the heart, and we will see the uselessness of our own efforts, and the advantage of trusting God.

> Now all the tax collectors and sinners were coming near to listen to him. 2 And the Pharisees and the scribes were grumbling and saying, "This fellow welcomes sinners and eats with them." (Luke 14:1–2)

Our Lord always graciously receives sinners because they are more open to receiving his Word than people filled with their own sufficiency. So we work to convert sinners to Jesus Christ. Some say they are unworthy to approach Jesus Christ but we pray that they receive the grace to approach him. If sinners are kept away, they will never be in a state to receive the Word.

Scripture says that these poor *sinners were coming near to listen to him*. My God! If the sinners approach him, they will be justified. But some said this was an error but we need to believe that this is good for sinners or we go against the gospel. Keeping sinners away from Jesus Christ is like keeping the sick away from their medicine. It is easy to see that Jesus Christ bore the most fruit among sinners. Many sinners were saved, who converted and followed Jesus Christ. The doctors and Pharisees did not do this, except for Nicodemus, because they wanted the respect of human beings.

> So he told them this parable: 4 "Which one of you, having a hundred sheep and losing one of them, does not leave the ninety-nine in the wilderness and go after the one that is lost until he finds it? 5 When he has found it, he lays it on his shoulders and rejoices." (Luke 15:3–5)

Our Lord tells us this parable so that we understand the love that he has for sinners and for whom he suffers when they are not with him. Because he will *search* with much goodness the sheep who has gone *astray*, can we doubt that he will find them with joy when they present themselves? O Love! You left the bosom of your Father and all the angels, to search on the earth for poor lost sheep! However, it seems that most humans stray away from you, who are the true way.

When our Lord *finds* this poor lost sheep, he *carries her on his shoulders* because she is too tired to support herself. This good pastor carries her himself but she must allow herself to be carried. If she starts to walk, she will again become lost. O weak and lost souls, let yourself be carried and you will soon be in a safe harbor. Your good master only asks this of you. If we through our faith let ourselves be carried, we will advance in the faith.

> "And when he comes home, he calls together his friends and neighbors, saying to them, 'Rejoice with me, for I have found my sheep that was lost.' 7 Just so, I tell you, there will be more joy in heaven over one sinner who repents than over ninety-nine righteous persons who need no repentance." (Luke 14:6–7)

If the conversion of a sinner gives joy to our divine pastor, then why don't we work to cause him happiness, either by our own conversion or the conversion of others? But in our blindness, we stop our pursuit of sinners, when we meet the least resistance. Sinners only convert through our patience and sweetness. When we act with bitter zeal and expect instant conversions, we will convert very few sinners. Instead, patience, sweetness, and perseverance will win their souls. This is the way our Lord did this when he was on the earth. O pastors! Act contrary to sinners and you will not gain souls for Jesus Christ. It is necessary to have the same patience that he had. Yet today when we have difficulty in the path of perfection, we stop. O sinners! Convert to your God; he strongly wants your conversion.

> Then Jesus said, "There was a man who had two sons. 12 The younger of them said to his father, 'Father, give me the share of the property that will belong to me.' So he divided his property between them. 13 A few days later the younger son gathered all he had and traveled to a distant country, and there he squandered his property in dissolute living." (Luke 15:11–13)

Here is a figure of a sinner who has received very singular graces from God and wastes them on creatures and external things. God gives us a large quantity of talents and gifts so we may love and serve others. To one he gives spirit and beauty, to another riches, and these gifts should give birth to acquired lights, such as giving us a great facility to understand science. We should use all these strong gifts and graces that our Lord has given us through his goodness to love and serve others, but instead we use these gifts for ourselves in the world of creatures. We lose these great goods in debauchery and are changed from a human being into a beast.

> "When he had spent everything, a severe famine took place throughout that country, and he began to be in need. 15 So he went and hired himself out to one of the citizens of that country, who sent him to his fields to feed the pigs." (Luke 15:14–15)

What happens to this sinner who abandons the house of his Father with all his benefits? He is in a *far country* that is far from God, as he approaches creatures. This is why scripture says, that he is *very far away* in considerable sin lasting a long time. This is the opposite of conversion. In conversion he approaches God, and leaves the world of creatures behind without even thinking about leaving creatures. What happens to this poor unfortunate person when he is far away from the strength of God and his father? In leaving the *house of his Father*, who is his heart where God lives, he loses grace, becomes dissipated, and caught in vices of the natural world. He is now destitute of support. The heart that strays away from God remains hungry with an unconceivable *famine*. He will find in the world of creatures nothing that will satisfy him. He needs to change his condition and find freedom from his slavery. He is sold into slavery and has nothing, which is how evil works. However, because of his sins, he is blind and prefers his slavery to his former freedom.

> "He would gladly have filled himself with the pods that the pigs were eating; and no one gave him anything." (Luke 15:16)

O unfortunate sinners! What advantage do they have to follow such a miserable master? When you are at the table of your father, you eat the bread of angels and now you would like to eat the pods that the pigs ate and no one will give you anything. This pig's food that this poor famished person desires are brutal pleasures that are compared to pig's food. They only have the appearance of pleasure and yet have nothing solid. The pleasures of the world are these pleasures like pig's food. They are without life and, when possessed, have nothing solid. They are the opposite of innocent pleasures that we taste in the house of our heavenly Father. There under the appearance of bitterness and a cross runs a deep marrow of pleasures and ineffable delicacies.

> "But when he came to himself he said, 'How many of my father's hired hands have bread enough and to spare, but here I am dying of hunger! 18 I will get up and go to my father, and I will say to him, "Father, I have sinned against heaven and before you; 19 I am no longer worthy to be called your son; treat me like one of your hired hands."'" (Luke 15:17–19)

Oh, if sinners paid some attention to the nobility of the human condition and the advantages they would have in their Father's house! How unfortunate it is to be subjected to sins and enslaved to their passions and how they suffer for their brutality! They would leave their unfortunate state where they reside and they would strongly resolve to go to their loving Father, where even the domestic servants are happy. Here is a child whose soul has received privileged graces but who has abused them. This is why in sadness caused by this unfortunate use of these graces given by his God and his Father, he says, "Truly I am an ungrateful child and the most unfortunate of sinners but my Father is very good. His goodness is a thousand times stronger than my malice. I no longer hope to be one of his children but I will go and speak to him to see if I can be one of his servants and if he will let me work for him. I have lost my inheritance through my own fault. I do not want to stay in this same place, *I will get up* from the state where I am. All my misfortune has happened because I turned away from God and I left the way on which he was leading me. I left his path and turned away from him and now I am taking my first steps to return to God. I will go to him and say, *My Father, I am not worthy to be called your son*. I have lost through my own fault your presence which I should prefer a thousand times over any other. But receive me as the rank of your servant."

> "So he set off and went to his father. But while he was still far off, his father saw him and was filled with compassion; he ran and put his arms around him and kissed him." (Luke 15:20)

Once the sinner resolves to convert a good effect happens. This poor sinner rises from his misery and *went to his father*. O misfortunate fortune! And you, O happy misfortunate! You only have the resolution to return to your father and begin to take the way to return, when your father full of love and tenderness sees you beginning to return to your goodness. O sinner, want to convert! Your resolve has to be as hard as a diamond. What do you fear? Do you fear that you will not be received? Your loving Father *goes ahead* to meet you in love. If you turn, he comes first to meet you, as he himself said, *Return to me, says the Lord* of hosts, and I will return to you, says the *Lord* of hosts (Zechariah 1:3). It is very wrong to say that only the just return to God and not sinners. Sinners who have turned away from the heart of God should return to God's heart. In this scripture we see how sinners convert back to the goodness of God who receives them and goes out to meet them. It is first necessary to break our unhealthy attachments that hold us in this strange country. He says in simplicity, *I will get up and go to the house of my father*. He gets up and he goes to his Father's house. In taking this way returning to God, he leaves without mystery or effort all the attachments that he has to sin. This way is strong and sure. O sinners who are far away from God, return to your heart. You only need to ask to return.

He only makes a few steps to return to his heart, and this Father, full of mercy, goes ahead to meet and guide him. This sinner has pain in his misery and the good Father has compassion on him. Does the Father wait a long time to give him grace? No, he embraces him, he *puts his arms around him*, he gives him the *kiss* of peace, and in his compassion wipes his tears away. O sweetness, O the patience of God! Oh! Is this the way that we treat sinners? The good Father does not even want to speak to him about his disorder so that pain does not mix with his joy. If this prodigal child had not considered his wicked state with horror, he would not have returned to God and he would have been unhappy, afflicted, and guilty for a long time. But when he got up and began the way of returning to God, God goes out to meet him. This place in the Gospel condemns the idea that prayer is not for sinners and that sinners must wait until they are entirely purified and renewed. The good Father does not wait to give the kiss of peace to his son so that all these things be done. The disposition which he wants is for the sinner return. If he returns, the Father is content. He does not ask for many years in penitence. He receives the sinner the very day of his sincere conversion. Not only is he received, but he is honored with a kiss. Oh, kindness without equal! Oh, what consolations for the sinner! Return, O sinner! You can. You have the ability to do this. You are invited. What will you do?

> "Then the son said to him, 'Father, I have sinned against heaven and before you; I am no longer worthy to be called your son.' 22 But the father said to his slaves, 'Quickly, bring out a robe—the best one—and put it on him; put a ring on his finger and sandals on his feet.'" (Luke 15:21–22)

True recognition of faults and the humiliation this brings is the best disposition in which to receive a pardon and to find favors. Nothing pleases God more than humility. God frequently permits certain people who have put virtues aside but are full of their own sufficiency to fall into faults caused by pride so that they may find humility. Whatever fault that we have committed, we do not worry, if we have humility within us. God never fails to forgive us. One cannot believe the confusion of a soul who abuses the strength of God's graces and goodness. The attachments to sin are strong and overwhelm him with confusion. What! He says, "I am so unworthy to approach you and have abused your graces, yet you will make me new! I cannot bear this. Oh, punish me and satisfy your divine justice on me! Oh! The greatest punishment you could give me is not to punish me. I ask you only for the grace to help your servants because I want to serve you." The Father without answering the questions treats the sins as something already forgotten, and does not speak to this point. The Father takes away the idea of who the sinner was and thoroughly consoles him. Finally, the Father does not want him to think of himself as a mercenary servant but as a true child, he gives him *the best robe* of justice and innocence, putting him entirely in purity. He destroys the robe of injustice and sin and gives him the robe of innocence and simplicity. He puts *a ring on his finger*, to mark that all his actions are holy; and sandals are given to him so he can hear. The Father captures all his affections so that they are reunited one to another.

> "And get the fatted calf and kill it, and let us eat and celebrate; 24 for this son of mine was dead and is alive again; he was lost and is found!' And they began to celebrate." (Luke 15:23–24)

The Father's generous love is still not satisfied and he wants his child to come feast at his table to mark their reconciliation. He wants to fill his child with grace and favors. He has a new robe made for him. He gives the best of everything he has to his dear child. From where does this come, O very loving Father, who has done very extraordinary things for your ungrateful child, who has used your first favors only to offend you? He has abused all the Father's goods that were given to him. You give him new favors and are you sure that he will not abuse these? If you receive him so easily, then will he take advantage of you again? Oh! God only consults his goodness in these things. He testifies to his love for the sinner and the joy he has at his return, that he does not measure out his love. O Love! Your love captivates the afflicted heart which would be harmed by miserly rigors. The generous mercy shows him again the grandeur of God's goodness and the happiness he will possess with his Father and makes him more aware of the wrongs he has done. He was *lost* and *is found*, and is *resurrected from death*. The sinner deplores this loss and death, and is astonished at the joy of the Father's possession.

If we wish to enter into the mystical now and pass from the sinner to the soul truly lost in God, we may say, that the more we are lost and the stranger the death, the greater the joy at being found and resurrected.

> "Now his elder son was in the field; and when he came and approached the house, he heard music and dancing. 26 He called one of the slaves and asked what was going on. 27 He replied, 'Your brother has come, and your father has killed the fatted calf, because he has got him back safe and sound.' 28 Then he became angry and refused to go in. His father came out and began to plead with him." (Luke 15:25–28)

The righteous who have always been righteous, and who have not tasted the weakness of sin are frequently like this child. They frequently have zeal full of bitterness, and they cannot endure the mercy that God gives to sinners. They are afflicted and angry. If sinners fall into their hands, they have only severity toward them. It is for this reason that Jesus Christ took sinners for his apostles and pastors. He allowed Peter to fall, so that he would understand the weakness of human beings and the compassion we must have for them. Usually people who have not sinned are not fit to help others. Some go even farther and want to be relieved of the service of God, because newly converted sinners have more favors than they do. But the goodness of the Father of the family is admirable, because he does not leave this soul in his agitation. The Evangelist says that the good and charitable Father *prayed* with his son to come, as if fortune depended on him. Frequently Jesus Christ himself prays that people have pity on sinners. This is easy to see in St. Bernard of Clairvaux's ninth letter to Suger Abbot of St. Denis after his conversion. St. Bernard writes, "A piece of good news has reached our district; it cannot fail to do great good to whomsoever it shall have come. For who that fear God, hearing what great things he has done for your soul." Bernard goes on to describe Suger Abbot's sins and the great gift of salvation that he has received.

> "But he answered his father, 'Listen! For all these years I have been working like a slave for you, and I have never disobeyed your command; yet you have never given me even a young goat so that I might celebrate with my friends. 30 But when this son of yours came back, who has devoured your property with prostitutes, you killed the fatted calf for him!'" (Luke 15:29–30)

This son measures only his reward for the service and does not look at the goodness of the one he serves. People such as this are so proprietary that it appears that they think that God owes them gratitude. In their minds, they should receive all the rewards for their service. They stand on this idea so strongly that it seems they think that God should only have graces for them. God engages sinners who have recently converted to his service with sensible graces. This attracts the jealousy of others, who think the sinners should not have the benefits after the faults they have made. Supporting themselves in their proprietary justice, they speak with contempt of the bad conduct of these sinners and they do not understand that the sins will be a shadow that will serve them eternally to raise them to God's eternal presence. The sins will also be a preservative against pride. When sinners look at themselves, the sight of what they see, causes them extreme humiliation. The more graces that God gives sinners, the more their former opposition and ingratitude appears dark.

> "Then the father said to him, 'Son, you are always with me, and all that is mine is yours. 32 But we had to celebrate and rejoice, because this brother of yours was dead and has come to life; he was lost and has been found.'" (Luke 15:31–32)

In these words we see that God bears a strong and constant love for the elder son. Felt love is for spiritual infants like milk that supports and nourishes. But true and real love, above all feeling because of its purity, is for souls who have already been with God for a long time and who are already strong in his service. A father is always the most tender with a small and young child but he has a firm love for his children and he gives them knowledge of who he is. Although he does not caress him, his life is incomparably precious and the father gives him abundantly out of his goods. However, if we are ignorant, we measure the devotion we receive by the standard of what an infant receives with grace and caresses, which do indeed show the mercy of God and his love, but do not show the most perfect and pure love.

God rejoices at the conversion of a sinner by pouring out generous love and considering only the good for this sinner's conversion. God brings them back to him through pain and regret, yet hastens to reward them when they come back. He slows down the chastisement and sends the touch of his grace to bring them to conversion.

> Then Jesus said to the disciples, "There was a rich man who had a manager, and charges were brought to him that this man was squandering his property. 2 So he summoned him and said to him, 'What is this that I hear about you? Give me an accounting of your management, because you cannot be my manager any longer.' 3 Then the manager said to himself, 'What will I do, now that my master is taking the position away from me? I am not strong enough to dig, and I am ashamed to beg. 4 I have decided what to do so that, when I am dismissed as manager, people may welcome me into their homes.' 5 So, summoning his master's debtors one by one, he asked the first, 'How much do you owe my master?' 6 He answered, 'A hundred jugs of olive oil.' He said to him, 'Take your bill, sit down quickly, and make it fifty.' 7 Then he asked another, 'And how much do you owe?' He replied, 'A hundred containers of wheat.' He said to him, 'Take your bill and make it eighty.' 8 And his master commended the dishonest manager because he had acted shrewdly; for the children of this age are more shrewd in dealing with their own generation than are the children of light." (Luke 16:1–8)

In order to keep us holy, the Lord tells us to watch the needs of our interior life with the same prudence and care that we employ for our temporal affairs. Who does not take the most care with our worldly affairs? Who would risk losing everything if we could take a small precaution that we believe would help? If we cannot take care of our affairs, we trust them to a capable and wise person who helps us. We take these precautions for situations that are not very important. Yet we neglect the matter of salvation which we must endure for eternity, and which is easy to assure. We should place ourselves in the hands of God who takes care of us. Our own self-understanding of our powerlessness shows us not to risk such an important matter. We must remain with God and let him guide us. Oh, then we are very secure, and we will risk nothing!

> "And I tell you, make friends for yourselves by means of dishonest wealth so that when it is gone, they may welcome you into the eternal homes." (Luke 16:9)

The way to *make friends for yourself with wealth* is to help the poor and your neighbor and to do so for the glory of God. We must not regard ourselves as owners of the wealth but as stewards. We are not attached to the riches but are ready to leave them as soon as God asks. When we are not attached to the wealth, we are ready to abandon it without pain. The same riches that frequently cause us to become lost will by this good use become an instrument of our salvation.

> "Whoever is faithful in a very little is faithful also in much; and whoever is dishonest in a very little is dishonest also in much." (Luke 16:10)

The whole affair of our salvation and the establishment of the interior consists in *faithfulness in small things*. The small things are always present and the large things are infrequently present. However, a thousand small occasions allow us to practice the virtues. We are falsely persuaded that we must only be faithful in the grand occasions when they present themselves. This is an abuse that holds most of humanity in its error. Because we are defeated in these small things like gnats, the whole army falls in defeat. It is necessary first to conquer the small things and to be faithful in all the little situations present with us from moment to moment. This is what God asks of us. This is why it is of serious consequence to be attentive to God, to know his movements, and to follow him both inside and outside. We need to be faithful and receive moment to moment what he wants us to do. Everything must be equal to us coming from the hand of God. If we do for God the *small things*, God will give us *large* occasions to work for him and the grace of success. It is the same with injustice and sin. When we neglect our small faults and we have small infidelities, we lose the grand things.

> "Therefore if you have not been faithful in the use of unrighteous wealth, who will entrust the true riches to you? 12 And if you have not been faithful in the use of that which is another's, who will give you that which is your own?" (Luke 16:11–12)

When we are detached from unrighteous wealth, we begin our true piety. The measure of our detachment is the measure of graces from God and progress in true spirituality. When we use our riches in almsgiving and we dedicate this to God, then anything is possible. In following God, we have a very great grace. Usually people who are very charitable sooner or later become interior people.

Yet there are people who work hard to take from others and do not mind the work they do to get these things. They are attached to what they have and must keep it for themselves. They imagine that they have only what they need and that they should give nothing of their own. They feel that they fulfill all the laws of charity by what they do. They are much mistaken in this. By thinking this, they are resting only in their exterior lives and are never in the interior, because they are very much attached to what they own. These people are also very attached to their desires of what they want. They are not about necessities but what they getting more. They are more devoted to themselves than the world. Because of this, they have very few graces, because they are attached to disorderly desires. Their attachments to these desires make them more proprietary, instead of becoming detached from their things.

> "No slave can serve two masters; for a slave will either hate the one and love the other, or be devoted to the one and despise the other. You cannot serve God and wealth." (Luke 16:13)

When one serves wealth and God, we see two excessive disorders. In one example, they serve God with embarrassment. Because they are still embarrassed, they sink lower and lower away from God. They die without ever doing anything for their salvation.

In the second disorder, others practice this by abandoning the care of their family and all of their temporal concerns to God. They believe that it is necessary to do this in order to *serve God*. Yet Jesus Christ does not say that money is not to be used, or that we should not care for our families or that we should not do our duties but he did say that we are *not to serve money*. We should serve God and then money serves us. Those who become enslaved to their passions, filled with avarice to which they show care and attention, are in a form of idolatry. This is why they cannot serve God.

But those who truly love God make God their principal occupation only. They are not concerned about temporal affairs but are dependent on his will. They do not hurry through service to God and they neglect nothing when it comes to service. They also do their duty and are indifferent to whether they have success. They do all things with peace and tranquility. They succeed more in life than those who are anxious to succeed.

> The Pharisees, who were lovers of money, heard all this, and they ridiculed him. 15 So he said to them, "You are those who justify yourselves in the sight of others; but God knows your hearts; for what is prized by human beings is an abomination in the sight of God." (Luke 16:14–15)

Nothing is more opposed to the Spirit of God than pride and *avarice*. This is why the Pharisees who are filled with these two passions had no benefit from the words of Jesus Christ. Their pride prevented them from submitting to his words. They had no humility which made Jesus Christ's word ineffective in them. Avarice hardened their heart, so that the word would not enter their heart. Those who *scoff at the word* and ridicule the truth of the word are usually possessed by one or both pride and avarice. These people *justify themselves in the sight of others*. They try to make themselves look perfect and to do nothing externally that will make others blame them. All their effort is trying to purify the outside and to be irreproachable before other people. But Jesus Christ assures us that this is not essential, and that God sees and *knows* the foundation of the *heart* because everything depends on the faithfulness of the heart. If the heart is true to God, all our actions are done for him and in him. Therefore, it is the interior that God wants and not the exterior. An exterior without an interior is of very little value before God. But an exterior that is ruled by the interior and a life that is animated by the vibrant principle of the interior, and which gives life to all its actions, is that which pleases God. Because God does not judge by external appearances, but only by what is real in the foundation of the heart. This is why Jesus Christ added, *For what is prized by human beings is an abomination in the sight of God.* Human beings stop at the bark and the exterior that is frequently ruled by pride and self-love. Therefore, all consists in the interior, which gives life to all our actions.

When I speak of living actions, I mean only the actions animated by justifying grace, which is common and ordinary grace, without which even the best actions are dead works. But I say that this living principle is only found in the interior and in the foundation of the heart. These people are made into a home for the presence of God in which God is the particular and true principle for all their actions. It is also good that God is their particular principle because they only act then by the movement of God's Spirit, to which they are very attentive. Instead of violating the action of God by their self-motivated actions, they follow the Spirit's movement, like a child who is led by sweet and easy actions from the hands of a loving parent. If the child does otherwise, he tries to force the hands of his parent and does false actions. We see that the master is stronger, yet God never forces the will of his children so everything depends on the suppleness of his child to let the hand of his parent guide him. If the child lets the parent lead him, all goes well but if he resists the parent, he will develop defective traits.

> "Until John the Baptist, the law of Moses and the messages of the prophets were your guides. But now the good news of the kingdom of God is preached, and everyone is eager to get in. 17 But that doesn't mean that the law has lost its force. It is easier for heaven and earth to disappear than for the smallest point of God's law to be overturned." (Luke 16:16–17)

Jesus Christ assures us that the rigors of *the law* and the testimony of *the prophets lasted until John*, which is the figure of penitence. All of this came through penitence and introduced the soul into the interior. But since that time, the interior kingdom, which is the preached kingdom of God, has its effect. Then the letter and the rigor of the law entered into the Spirit and love of the law. Containing a strong exterior and letter of the law, the interior Spirit of the law must accomplish everything before the end of the world.

> "There was a rich man who was dressed in purple and fine linen and who feasted sumptuously every day. 20 And at his gate lay a poor man named Lazarus, covered with sores, 21 who longed to satisfy his hunger with what fell from the rich man's table; even the dogs would come and lick his sores. 22 The poor man died and was carried away by the angels to be with Abraham. The rich man also died and was buried." (Luke 16:19–22)

Jesus Christ tells us this story so that we see the difference between the poor who have no help or good things in life, while living under a cross with misery, as opposed to the rich, full of pleasures and satisfactions, who have everything they wish. Oh, their strength is so different from this life and the next life! In this life the rich man had an abundance of all goods, and in the next the assembly of all evils. These goods were terminated and now he entered into inconceivable evils. Oh, the abuse he made of his goods! But the poor man, whose strange sorrows cause this story, finds his evils terminated and infinite goods follow his suffering. He has great abundance in proportion to the sorrows he has known. O God! To what happiness do the crosses, bitterness, persecutions, sufferings and poverty lead us! And what horrible misfortune do pleasures, sensualities, and abundance lead us.

> "In Hades, where he was being tormented, he looked up and saw Abraham far away with Lazarus by his side. 24 He called out, 'Father Abraham, have mercy on me, and send Lazarus to dip the tip of his finger in water and cool my tongue; for I am in agony in these flames.' 25 But Abraham said, 'Child, remember that during your lifetime you received your good things, and Lazarus in like manner evil things; but now he is comforted here, and you are in agony.'" (Luke 16:23–25)

The mercy of God is infinite but it is only the time of this life that can bring this to us. When God's goodness has been rejected, we are not certain that we are pardoned. If we have scorned God, we may not be received in him. As long as we live, we may and must always hope in the mercy of God. But after this life, there may be nothing left for us. If we have in this life *received good things*, pleasures, and success, we may in the next life have inconceivable *torments*. But if our portion is to receive the *cross*, we shall have in the next life goods and glory.

> "'Besides all this, between you and us a great chasm has been fixed, so that those who might want to pass from here to you cannot do so, and no one can cross from there to us.'"(Luke 16:26)

This is an inconceivable *chasm* and an almost infinite space between a justified and predestined soul and an unrepentant sinner. It is entirely incompatible that they remain together. One may not go with the other. It is impossible for them to have rapport: justice with injustice; simplicity and innocence with propriety; truth with lies. And if, though impossible, a demon went to heaven, he would change this place into hell for himself, and the blessed would suffer from the extreme disorder caused by the demon. If a saint went to hell, her purity would increase the torment of the damned by heightening their sense of impurity.

> "Then he said, 'I beg you therefore, father, that you would send him to my father's house, 28 for I have five brothers, that he may testify to them, lest they also come to this place of torment.'" (Luke 16:27–28)

This unhappy man's request was not a prayer of charity, of which the damned are incapable, but a prayer of rage and chagrin. The sight of Lazarus in his glory increased the rich man's torment because he saw how different their fates were. His rage and jealousy caused him to ask that Lazarus be sent to his brothers, not that he desires the salvation of his brothers, but that he wants to deprive Lazarus of the happiness that he enjoys. Often sinners are the same. They try to draw the saints away from the good that they enjoy under the pretext of charity and care for others. They cannot endure the saints' retreat and solitude. Under a pretext of public charity, they deprive them of their solitude so that these interior souls are tormented.

> "Abraham replied, 'They have Moses and the prophets; they should listen to them.' 30 He said, 'No, father Abraham; but if someone goes to them from the dead, they will repent.' 31 He said to him, 'If they do not listen to Moses and the prophets, neither will they be convinced even if someone rises from the dead.'" (Luke 16:29–31)

Those who are not converted by the ordinary ways that God send them every day, will also not be converted by extraordinary ways. This is why Abraham does not do as the rich man asks. Jesus Christ himself did not perform miracles as people asked him to do, because those who do not let themselves be touched and loved by the Word, will not be won by miracles. The miracles support and confirm the word but the word alone must operate the conversion. Throughout history we see the necessity of discipline and spiritual poverty for our spiritual growth. Having a rich exterior and interior are damaging if we do not remain in need and allow ourselves to lose our propriety.

> The apostles said to the Lord, "Increase our faith!" (Luke 17:5)

The apostles understood how very necessary faith is. With faith they will persevere in their way and succeed in their ministry. The apostles pray that their faith increases more and more. Nothing works in ministry except through faith. The whole interior does not begin, or continue, or reach perfection except through faith. At the beginning, with a strong and sustained faith, faith multiplies our ministry. Next comes our passive faith. Then a naked faith deprived of all support, maintains us and we taste and experience faith. Faith might be no longer known to the person who possesses it. Nevertheless, the person has a strong faith, even though the faith does appear to her to be small.

> "Who among you would say to your slave who has just come in from plowing or tending sheep in the field, 'Come here at once and take your place at the table'? 8 Would you not rather say to him, 'Prepare supper for me, put on your apron and serve me while I eat and drink; later you may eat and drink'? 9 Do you thank the slave for doing what was commanded? 10 So you also, when you have done all that you were ordered to do, say, 'We are worthless slaves; we have done only what we ought to have done!'" (Luke 17:7–10)

If we have done what we are *obliged to do*, we will be very happy. But which of us feels this way? Why in our vanity do we feel that we do so well? God in his mercy accepts our services. It is this understanding of the uselessness of creatures that persuades truly interior people to regard their work as nothing. They are useless to the accomplishment of all good and they do not believe that they have done anything good. This view of their uselessness does not, however, lead them to neglect their duties as some imagine. To the contrary, they see themselves as little, and they do as much as they can, believing that they always do too little. They do not rely on their works and their works do not carry them.

> On the way to Jerusalem Jesus was going through the region between Samaria and Galilee. As he entered a village, ten lepers approached him. Keeping their distance, they called out, saying, "Jesus, Master, have mercy on us!" When he saw them, he said to them, "Go and show yourself to the priests." And as they went, they were made clean. (Luke 17:11–19)

Lepers here represent sinners: the one who is healed and returns to Jesus Christ has contrition and receives the secret and divine virtues of Jesus Christ that enter him at the time of conversion. Jesus Christ sent them to the priests to confess and on the way they were made clean. Jesus wanted the others to yield to him also, yet they refused to submit, and they refuse their healing. To go *show themselves to the priests* is no other thing than to show the leprosy of our sins so we can be healed. Yet if this way of sincere resolution is taken, we are healed. When we ask forgiveness from God with good faith and the melting of our heart, like the lepers, then we have the disposition to show ourselves to the priest. Our brothers and sisters who deprive themselves of this benefit also deprive themselves of true healing. Instead, they should go show themselves to the priests to confess, to be done according to the ancient law in a particular way, to be confirmed and established by Jesus Christ, as the apostles have taught. *Confess your sins to one another* (James 5:16).

> Then one of them, when he saw he was healed, turned back, praising God with a loud voice. He prostrated himself at Jesus' feet and thanked him. And he was a Samaritan. Then Jesus asked, "Were not ten made clean? But the other nine, where are they? Was none of them found to return and give praise to God except this foreigner?" Then he said to him, "Get up and go on your way; your faith has made you well." (Luke 17:15–19)

There are many who are healed from their sin and become converted, but there are only a few whose conversion lasts. Those who leave have a lack of gratitude. They do not attribute everything to God alone for his power to heal that they have received. God uses many means to heal us and we frequently attribute most of everything to the creature and very little to God. This is an abuse and a very great wrong toward God. We do not show God the gratitude that he deserves. Only a foreigner gives thanks for the healing, and he was not under the authority of the law. Who was this man? He glorifies God with all his power in a loud voice. He attributes his healing to the mercy of God. He falls down at Jesus' feet, his face against the earth, for a profound annihilation in which he reenters in the dust of his meanness and his baseness. He remains in this position at the feet of Jesus Christ, content to give thanks in his baseness and meanness with his profound silence, with no words. He was not only healed, but confirmed in his healing. Go, says Jesus, your *faith has saved you*, your health is confirmed, and your health has come because of your faith. You have not attributed your healing to any human being, but to me only.

> Once Jesus was asked by the Pharisees when the kingdom of God was coming, and he answered, "The kingdom of God is not coming with things that can be observed; 21 nor will they say, 'Look, here it is!' or 'There it is!' For, in fact, the kingdom of God is among you." (Luke 17:20–21)

The *kingdom of God is within us* is a natural and true explanation. How can we doubt this? Where should we search to find the reign of God and do we need anything extraordinary to find this? This passage confirms what is said: we search for God in our hearts. Nothing extraordinary needs to light our way to find the kingdom of God. We do not need to seek outside of ourselves for the kingdom of God, neither do we need to seek in another place for the kingdom of God. The *kingdom of God is within us*. It is within that we must search. It is the easiest thing in the world to have this strength. We stand within before our King to be united with him and have part of his kingdom. If the kingdom of God is within us, it is necessary to let him reign in us with the righteousness of the sovereign King, giving him everything we have, and letting him guide and govern us. O my Sovereign King! I will do nothing else but to stand in my foundation in silence and peace, waiting for what you command us to do. All my pleasure is obeying you and I will do your will without reserving anything. Jesus Christ is truly the King within us, and when my Sovereign commands, I obey without resistance.

> Then he said to the disciples, "The days are coming when you will long to see one of the days of the Son of Man, and you will not see it." (Luke 17:22)

The state that Jesus Christ describes to his disciples is one of a sensible and perceptible presence of Jesus Christ. Therefore the soul suffers a strange grief when she loses this and ardently desires to have this. However, this loss must happen. "If I do not go away," he says in John 16:7, "*The Advocate will not come to you; but if I go, I will send him to you.*" It is necessary therefore to lose this sensible presence. The afflicted soul who does not understand this loss is at a disadvantage. She ardently longs to *see one of the days of the Son of Man* but she *will not see it*, because if the Lord grants this, she will have an inferior grace which will be communicated to other souls.

> "For as the lightning flashes and lights up the sky from one side to the other, so will the Son of Man be in his day. 25 But first he

must endure much suffering and be rejected by this generation."
(Luke 17:24–25)

Jesus Christ's days of light disappear little by little. But when he comes as a second advent in the soul, it is a day different from the first. He comes with promptitude and surprises us when we least expect it and enters the entire soul. Everything in the soul is filled with Jesus Christ when he enters the soul as Word and he becomes mystically incarnate, which is *the last advent*. This day is prompt and sudden, yet he remains for eternity. But before this great happiness arrives, the soul must first have carried Jesus Christ crucified, she must have *suffered* with him in his passion, or rather, carried the states of his suffering. She must have been *rejected*, condemned and despised through all the world.

> "On that day, anyone on the housetop who has belongings in the house must not come down to take them away; and likewise anyone in the field must not turn back." (Luke 17:31)

This view is important for the whole spiritual life. It is what can strengthen or prevent the interior life when one is in the midst of crosses, sufferings and when one carries the states of Jesus Christ. As we are in a state of entire naked openness and vulnerability, it sometimes appears good to, already being raised to a very sublime level of loss and stripping, *descends* to lower degrees because they are more satisfying. It is *coming down to take them away*, the gifts, virtues, graces, and favors, and obtaining them by our own work. This is what ought never to be done and what most do, for lack of understanding the counsel of Jesus Christ. *Then the one who is in the field*, that is to say, the one who is already in freedom, *must not turn back* under a pretext, and wanting to return to his first slavery and captivity. All the disorder and evil in the spiritual life comes from these two things.

> "Remember Lot's wife." (Luke 17:32)

Our Lord gives us an example to know that we must never look back under any pretext, either out of fear or curiosity. These are the two things that will make us turn back. In fear we doubt and hesitate, and we return because we are looking for assurance. In curiosity, we want to know where we are, and the way that we have gone. All these returns or reflections are to be avoided. However, as it is said, it is prudent to use our strength. *Lot's wife* was changed into a statue of salt, to mark, that being too wise is to lack real wisdom. Human wisdom stops and prevents the soul from advancing.

> "Those who try to make their life secure will lose it, but those who lose their life will keep it." (Luke 17:33)

Jesus Christ confirms in these last words all that he has said in this passage. If someone fears, doubts, or hesitates in the way of abandon and searches for a way to *save* herself, then inevitably she will lose herself and experience a heavy fall. God permits this as a consequence for her defiance. But if someone *loses her life* by abandon into the hands of God, without care or worry about herself, without fear, doubt, or hesitation, and no self-concern, then she will be revived. She will enter into a new life where her death will be assured and her salvation will be more assured. She will find salvation in her total loss. The bosom of death will be a source of life. Notice what Jesus Christ says, *Those who lose their life*, freely and generously, *will find life for their souls*, and enter through their loss into new life.

> Then Jesus told them a parable about their need to pray always and not to lose heart. 2 He said, "In a certain city there was a judge who neither feared God nor had respect for people. 3 In that city there was a widow who kept coming to him and saying, 'Grant me justice against my opponent.' 4 For a while he refused; but later he said to himself, 'Though I have no fear of God and no respect for anyone, 5 yet because this widow keeps bothering me, I will grant her justice, so that she may not wear me out by continually coming.'" 6 And the Lord said, "Listen to what the unjust judge says. 7 And will not God grant justice to his chosen ones who cry to him day and night? Will he delay long in helping them? 8 I tell you, he will quickly grant justice to them." (Luke 18:1–8)

This parable of Jesus Christ shows us that prayer of the heart, interior prayer, and faith are good. We must *pray continually* without getting tired. This Gospel expresses this with strength, yet it is impossible to pray continually without wearying if we use vocal prayers or reasoned discourse. It is necessary to pray continually in a way compatible with all the states of being. This prayer begins in the heart and becomes stronger. Slowly but surely this prayer of faith becomes continual. The soul becomes stronger and obtains all it desires and only desires what is given to it. Jesus Christ assures us that God becomes the both the avenger and support of these souls. What manner does he use to avenge us? He defends us against our enemies and removes us from sin. He defends us against demons. Sooner or later, he avenges our persecutions and outrageous abuse from other people. He assures us that he does not desert us, that is to say, he is always ready to help when we are in need. We are to remain in our continual prayer and abandonment to him without reservation. *He will quickly grant justice* to us from our enemies. His help will be as prompt as our need is urgent.

> "And yet, when the Son of Man comes, will he find faith on earth?" (Luke 18:8)

Jesus Christ confirms here in this place what he has said about the prayer of faith. The one who does not pray continually has no excuse; it is a defect of faith. Jesus Christ *will not find faith on earth*. But if we take another way and enter into prayer and in the way of faith, this prayer obtains all that we desire. The prayer of faith is more like a state of being than a prayer because it is continual in all situations.

> He also told this parable to some who trusted in themselves that they were righteous and regarded others with contempt. (Luke 18:9)

Jesus Christ also addressed those who trust in their own goodness and their exterior life, while easily condemning others and having *contempt* for them in their hearts. They elevate themselves with complacency about how good they are and against those they despise. They are filled with pride and think they are justified before God. They do not praise themselves, yet they praise all those who are like them. They take every occasion to debase others and tear them down. Oh, what pride and lack of charity in these bright and extraordinary lives! They rely on their own justice. They place all their *trust* in their works and diminish the trust they must have in God.

> "Two men went up to the temple to pray, one a Pharisee and the other a tax collector. 11 The Pharisee, standing by himself, was praying thus, 'God, I thank you that I am not like other people: thieves, rogues, adulterers, or even like this tax collector. 12 I fast twice a week; I give a tenth of all my income.'" (Luke 18:10–12)

This prayer, according to the common prayer, appears to the most just in the world because finally, what is more just than to thank God for the mercy he has done? Thinking about ourselves is never perfect, although it is not always criminal. If we reflect on graces with good reason, often we are raised up. If we on think on misery, we are discouraged. If we do not see God and see all the good he has made in relation to others, we prefer ourselves in our heart. We take occasion to blame and condemn others. The greatest mark of pride is to support our manner of extraordinary life on the debris of others. What could be more just than *to fast twice a week*, to be exact in their duties, to do good and not to do evil? However, these things, even if good and true in themselves, serve only to support their own self-love. This is condemnable because they trust in their works and in themselves, which are nothing. But the works on which we rely and which support our own understanding of justice are corrupt and dirtied. True and pure works are those which are done out of faith.

> "But the tax collector, standing far off, would not even look up to heaven, but was beating his breast and saying, 'God, be merciful to me, a sinner!' 14 I tell you, this man went down to his home justified rather than the other." (Luke 18:13–14)

O my God! This is true goodness that you do not ask for an arrangement of speeches in prayers, but a humble and sincere prayer pleases you! Who speaks the most, the Pharisee or the tax collector? It is easy to see. The tax collector says only one thought in his profound humility. He says to God, *Be merciful to me, a sinner!* He expects everything from God's goodness. Following this he remains abased and in humility; he *would not even look up to heaven*. That is to say, not even daring to consider God, but to remain annihilated. He remains content in his single prayer and does not consider himself worthy of being noticed. He says only, *God, be merciful to me, a sinner!* These words with this disposition of profound annihilation instantly turn the sinner into a saint. Will it be possible after this to find it wrong that sinners pray in this way? O poor sinners! Pray only like this and you will be justified. A heart persuaded of its misery and annihilated under its weight can only pray in this way when abased in the dust of its nothingness. Oh, this prayer is efficacious! If Jesus Christ had not said this, who would have thought about this difference between prayers? Who would not regard the tax collector as a criminal? Yet the tax collector receives the graces of God, and also receives the glory of God.

> "For all who exalt themselves will be humbled, but all who humble themselves will be exalted." (Luke 18:14)

Oh how good it is to rest in our annihilation before God! This prayer is efficacious in all things. Whoever stands in her nothingness, will be exalted. But whoever exalts herself and her own understandings will be humbled. We are mistaken if we pretend to be annihilated before God so that we will be carried to extraordinary things.

> People were bringing even infants to him that he might touch them; and when the disciples saw it, they sternly ordered them not to do it. 16 But Jesus called for them and said, "Let the little children come to me, and do not stop them; for it is to such as these that the kingdom of God belongs. 17 Truly I tell you, whoever does not receive the kingdom of God as a little child will never enter it." (Luke 18:15–17)

This passage is placed in the gospel following this parable to mark the simplicity with which God wants us to go to him. *When the disciples saw it, they sternly ordered them not to do it.* This happens today when people say, this path is not for the children of grace. But Jesus Christ defends them and assures them saying, *For it is to such as these that the kingdom of God belongs.* This includes both the interior kingdom, which they want to make inaccessible, and heaven. The best disposition to find God is to be simple and childlike, and to go to him in this way. God asks nothing extraordinary of us, and he even *swears by this truth*, that *whoever does not receive the kingdom of God as a little child will never enter it.* It is impossible to taste the interior kingdom if we are not humble and do not enter into a spiritual childhood. Those who are sufficient in themselves do not enter into the interior kingdom.

> He entered Jericho and was passing through it. 2 A man was there named Zacchaeus; he was a chief tax collector and was rich. 3 He was trying to see who Jesus was, but on account of the crowd he could not, because he was short in stature. 4 So he ran ahead and climbed a sycamore tree to see him, because he was going to pass that way. 5 When Jesus came to the place, he looked up and said to him, "Zacchaeus, hurry and come down; for I must stay at your house today." 6 So he hurried down and was happy to welcome him. (Luke 19:1–6)

This man was the *chief tax collector* and he was very *rich*. To be the chief tax collector is to have work that appears to be opposed to all conversion. In terms of being rich, Jesus Christ says that it is very difficult for the rich to enter into the kingdom of heaven. However, this chief tax collector wants to see Jesus Christ and puts himself in a place where Jesus Chris can see him. O divine Savior! You desire nothing else but to save human beings! However, we might falsely tell ourselves that this is too difficult. How does Jesus Christ save a sinner? First, he *climbed a sycamore tree to see* Jesus. He wants to know and deepen his understanding of who Jesus Christ is. It is a very good disposition for a beginning. What does Jesus Christ do? He said, *Zacchaeus, hurry and come down* and enter into the interior of your heart, in smallness where you will dwell naturally in annihilation. He says, *I must stay at your house today*. Oh, what advantage! We must note that scripture says, he was *rising up*, because he was small, rising up in consideration and reasoning. A soul that remains in its smallness and in its annihilation is good to receive Jesus Christ. Then is why he tells Zacchaeus to *Come down*, that is to say: "Place yourself in your state of smallness and in your natural state. You will find happiness in me and happiness to see me at your home. It is not necessary to make an extraordinary effort to find me. You find me when you will be in your place." Jesus Christ tells him to come down in a *hurry* because we must not delay a moment when Jesus Christ calls us. Otherwise, the call passes away.

First, Zacchaeus watches for him and then attracts him. Oh, happy watching! He joins this watching with the anointing of his word, which is a sweet peace that invites the soul to enter into its smallness, and to come promptly. He comes into recollection to receive Jesus. This prompt correspondence without waiting a moment works in the economy of grace. This is why scripture adds, *So he hurried down and was happy to welcome Jesus with great joy*. He does not wait a moment to descend. And his descent causes a great good! He is ready to receive Jesus Christ. With what joy does this poor sinner receive such a great good! He is all outside of himself. What, he says, O divine Savior! O Love that I love forever! Even if I know you only a little, you will come to my house and fill my heart with joy. Joy makes me quiet and respect for Jesus rescues me. Zacchaeus does not apologize for his indignity and does not say, like St. Peter, "Depart from me, for I am a sinful man" (Luke 5:8). He forgets everything about who he has been and thinks only of receiving Jesus Christ. He is persuaded that whatever miseries he has, Jesus Christ is all-powerful and can rescue him from all of them. He has given the necessary dispositions and states to received Jesus Christ.

> All who saw it began to grumble and said, "He has gone to be the guest of one who is a sinner." (Luke 18:7)

It seems that even as Jesus Christ has only goodness for sinners and a desire to save them, while people oppose the salvation that Jesus Christ communicates to them. They *grumble* and are scandalized that sinners go to Jesus and think there is a risk in saving sinners. Jesus Christ came to search for sinners with care. They began to murmur against Jesus who searches for sinners and gives himself to them, and *he goes home with them*. We must not be surprised if we still find people today who murmur against people who ask sinners to let Jesus Christ enter their hearts. But as the murmurs of the people did not stop Jesus Christ from going with Zacchaeus, all the noise from people does not stop us from inviting sinners to let Jesus enter their heart. Come, poor sinners, whoever you are. Do not be afraid to approach him. He is your sovereign medicine. He will heal you of all your illness. If you wait to approach him for healing, you might never approach him. For how will you be healed if you do not approach Jesus Christ who is the medicine and the remedy?

> Zacchaeus stood there and said to the Lord, "Look, half of my possessions, Lord, I will give to the poor; and if I have defrauded anyone of anything, I will pay back four times as much." (Luke 19:8)

O wonderful effect of the presence of God, when it is manifest and discovered in the heart! If they would have preached a lot to Zacchaeus, would he have done this? Who advised him to do this? In the strictest sense, he would have only been obliged to repair the wrong he had done. O Love! When you give yourself, you find a superabundant mercy that works a superabundant penitence! It is necessary to note these two things. First, restitution and perfect conversion were made in Zacchaeus only after he received Jesus. Secondly, we see his conversion in his works, yet Jesus did not tell him in exterior words to do any of these things. Only Jesus Christ's presence inspired these sentiments. Those who believe that Zacchaeus must be free of faults before looking for Jesus, occupying with his presence, standing with him and receiving him in his heart, will see that Jesus Christ did not do this with Zacchaeus. The conversion is not done externally and is not accomplished with external perfection, but is done well in his interior. Oh, if an interior conversion is done it is durable and permanent! If we require sinners to stop a thousand things to which they are attached, without attaching their heart to Jesus Christ, conversion is impossible. Attach the heart to God and nothing else will cost anything to do. We should also note that it is the conversion which God's presence makes abundance.

> Then Jesus said to him, "Today salvation has come to this house, because he too is a son of Abraham. 10 For the Son of Man came to seek out and to save the lost." (Luke 19:9–10)

O God! When you *come* in a heart, and make your presence known, it is then that the soul *receives salvation*, and a very abundant salvation, that is durable and lasting, because it is not supported on the weakness of the creatures. The soul melts into God alone. When the soul discovers God in her foundation, and she searches for God with all her heart, her salvation is durable and permanent.

This man, says Jesus Christ, *is a son of Abraham*, but not because he is Jewish. He is a child of Abraham because he has faith. According to Paul, Abraham is the father of all those who believe. Jesus Christ then assures us that he has *come to save and seek those who are lost*. According to this, would he reject sinners and the lost when they present themselves to him?

> So he said, "A nobleman went to a distant country to get royal power for himself and then return.... 14 But the citizens of his country hated him and sent a delegation after him, saying, 'We do not want this man to rule over us.'" (Luke 19:12, 14)

We are frequently like these rebellious subjects who do not want to acknowledge Jesus Christ as king, though he came from heaven to reign in us. He does not ask anything else except to reign in our heart. And yet we resist him! He *rejoices in his inhabited world and delights in the human race* (Proverbs 8:31) and yet we prevent his reign in us. He comes to be King, and his people did not receive him. But who are these people who do not submit to his sweet empire, though this kingdom belongs to him with many titles? Listen to him.

> "'But as for these enemies of mine who did not want me to be king over them—bring them here and slaughter them in my presence.'" (Luke 19:27)

They will die like criminals. It is therefore to be criminal not to submit to Jesus Christ and let him reign within. O divine King! Reign in our hearts! You are born king. You have bought the kingdom with your own blood. You have the kingdom as a conqueror. We give you all the rights over us.

> As he was now approaching the path down from the Mount of Olives, the whole multitude of the disciples began to praise God joyfully with a loud voice for all the deeds of power that they had seen, 38 saying, "Blessed is the king who comes in the name of the Lord! Peace in heaven, and glory in the highest heaven!" (Luke 19:37–38)

The soul that is in *descent*, that is to say, in the way of annihilation, begins to know and discover the *miracles* of God. She sees then that everything is of God and the miracles he has made. God operates in the soul in such a wonderful way that our losses come from the hand of God as a favor and as a means for salvation. It is then that she sings this hymn with all her heart, *Blessed is the King who comes in the name of the Lord*, who brings *peace in heaven*, that is to say, in the foundation of the soul. *Glory in the highest heaven* is in the highest part of the same soul.

> Some of the Pharisees in the crowd said to him, "Teacher, order your disciples to stop." 40 He answered, "I tell you, if these were silent, the stones would shout out." (Luke 19:39–40)

The Pharisees could not suffer the disciples of Jesus Christ giving him glory in all things and attributing everything to his power. This is why they ask Jesus Christ to silence his disciples. But the divine Master teaches them how pleasing and right the disciples' conduct is. He assures them that if his disciples, who are his true children, do not publish his glory, inanimate objects, signified by *stones*, will publish his glory.

> As he came near and saw the city, he wept over it, 42 saying, "If you, even you, had only recognized on this day the things that make for peace! But now they are hidden from your eyes." (Luke 19:41–42)

Jesus Christ cries over Jerusalem but the tears of the Savior were not only for this certain city. They were also for all the souls who did not benefit from these days and times of grace. It is so easy to have interior faith and yet many do not want it. We do not know how to take advantage of the day that is given to us, which is a day of *peace*. Oh, if we knew how to profit from this day and discover this in our interior, what peace would we taste? But because we do not profit from grace in the interior, we fall into some blindness and we are incapable of comprehending the things of the Spirit. The Jews ardently desired the Messiah that had been told them by the prophets, but he was neither received nor known by them when he came. We frequently do the same. We spend all of our life in desire for him and when Jesus Christ comes and is in the middle of us, that is in our heart, where he asks no other thing that we receive him as King and Savior, we do not want to recognize him. We content ourselves with just wanting him.

> "Indeed, the days will come upon you, when your enemies will set up ramparts around you and surround you, and hem you in on every side. 44 They will crush you to the ground, you and your children within you, and they will not leave within you one stone upon another; because you did not recognize the time of your visitation from God." (Luke 19:43–44)

There comes *an unhappy time for souls* who have not given themselves to God and not received God within, when *your enemies besiege and surround you*. They then necessarily perish because they have no place of refuge. When there are *ramparts* around them, and the enemy besieges all parts without a place of refuge, they will perish. We often place our refuge in our own work, which is a weak wall that the enemy easily destroys. But if we have an interior refuge where we are accustomed to follow God when we are attacked, we have in God a strong and impenetrable citadel, equipped with everything that is needed, where we can rest in peace. We respond with perfect assurance, while our enemies make vain efforts to try to take us and harm us.

> "Therefore settle it in your hearts not to meditate beforehand on what you will answer; 15 for I will give you a mouth and wisdom which all your adversaries will not be able to contradict or resist." (Luke 21:14–15) New King James translation

This wisdom of Jesus Christ shows the wisdom of abandonment into his hands, which he wants all people to have. We need to let him lead us in all things. *I will give you a mouth* and not only a word. The Word himself speaks through this mouth. By means of this mouth he communicates in souls. When speaking with continual wisdom, all her enemies remain mute, because they are convicted and terrified by this word of truth. But to whom does God give this mouth and wisdom? It is not to those who have their own proper wisdom but to those who *do not prepare their defense in advance* and who abandon themselves to God in all things.

> "You will be betrayed even by parents and brothers, by relatives and friends; and they will put some of you to death." (Luke 21:16)

All those who truly want God must expect persecution. Of all persecutions, there are no stronger ones made than against abandoned souls. All seem to have the right to persecute and cause pain to abandoned souls, even friends and relatives. The faithful should have the docility to receive the movements of grace. The world regards this as a defect of the mind not to prepare what one ought to say and not to defend oneself against persecution and calumny. It suffices, though, to be with God and to considered the refuse of the world.

> "You will be hated by all because of my name 18 but not a hair of your head will perish." (Luke 21:17–18)

If we are hated by the world, and struggle with all their lies and contradictions, then we are to rejoice and be happy. Jesus Christ assures his apostles and his true children that he will care for them. But also, they are assured that our good God will let no evil be done to them. Frequently apostles lose their lives in their ministries. This would seem repugnant to what Jesus Christ says, *But not a hair of your head will perish*. We will not lose a hair by the persecution of which God keeps a very exact account. God will not let us perish. He remembers everything to reward us. He keeps records of even a small circumstance and rewards us with interest on it. Yet God does not examine our faults with rigor. He closes his eyes. He forgets our sins which we have converted to him. Alas! If he looked at our iniquities, who could stand before him? God knows our weakness and has compassion. He does not punish us but he rewards even the smallest good that we have done, although he is the one working this in us. Human beings do the opposite. They forget all the good that has been for them after even the smallest injury. They do not forget the injury but they do forget the good.

> "By your endurance you will gain your souls." (Luke 21:19)

The theological virtues of faith, hope, and love are essential because they carry us, yet we need the virtue of patience in the spiritual life of repose. Patience brings the reward because patience carries and presupposes many other virtues. To be patient we need faith and hope as well as being animated by love. Patience is always accompanied by humility, gentleness, and modesty. We need to be humble to be patient. This is why it is written, *The learning of a human being is known by patience and his glory is to pass over wrongs* (Proverbs 19:31 Douay Reams Translation). Only a person with a generous heart will pass over wrongs done to her.

We see that patience is a chain of virtues. We all agree that patience is beautiful and necessary; when we acquire it we *gain our soul by endurance* and patience.

Patience is difficult because it is the daughter of humility. As there is very little humility in the human race, there is also very little patience. We cannot obtain patience through intellectual efforts or power. Even if we have patience, we may become irritated and lose it.

The way to acquire patience is to collect ourselves in our interior faith and sink deeply into this when we have an attack of impatience. In this recollection or contemplation for souls who are still weak, impatience is suddenly extinguished without any additional effort except to hold oneself close to God. Patience is substituted in place of the growing impatience. Impatience frequently changes into anger when it is not caught in its early stages. We must not fight against impatience directly or it will never end.

We must extend patience to God, to our neighbor, and to ourselves. It might seem strange to say we need patience with God, yet without this we will not advance. We must suffer God's absences, rigors, and the weight of his justice. David said, *I waited for the Lord with great patience, and at last he humbled himself to me* (Psalm 40:1). We must suffer all the crosses, illnesses, and interior pains that God sends us. Patience with God is the most difficult to have.

We must also have patience with our neighbor, suffering all that he does to us, all the moods, all the faults and weaknesses, and all the persecutions.

We must also have a lot of patience with ourselves, to suffer our own weakness, misery, poverty, and things that happen to us by our own lack of wisdom and folly. We must have patience for the crosses that we bring on ourselves. This patience is necessary because we are always with ourselves. We can get rid of other creatures, but we cannot get rid of ourselves.

When we are patient in these ways, we *gain our souls* in a perfect peace. We may only possess our soul in peace and tranquility. Without peace, we may not even know our soul for it is agitated.

> "Be on guard so that your hearts are not weighed down with dissipation and drunkenness and the worries of this life, and that day does not catch you unexpectedly, 35 like a trap. For it will come upon all who live on the face of the whole earth. 36 Be alert at all times, praying that you may have the strength to escape all these things that will take place, and to stand before the Son of Man." (Luke 21:34–36)

Jesus Christ asks us here to *be on guard* so that we do not fall into *dissipation of the heart* and become involved with weakness and sins. But how does he want us to take precautions? He wants us to *be alert at all times* and *pray continually to God*. The heart becomes dissipated because it is not exercised in the dispositions of God. Sadly when our heart moves, it sometimes enters into contrary dispositions and does not exercise its love by occupying itself with the presence of God and becoming united to him.

Jesus Christ wants us to stop from applying ourselves to the *worries of this life*. He wants us to abandon everything to him and to be occupied with only one thing that is to watch and to pray. Death surprises us when we least expect it. We must put ourselves in a state where we can *appear without fear before the Son of Man*. We can only have this freedom and favorable access with him in the next life by the familiarity we have had with him in this life. We can only have this familiarity through continual commerce. God's strong and powerful love, a great presence, teaches us how to talk with him. God's love makes us equal friends. This passage is well supported in Paul, who tells us to *pray without ceasing* (1 Thessalonians 5:17). To pray without ceasing is to love without ceasing. Our love causes us to be occupied continually with God. We stand by him and tell him our needs. We give ourselves to him and speak with him. It is to do as David did when he says, *For God alone my soul waits in silence* (Psalm 62:5). By doing this, we avoid evils with which we are threatened because God keeps and sustains us when we are faithful to watch him. God thinks about us and delivers us from all evils. God gives us all good. As we watch God during the day, God watches us. It would be vain for us to watch before daybreak, if God did not watch over us. When we watch with God and for God, God watches us. Let God do this and we content ourselves to watch God.

> Every day he was teaching in the temple, and at night he would go out and spend the night on the Mount of Olives, as it was

called. 38 And all the people would get up early in the morning to listen to him in the temple. (Luke 22:37–38)

True apostles exercise their ministry by associating themselves with Jesus Christ's ministry. Apostles imitate Jesus Christ in all things. They *teach* and instruct the people in the *day*, which is to say in the divine light *in the temple*. We should not only teach in the church, but also instruct when in the state of listening. Jesus Christ speaks to them in the temple, which is the most profound place in their being. This is where he desires to teach if they are faithful enough to withdraw to the temple. We cannot always be in the church, but we may always retire into our interior temple. This is why he says, *I will listen to what the Lord my God says within me* (Psalm 85:8). This is the secret of the whole spiritual life. This is what we are assured of in *The Imitation of Christ* by Thomas à Kempis who shows us how to listen to God within ourselves. This is what the apostles teach to people and this is a truth that should be understood throughout the world. However, this is not taught.

At night, we must retire like Jesus Christ *on the mountain*. All these circumstances are to be noticed. In the night we may hear in two ways both natural and spiritual. The true apostle should use these two nights like Jesus Christ used them. In night in the natural, when all the world is in silence, it is good to repose, and it is only right that the true apostle be delighted in the midst of his labors in the divine repose. In the spiritual night, we need to repose in the same way. There are moments of repose where God does not want us to speak or to act because God wants to maintain and possess the soul in a particular way. Then God interrupts the actions of the apostolate so that we can think only of God.

Jesus Christ *went out and remained on the mountain*. His occupation was to remain in repose on the mountain of divinity. This could not be seen in Jesus Christ's exterior because it was in his interior that he always stayed on this mountain. He stayed there because he always stayed close to his Father's heart and when he came out, he never left the Father but brought the Father to the waiting people. Because of Jesus Christ's union with the Father, he can meet the needs of his sheep. For Jesus Christ, to go out is to enter and to enter is to go out. It seems that in this time he had the freedom to enjoy the presence of his Father, always permanent and durable by the hypostatic union that was in Jesus Christ. This union of Jesus Christ with his Father is imitated in the union between Jesus Christ and the church, the Beloved and his spouse, in which the soul is placed in an essential union. This is union is the repose of the soul in Divinity. This is why scriptures says, he remained *on the Mount of Olives*, to show the peace he had when separated from all creatures. The true apostle must also spend time resting alone with God.

Scripture adds that, *all the people*, without exception and without distinction, *went to listen to him in the temple*. We notice that after our conversion we must without exception in the morning enter into ourselves and hear Jesus Christ and listen to him speaking. Everyone can do this. This is why the divine Word spoke to the prophets, saying, *Speak to the heart of Jerusalem* (Isaiah 41:1–2). To the heart: we must always speak to the heart. And what is it we must do? *Comfort my people*, because God says this. God will console and visit them. God will speak his voice in their hearts when they are ready to listen. This is why they are all invited to listen to the divine word.

> "Listen," he said to them, "when you have entered the city, a man carrying a jar of water will meet you; follow him into the house he enters 11 and say to the owner of the house, 'The teacher asks you, 'Where is the guest room, where I may eat the Passover with my disciples?" 12 He will show you a large room upstairs, already furnished. Make preparations for us there." (Luke 22:10–12)

Jesus Christ *eats the Passover* with us and we must eat this with him. He eats the Passover within us when the soul is in the state of being united with him. We eat with him when the soul enters into God and remains hidden in God. He is only content when he is our Passover and we lose ourselves in him in the bosom of his Father.

But for all these Passovers we must have the disposition that Jesus Christ asks. First, the first disposition is the *jug* that is the soul that is emptied of herself or of the rigors of sin but *full of the water* of grace, or the living water Jesus Christ. This disposition is the most perfect. It suffices to commune and be emptied of sin and to be full of the water of grace so that Jesus Christ eats his Passover *with us* and we pass with him into the bosom of his Father. This disposition is enough. It is necessary that we be emptied of ourselves and filled with God. We need the Word that is the source of the living water to be with us in abundance because he fills us with himself. Then he leads us and we lose ourselves and are annihilated with him in God. It is necessary moreover that the *room be covered*, that means that the soul be adorned with all virtues and that she wears everywhere the marks of the One in whom she lodges.

> He said to them, "I have eagerly desired to eat this Passover with you before I suffer; 16 for I tell you, I will not eat it until it is fulfilled in the kingdom of God." (Luke 22:15–16)

There are many Passovers to eat but if we have an inconceivable happiness in their possession, they always presage future sufferings. Jesus Christ wants *to eat this Passover with you before I suffer* and *eagerly desires* to eat before this time. He teaches us in this, that those who have the advantage of frequent communions are preparing to suffer because they are strengthened for their suffering. Every Passover in the spiritual life always carries this delicate joy but it is followed by the cross and suffering.

Jesus Christ assures us, *he will not eat it again until it is fulfilled in the kingdom of God*. Oh, this is a great mystery! We will be deprived of the wonderful Passover when the cross and suffering arrives, yet next we will be fulfilled in union in the kingdom of God. When the soul passes into God and finds the fulfillment of the Passover, she herself is in the fulfillment of these scriptures and the Passovers. Everything is fulfilled and reunited in the end.

> A dispute also arose among them as to which one of them was to be regarded as the greatest. (Luke 22:24)

Pride is a strange thing. It enters and intertwines among everything. Was there any company that would have been more special than Jesus Christ? However, when Jesus Christ spoke to the apostles about his suffering and passion that he will exercise among them, instead of being in pain, confusion or even defiance, they amuse themselves in a dispute about vanity. Our Lord allows these strange weaknesses in the apostles so that we are not discouraged by our own weaknesses and that the torment of vanity and self-love do not prevent us from following the path of virtue.

> "For who is greater, the one who is at the table or the one who serves? Is it not the one at the table? But I am among you as one who serves." (Luke 22:27)

O Jesus! You serve your servants and serve them yourself. If we measure our greatness by the actions we have done, we will easily be misled. Instead, we should discern your greatness by your excessive love. You took lowered states for us, by hiding who you are, so that we understand that such a perfect, great, and disinterested love can only come from God. The more love is pure and disinterested, great and strong, giving everything to God and leaving everything for God, the more we love God. The more we love, the greater we are; the greater we are, the more we look small in our own eyes and in the eyes of others.

> "You are those who have stood by me in my trials; 29 and I confer on you, just as my Father has conferred on me, a kingdom, 30 so that you may eat and drink at my table in my kingdom, and you will sit on thrones judging the twelve tribes of Israel." (Luke 22:28–30)

With these words, Jesus supports what has been said, pointing out that their greatness only comes from faithfulness and perseverance in love.

You are those who have stood by me in my trials. Jesus Christ in this word speaks of two types of persecutions. Those that he himself suffers, when his faithful disciples are removed from him and those his disciples suffer, whom he calls friends, and they suffer only because of him. Their faithfulness in suffering was a strong sign of love and is also true greatness. This is why they were speaking of greatness. While they were still weak, he promised them the greatest of grandeur, which is to possess *the kingdom that Jesus Christ has prepared* for them *as his Father had prepared the kingdom for his Son.* Jesus Christ wants that they *may eat and drink at my table.* This means that they are in the fullness of God as much as they are capable of, as he is himself. This is explained when Jesus Christ says, *The glory that you have given me I have given them, so that they may be one, as we are one* (John 17:22). Following this, he promises that they will *judge* all humanity signified by *the tribes.* This is what will satisfy the love of greatness. Jesus Christ is admirable here in his sweetness. The apostles are astonished that when he corrects them about their pride, he does not speak to them with severity. To the contrary, Jesus Christ shows them what real greatness is and gives them promises. But at the same time, they understand that what they think of as greatness is only baseness.

> "Simon, Simon, listen! Satan has demanded to sift all of you like wheat, 32 but I have prayed for you that your own faith may not fail; and you, when once you have turned back, strengthen your brothers." (Luke 22:31–32)

The Devil wants only to sift and destroy apostolic souls, to tempt them and stir up thousands of persecutions, in order to shoot them down and force them to stop their enterprise. But Jesus defends them from persecution and supports them against temptation. Jesus Christ prays for all apostolic people, but particularly for Peter, *that your faith may not fail*. Jesus Christ tells him at the same time that he will fail and betray him. Jesus Christ adds, *When once you have turned back, strengthen your brothers.* That is to say, he asks that Peter's faith not fail when he confirms him as pastor, which is after the sins of Peter and the resurrection of Jesus Christ. Jesus Christ says to him, *Feed my sheep.* Since that time, his faith never failed. This does not mean that as a particular man Peter never failed, but his faith never failed. Jesus Christ does not assure him that there will be no personal faults but only that he will not lack faith.

> And he said to him, "Lord, I am ready to go with you to prison and to death!" 34 Jesus said, "I tell you, Peter, the cock will not crow this day, until you have denied three times that you know me." (Luke 22:33–34)

The temerity of this man is a strange thing. Peter has not had an experience of his weakness yet knows that his heart loves. He only consults the power of his love and does not look upon his weakness. If he leaned only on God himself, his powerlessness would be useful to him. But as he believes that the vigor of his love is his own power, he leans on this love and is usually wrong. Such is the disposition of Peter when taking the heart of love for a force, he responds to his Master's prediction of a future fault in which will fall, *"Lord, I am ready to go with you to prison and to death!"* O Peter, what did you say? You know very little. You told your master you would be strong. He knows what you will be and all that you will do. So Jesus Christ assures him, *"The cock will not crow this day, until you have denied three times that you know me."* Peter does not care about these words. To the contrary, he protests that this will not be. Those who rely so strongly and rest in sensible love are always deceived and usually fall.

> He said to them, "When I sent you out without a purse, bag, or sandals, did you lack anything?" They said, "No, not a thing." 36 He said to them, "But now, the one who has a purse must take it, and likewise a bag. And the one who has no sword must sell his cloak and buy one. 37 For I tell you, this scripture must be fulfilled in me, 'And he was counted among the lawless'; and

indeed what is written about me is being fulfilled." 38 They said, "Lord, look, here are two swords." He replied, "It is enough." (Luke 22:35–38)

This passage appears very obscure. However, it is very clear in the mystical sense. When we go under obedience under Jesus Christ and practice the works of charity and live the apostolic life, we must go in entire humility and in total nothingness. We go without strange affection, without provisions, in a grand poverty. This state is very perfect. But when we go to suffer with Jesus Christ, not only the passion, but also the ignominy of the passion, Oh, the method is changed! We are now garnished with the same things that were taken away and this is why he says *take a purse*, which is to say, you can now be dressed, you will have what has previously been taken away, because the Son of Man is counted among the lawless. It is just that you also have this state of being counted among the lawless in your eyes and in the eyes of others, seeing that you are dressed in the same things that you have been stripped away of. This proposition is what the bridegroom said to the bride, *I had put off my garment; how could I put it on again?* (Song of Solomon 5:3). It seems that we are given what we have taken off for God. It is one thing to be before the Passion and this last Sacrifice but it is good to look at all of these circumstances.

First, Jesus Christ gives us a precaution, that the thing appears more natural. *"When I sent you out without a purse, bag, or sandals, did you lack anything?"* We must note that Jesus Christ does not want them to have support in things. To the contrary, they are to lose all of their support in things. He wants them to see that if they walk without support, their poverty is not their fault. But only because as he *was counted among the lawless* and all those who follow the way of the Passion must also pass as guilty. This is why these people must take these things they have left and they are released from extreme rigor. He then orders them *to provide for arms* to defend oneself and to fight; he wants them to have weapons. But what weapons? Useless weapons, those that serve only to make them more aware of their weakness because Jesus says that *it is enough* to have two swords. What is this against so many enemies? When one thinks of using the sword, he does not even want it, saying, *He who lives by the sword, dies by the sword.* Where does it come from that you want us to have weapons? It is enough to be placed in the rank of the malefactors, and those who use their weapons to attack and defend. These weapons are useless because you have proven this when you did not have weapons, you needed nothing. The weapons serve only to help you know yourself, in order to further show your powerlessness. It is necessary to have these weapons, but weapons that you will want to use in the heat of the moment after you fall into infidelity. This defense only serves to make us feel stronger than one is because we do not feel our weakness when placed in a test. We need to be placed in the ranks of the lawless and that we appear lawless to such people to proper eyes. When we have been without arms and provisions, we did not miss anything and we did not suffer injuries or attacks. But as we could attribute this faithfulness to the creatures, this creature must be, who without arms was victorious, be defeated with his arms, so that strength is not attributed to human beings, but to God. It is necessary that people who had no lack when they had no provision also have no lack when everything is provided. Oh, how glorious is God! This is the state that preceded the passion. This place is the hardest of all because no one wants to be seen as guilty. What people want to pass as guilty when they are innocent? Who wants to feel guilty and pass for such? Oh, this is rare!

> "Father, if you are willing, remove this cup from me; yet, not my will but yours be done." (Luke 22:42)

Oh, how it is easier to carry the cross than to carry the infamy of the cross! When this chalice of suffering is proposed to the soul, we defend ourselves against this. Like Jesus, we pray, *Father, if you are willing, remove this cup from me*. However, we do not want to be released from the will of God. Nothing happens in the interior states that Jesus Christ does not want to test. This is why he wanted to experience the circumstances of this last sacrifice, and to carry them in all he could, bearing the weaknesses and appearances of the sinners, when he himself was infinitely holy and raised far above sin. Although nature is strongly opposed to drinking the chalice, our will submits, as in Jesus Christ. For Jesus Christ prayed in this way so we could see the dispositions of his soul.

> Then an angel from heaven appeared to him and gave him strength. (Luke 22:43)

God never abandons the soul in this state but send some light so that he knows the will of God. It is not an illusion, but a true light that strengthens. But what does this angel do? He confirms and makes it clear that he should drink the chalice and he must pass through this state according to the will of God. When the soul is strengthened, he is fortified to suffer. What is most surprising is that this happens when the pain is most profound, and when we are more committed to God and with more strength. The soul is never more united to God than in the most extreme agonies.

> In his anguish he prayed more earnestly, and his sweat became like great drops of blood falling down on the ground. (Luke 22:44)

The pain must be strong and profound to cause such an effect. This points to a physical pain equal to the pain of the spirit. Of all the spiritual pains, there is none like this last sacrifice, and the mortal agony that precedes this last and most painful of all sacrifices. In comparison, all the crosses together are only a shadow of this one cross. There is nothing even close. He must swallow this bitterness. He must be placed in the rank of the lawless and criminals. This is why he acts this way.

> While he was still speaking, suddenly a crowd came, and the one called Judas, one of the twelve, was leading them. He approached Jesus to kiss him; 48 but Jesus said to him, "Judas, is it with a kiss that you are betraying the Son of Man?" (Luke 22:47–48)

We often betray Jesus Christ with a kiss, either in the bad communions or in the abuse of his grace. The true sense of these words is the mystical one. The ones who have his friendship, and have more obligations to him, are the ones who torment and persecute him. To torment and crucify simple souls, persecutors use their simplicity and charity to betray and persecute them. One who dares not persecute and does not have the strength provokes the persecutions. All is good in the will of God.

> Then one of them struck the slave of the high priest and cut off his right ear. 51 But Jesus said, "No more of this!" And he touched his ear and healed him. (Luke 22:50–51)

Peter who is the most courageous in appearance will be the first to fall. Jesus says to him, *"No more of this!"* This is as if to say, this effect of your strength suffices. It is necessary that in a short time, you should feel your weakness. Why was *the ear* of the slave of the high priest cut off? To show that all done by these miserable men came only because they did not want to listen to this voice of the Word, which convicted them of crime and misery. The death of Jesus Christ came only because they would not listen to his Word, and they hardened their heart. We only sin because we do not want to hear his word. Jesus Christ heals, however, to show that he always gives a way to hear. Oh, my brothers and sisters, listen always to God speaking within you and you will never sin.

> Then Jesus said to the chief priests, the officers of the temple police, and the elders who had come for him, "Have you come out with swords and clubs as if I were a bandit? 53 When I was with you day after day in the temple, you did not lay hands on me. But this is your hour, and the power of darkness!" (Luke 22:52–53)

Jesus Christ in these words says that the cross and the persecution they are doing comes from *the power of darkness*. This is so well said: as the submission and the abandon we have to the spirit of Jesus Christ makes us friends and the defenders of truth because his light like a beautiful day surmounts and dissipates little by little the dark, and the light becoming stronger, it surmounts little by little. All the persecutions done to Jesus Christ come only because the power of darkness has won little by little by taking away the light in others. When the power of darkness arrives in power, it is then that persecutions come and they want to kill Jesus Christ in souls and to extinguish his spirit.

> Now the men who were holding Jesus began to mock him and beat him; 64 they also blindfolded him and kept asking him, "Prophesy! Who is it that struck you?" 65 They kept heaping many other insults on him. (Luke 22:63–65)

The greatest outrage we have done to Jesus Christ was to blindfold his eyes and hit his face. In doing this, God was very dishonored. The reason is that the Word is the place of all-knowledge of the Father, we cannot want to blind Jesus Christ, *to blindfold his eyes*, without committing the outrage of wanting to make the Word blind. The second outrage is to *hit his face*, which is the image of his Father, who seeing himself in his Son is pleased, admired, and loved with strength, that God the Father proceeds from that love from which he loves the Son and send this same love through his Son to human beings, the great God of the Father and the Son. They dishonored and disfigured the Son and therefore also the image of the Father. Although this is not written directly, in this passage they outraged God in the strongest possible manner. They were trying to destroy God in his origin so that the Father could not be seen in the Son or God the Father would not be pleased in him. *"You are my Son, the Beloved; with you I am well pleased*" (Luke 3:22). God the Son can love only in the Holy Spirit and this Holy Spirit is produced through the mutual communion between the Father and the Son. So as they attack Jesus Christ, they want to attack the Father and the Holy Spirit.

These are the two forms of outrage done to Jesus Christ. Those who oppose the interior faith also practice outrage against him. First, they want to blindfold his eyes and keep their own understanding instead of the light communicated by Jesus Christ. They prevent Jesus Christ from recovering his image in them, which has been overcome by sin. No one other than Jesus Christ can repair this image. This prevents the soul from being healed and the image of God restored within him. They try to take away the glory of God and the communion that God had with humanity since the time of creation. They also attempt to destroy all the glory and delights that God shared with humanity. God shared with them the image of his Son and wants this image retraced and restored. God the Father is pleased with God the Son and is also pleased with those bear the character of his Son. Doesn't Paul assure us that God created us to be *conformed to the image of his Son* (Romans 8:29) ?

This image may only be in the interior, where the soul may imprinted with this beautiful image, when the soul is empty and devoid of content. Then the soul is like pure and beautiful ice which necessarily imprints that which is applied to it. As soon as our soul loses its former content from Adam, it is impressed with the image that was given to it in creation. This image is none other than the Word, which was printed in all creatures. This is why David, having found himself in this state, was delighted by grace, and had no prayer to ask for his salvation or other interests. He asked God for only one thing, *To look on the face of your anointed* (Psalm 84:8), as if wanting to say to God, "Regard my soul. You will not be angry with me and you only love me, because when you look at me, you will see the face of your Christ." This face is no other than the Divinity of Jesus Christ, which is imprinted in all human beings. But they wiped away the face by their sins, and the image cannot be repaired except by Jesus Christ. A mirror cannot be printed by a species that it had formerly and of which it is deprived, except by the approach of this same image. That is the secret of the incarnation. Jesus Christ had to retrace this image, and he has united with human nature so that humans will not lose this image anymore. Oh, the inconceivable advantage of human beings, who always carry the image of God in their movement, life, and action though Jesus Christ; we let God retrace in us his image!

We have been predestined to be conformed to his image. God's only design is to do good to people by letting his image be traced on them. This cannot be traced on a moving board, or on an agitated and troubled foundation but only on a peaceful and tranquil soul. In a like manner, troubled water in a turbulent state cannot receive the image of the Sun but only when it is clear and peaceful. The water, though, does not clarify by effort which would only disturb it further. It must repose and calm down. A small stone thrown in calm water, serves only to disturb it and make waves. Likewise in our soul, a distinct action blurs this peaceful foundation. The stronger the action, the more the foundation and its beauty is troubled. But when nothing stops the beautiful Sun from imprinting in us, it is then that we fear nothing, and we say with assurance, "Lord, look on the face of your anointed." See how natural and clear the face of our anointed is when imprinted on us. David speaks as a prophet and as the father of Jesus Christ and as a strong interior human being. As a prophet, he says to God, *Look on the face of your anointed* (Psalm 84:8) that was imprinted throughout the earth by the grace of redemption. Do not look upon human sins. Do not be angry with human beings but see everywhere the face of your Christ. What will happen one day is *Thou shalt renew the face of the earth* and fill it with joy. This is as if he said, "O God, you will receive the greatest glory you can have out of yourself, which is, you will see in all humanity the face of your Christ." This is what he said as prophet. But as ancestor of Jesus Christ, he says, "Regard my blood for the future image of your Christ, and do not lose me as the one who contributes to his temporal formation." As an interior human being, he says to God, "Look at me and you will see no other traces than the image of your Son." As soon as we come to this state, there is nothing left in us that can displease God. Therefore, let us allow God to repair the image of God within us. The greatest outrage we can do is to prevent the image from being retraced in ourselves and in others.

> When day came, the assembly of the elders of the people, both chief priests and scribes, gathered together, and they brought him to their council. 67 They said, "If you are the Messiah, tell us." He replied, "If I tell you, you will not believe; 68 and if I question you, you will not answer. 69 But from now on the Son of Man will be seated at the right hand of the power of God." (Luke 22:66–69)

In general, we believe enough the truths of the interior and the reign of Jesus in souls, but we do not believe them in the particular. When he testifies of himself in the interior of the great graces he makes there, they do not want to believe him. When he give us this testimony by letting us conform to his states, imprinting in them his own states, his crosses, his poverty, his destitution, his humility, they do not wish to believe him. This is why Jesus Christ says to the Jews, *If I tell you that I am the Christ, you will not believe*. Also, if we say that Christ is in our interior, operating all things, they do not want to believe.

But where does this come from, "*If I question you, you will not answer.*" He saw that they were held captive in their souls and how they would remain this way. He says, "If I question, you will not answer, and you are not convinced to the truth that I am, yet you will not win, neither will you let me go, that is to say, you will not let me free to operate in yourself and in others." However, Jesus Christ adds, "Your efforts will not stop the Son of Man from being *seated at the right hand of the power of God*, to judge all that you and others have done by preventing me from retracing the image in you and others, yet I will retrace this image in a large number of souls by an effect of God's power."

> All of them asked, "Are you, then, the Son of God?" He said to them, "You say that I am." 71 Then they said, "What further testimony do we need? We have heard it ourselves from his own lips!" (Luke 22:70–71)

We often urge others to speak the truth, and when it is said, we do not believe it. We take the truth for blasphemy and condemn it. There are people who do this to interior people. They ask them to speak the truth, and when they do this, they are condemned. They take their true words and yet declare them guilty and liars.

> And when he learned that he was under Herod's jurisdiction, he sent him off to Herod, who was himself in Jerusalem at that time. 8 When Herod saw Jesus, he was very glad, for he had been wanting to see him for a long time, because he had heard about him and was hoping to see him perform some sign. 9 He questioned him at some length, but Jesus gave him no answer ... 11 Even Herod with his soldiers treated him with contempt and mocked him; then he put an elegant robe on him, and sent him back to Pilate. (Luke 23:7–9, 11)

We esteem people for what is extraordinary in them and not for the very thing that is the reality and truth of their states. Herod only wants to see our Lord for his miracles, and not to be instructed by his doctrine. This is why we do not profit when we see Jesus Christ in apostolic souls because we are only searching for the extraordinary. If we went to be instructed and edified, we would always be content and full. Without these desires, often we gain nothing. To the contrary, Jesus Christ *gave no answer* to the interrogations of Herod. Likewise, he frequently does not say a word in apostolic souls to those who come to them with the motive of looking for the extraordinary. Often we are surprised that we have a great facility to speak with some and yet have nothing to say to others. This is a problem with disposition on the part of the person who comes to receive the word. They have come out of curiosity or with a bad motive. They try to use apostolic souls for their own motives, just as Herod tried to use Jesus Christ, and then *despised* him, calling him a dreamer, crazy and deceived. But who will grieve at having faith that causes this treatment, after Jesus Christ has gone through this? Who will be surprised at the mockery of creatures and their bad treatment of them, after Jesus Christ has experienced all of these things?

> That same day Herod and Pilate became friends with each other; before this they had been enemies. (Luke 23:12)

This is an astonishing thing, that people who are far apart in sentiments, who are opposed in feelings and inclinations, and are declared *enemies*, almost always agree at this point of persecution and condemnation of the servants of God: the good and the bad, all in a common voice condemn them.

> Pilate then called together the chief priests, the leaders, and the people, 14 and said to them, "You brought me this man as one who was perverting the people; and here I have examined him in your presence and have not found this man guilty of any of your charges against him." (Luke 23:13–14)

It is an ordinary thing to accuse apostolic souls, those in whom Jesus Christ has placed his character traits, as they accused Jesus Christ, to prevent people from doing their duty. There is no state which is so good at fulfilling obligations than the interior state, which is a continual dependence on God. And as God is at no point contrary to himself, when he calls to a state, he gives the dispositions and the necessary ways to fulfill what the state to which he calls us requires. If we do not fulfill it, it is because we have left the state of abandonment and dependence on God and union with his will.

When people in authority hold justice in the hand because of their work, at times they receive a warning, a ray of the justice of God which shines on them. They say they *have not found any reason for death or condemnation* to the persons they are addressing. They cannot help seeing that envy causes this persecution that brings suffering to some. This ray of justice happens frequently to bishops and people in authority.

> "Neither has Herod, for he sent him back to us. Indeed, he has done nothing to deserve death. 16 I will therefore have him flogged and release him." (Luke 23:15–16)

If this man is innocent, they why the *flogging?* However, people in authority understand through the light of God the innocence of the accused people. They know they are not supported by justice, if they make the punishment go as far as the enemies want, yet they still condemn them in something. They pretend to want to justify them, and they have the desire to justify them, yet they are still condemned. They are the party based on strength, not on human righteousness.

> Pilate, wanting to release Jesus, addressed them again; 21 but they kept shouting, "Crucify, crucify him!" (Luke 23:20–21)

Pilate did not find any reason to kill Jesus Christ, however he condemns him. He *wants to release him* but he does not have the courage. Vanity and respect of humans cause the evil against these accused people, when it would be natural enough to render justice. He asks, What reason is there to kill Jesus Christ. Without saying anything in response, they cry, *Crucify him!* People who bear his name and justice are treated in the same way. Others treat them ruthlessly and cry out against them with all their strength so that they become infamous. When he asks what good reason they have for these persecutions and their outcry against him, they do not say anything except, *Crucify him!*

O souls who are happy to be the stigma of people, the abjection of all people, the subject of their contradiction, rejoice to be treated like your Master. There are a lot of people crying *Crucify him!* and who believe they are doing service to God by sending people to many crosses. All is good, I admit, in the ordering of the will of God for these accused people who by suffering these outrages patiently bring great glory to God. It is a terrible thing to see the whole world without reason arrayed against these pious people. They cry *Crucify him!* Without knowing why, they still cry this. They are a pack of dogs, which bark together without knowing why, because they are panicked in terror.

> So Pilate gave his verdict that their demand should be granted. 25 He released the man they asked for, the one who had been put in prison for insurrection and murder, and he handed Jesus over as they wished. (Luke 23:24–25)

This is horrible cowardice to condemn an innocent man when he recognized his innocence and to *deliver* this man into the hands of his enemies and unfair witnesses and his poisonous opponents and to give judgment that *their demand should be granted*. They treat Jesus Christ and all his true servants as if they were humanity's worst and most infamous of criminals. They have compassion for men who have committed crimes. They condemn without good evidence. They should choose neutral people to arbitrate justice. They expect irreproachable evidence. But when they act to condemn Jesus Christ or his servants, his declared enemies are believed as well as those without any knowledge of the situation. They take for judges the most ruthless persecutors. They treat him with more cruelty than they would wicked people. Those who naturally have an inclination for justice and compassion are stopped by their respect for human beings, and they let themselves condemn what they secretly approve of. It seems that they are ashamed to hold the part of justice, because everyone violates it. O horrible evil that holds such respect for others! Jesus Christ was condemned because of the idolatry of humans and already his servants are treated the same.

> A great number of the people followed him, and among them were women who were beating their breasts and wailing for him. 28 But Jesus turned to them and said, "Daughters of Jerusalem, do not weep for me, but weep for yourselves and for your children." (Luke 23:27–28)

Among this general condemnation there are many good, innocent souls, the *women* and devout daughters, who *mourn* over the persecution that is done to the servants of God, as they weep for Jesus Christ. They are convinced in their heart of his innocence by the experience of God's mercy. But alas! They can give only tears for such a strange disaster.

Jesus Christ says to them, do not weep *for me* or for his servants because they are happy to suffer all things. These are people who feel easily touched by all the tragic events and are not engaged in many sins. Jesus Christ tells them not to cry for him because these tears are not efficacious, but to *weep for themselves*, for their disorders, and to *weep for their children*, and any disorders in them.

> "For the days are surely coming when they will say, 'Blessed are the barren, and the wombs that never bore, and the breasts that never nursed.' 30 Then they will begin to say to the mountains, 'Fall on us'; and to the hills, 'Cover us.' 31 For if they do this when the wood is green, what will happen when it is dry?" (Luke 23:29–31)

Jesus Christ assures us that we must cry over the strange persecutions that will happen to his true servants, because if he, who is always *green wood* and without fault is *treated* with injustice and cruelty, what will they do to *dry wood*, that is to say, to weak and imperfect souls in their nature, yet doing good and holy things because of his mercy? They must not be surprised if they are mistreated and condemned, and they pass for guilty, because Jesus Christ has passed for this and is treated the same.

> When they came to the place that is called The Skull, they crucified Jesus there with the criminals, one on his right and one on his left. 34 Then Jesus said, "Father, forgive them; for they do not know what they are doing." And they cast lots to divide his clothing. (Luke 23:33–34)

The true disposition of apostolic souls who are the ones whose crosses are the strongest are ones who *pray* like Jesus Christ, and with him, *for the persecutors*. They do not will to do evil, yet they have pity on their ignorance to even think of doing evil, when they could be doing good. For their salvation, they expose themselves to all possible evil and they receive persecutions. The blindness of humanity is strange, to declare themselves against those who are only working for good and who provide goods for others. We pity outraged enemies who in their violent hatred double the furor against an innocent and persecuted person. But, O God! *Forgive them; for they do not know what they are doing*. They are more worthy of compassion than of anger. They themselves offend by obtaining the ruin of the one who comes to save them. If we see everything in God, we easily pardon injuries and we would not seek pain for those who make these crosses for others. It is they who offend, while those receiving the crosses enjoy a great advantage, that is, suffering for God.

> One of the criminals who were hanged there kept deriding him and saying, "Are you not the Messiah? Save yourself and us!" (Luke 23:39)

To be crucified when innocent would be little in comparison to be crucified as guilty. It is a thing most strange to be crucified as guilty. To carry infamy and torture and to be counted as criminals, to have the outrage of even those who are punished for crimes, and to whom you are compared, are the circumstances of the cross all along with the most extreme pain. This is what they did to Jesus Christ and his faithful servants. They are trying to stain them with darkness throughout the world. Their story becomes one of a life filled with horror. These comparisons are used to scare the mind and spirit, surprise the simple, and give power to the accusers. What is even more amazing is that criminals get involved with this game and judge the holy and simple people unjustly. The criminals are to be pitied but they willingly outrage the servants of God. This is horrifying.

> But the other rebuked him, saying, "Do you not fear God, since you are under the same sentence of condemnation? 41 And we indeed have been condemned justly, for we are getting what we deserve for our deeds, but this man has done nothing wrong." (Luke 23:40–41)

Among the guilty, we always find some who have penetrated into the light of truth. A thief who was crucified with Jesus Christ becomes his defender and eulogist. He is on the cross as if he were on a throne and declares the truth of Jesus Christ and his innocence, at the same time that he is accused and condemned for his sins. This is the use of the cross, to convert and touch those to bring them to repentance. He suffers with Jesus Christ, that is to say, with conformity and unity in their sufferings. Jesus Christ brings the conversion, salvation, and very great graces. A crucified sinner becomes in one moment a convert who confesses his crime and sees the goodness of God. He instantly becomes an apostle, a Preacher, and a Martyr!

> Then he said, "Jesus, remember me when you come into your kingdom." 43 He replied, "Truly I tell you, today you will be with me in paradise." (Luke 23:42–43)

These words show that the thief had been enlightened by the true light that is given in the knowledge of who Jesus Christ is. He recognized

Jesus Christ as King, as God, and as Savior. To Jesus Christ as King, he prays to *remember me when you come into your kingdom*. To Jesus Christ as God, as the thief died on the cross in infamy, he recognized that Jesus Christ's reign was not in this world, but in the other, where God alone has the right to reign. To Jesus Christ as Savior, the thief confessed him as Savior, because he prays that Jesus Christ will remember him and save him, not for this life, but for the next. The thief also recognizes at the same time his unworthiness of the mercy of God but after seeing that God is crucified for his sins, he waits with a perfect confidence that Jesus Christ has merited salvation for him, despite all his unworthiness. These are the characters of a true repentance, a person who does not ignore his crimes but sees them and feels the pain of them. This does not discourage him but makes him hope even more in God. Discouragement and depression in penitence come only from self-esteem, but trust and abandon to God come from pure love. Also, public repentance in confessing his crimes before all this witnessing his torture, did he merit Jesus Christ assuring him of his truth when he said that *Today you will be with me in paradise*. He does not tell him that he will be with him in heaven, because heaven was not open until his Ascension but that he will with him today in paradise. To be with Jesus Christ is to be in paradise. As soon as we are united with him. We are in a true paradise. Your presence, O lovable Savior, makes a paradise in this world, and your absence make hell.

> It was now about noon, and darkness came over the whole land until three in the afternoon, 45 while the sun's light failed; and the curtain of the temple was torn in two. (Luke 23:44–45)

This is darkness with the pains of death that consume and finish death. As long as he can rest in a flash of light, the darkness is not perfect. The sacrifice of Jesus Christ is the model for all sacrifices and the death of Jesus Christ merits the life of grace. This is the model of the mystical death that provides a superhuman life lived in him only. All who arrive at the death of Jesus Christ arrive at the mystical death of souls, who conform and sacrifice their life of Adam for Calvary and are prepared for God. It is necessary that all souls are covered with thick *darkness* so she is covered with neither light nor truth. She sees nothing; she knows nothing. She only feels the grief of death that consumes and devours. Next the soul, like the *veil* of the temple *is torn in two and divides*. Then the soul divides entirely into two parts, the superior and the inferior, then the soul is pulled from herself: and then operates the mystical death, very real and true, and consumed by the sacrifice. The mystical death is like the very real and true death of Jesus Christ. His sacrifice was perfect.

> Then Jesus, crying with a loud voice, said, "Father, into your hands I commend my spirit." Having said this, he breathed his last. (Luke 23:46)

All of these things happened at the death of Jesus Christ, that Jesus Christ said, *"Father, into your hands I commend my spirit." Having said this, he breathed his last.* The soul in this state finishes her sacrifice by a total abandonment of herself and dies happily in the arms of love. But why does Jesus Christ say in dying these mysterious words: *Father, into your hands I commend my spirit*? This happens also to abandoned and sacrificial souls when they cease living in themselves. Their soul then passes into God who receives this soul. The inferior part remains abandoned in the paleness and weakness of death. We see this as the soul of Jesus Christ was received into the bosom of God, in the same time that his body was cold and abandoned of life and feeling. He is the same as the soul in this state. The superior part is united with God, while the inferior rests in the coldness of death. Likewise, once the mystical death is achieved, the soul without delay is received into the hands of God, where she is transformed through a total annihilation after death. There is a difference from union to transformation. It is to show that as notwithstanding the body of Jesus Christ died, the Divinity was not separated, and the division of the soul and body of Jesus Christ was not separated from Divinity, who always remained united to the body and the soul. Even thought the inferior part remains in death, it does not fail to participate in the union with the superior part. But he is in total death and does not know or distinguish anything.

> And when all the crowds who had gathered there for this spectacle saw what had taken place, they returned home, beating their breasts. (Luke 23:48)

Those who find themselves in this state of death, and seem to have nothing, operate admirable conversions. We cannot say what it is that touches these conversions more that are more efficacious.

> Now there was a good and righteous man named Joseph, who, though a member of the council, 51 had not agreed to their plan and action. He came from the Jewish town of Arimethea,

and he was waiting expectantly for the kingdom of God. (Luke 23:50–51)

There are always some virtuous people among the crowd who condemns Jesus Christ, who *did not consent to their plan* and react with horror to this. Joseph of Arimethea hopes and *waits* for the reign of *God and his kingdom*, to whom this will be manifested and experienced in secret. He is not strong enough to defend these actions and prevent the evil against Jesus from happening. He can do some things in secret and wait for the manifestation of Jesus Christ. He will discover the truth of this kingdom within his soul.

> This man went to Pilate and asked for the body of Jesus. 53 Then he took it down, wrapped it in a linen cloth, and laid it in a rock-hewn tomb where no one had ever been laid. (Luke 23:52–53)

All these circumstances surrounding the death of Jesus Christ are admirable and truly happen with people who die mystically. God always destines some to go through this by an effect of his goodness. When the cross produces an effect that he desires then he *is taken down from the cross*, repairs the outrages that were done and repairs his destroyed reputation. But how is this done in the interior? God himself draws this person off of the cross. He *envelops him in linen*, he gives him a new exterior of purity. Then he puts him in a *rock*, an immovable place, where he is not vulnerable to pain, and only those come who are sent by God. He is in a place where *no one had ever been laid*, except to arrive there by death.

> The women were terrified and bowed their faces to the ground, but the men said to them, "Why do you look for the living among the dead? He is not here, but has risen." (Luke 24:5)

The human condition includes weakened souls who are in the state of death. They surround us and at times we cannot discern the difference between those who are dead or alive. Then we *look among the dead* for those who are alive. In mistake, we regard those who are alive as if they were dead and those who are innocent as if they were guilty. Scriptures say, *Do not search among the dead for those who are alive*. If we do this, we are wrong in our search. It is important to remember that these holy women were searching for Jesus Christ among the dead to embalm him and to preserve him from corruption and they did not see that he was more incorruptible than they. Sometimes good people search because of charity among the dead for interior souls, who are very alive in God.

People want the perfume of a thousand exterior practices to stop corruption, as they say, because they do not see that interior souls are the most incorruptible. Interior souls are the most confirmed in grace and in strength, because they have passed into God, in whom they live.

> "Remember how he told you, while he was still in Galilee, 7 that the Son of Man must be handed over to sinners, and be crucified and on the third day rise again." (Luke 24:6–7)

One does not resurrect until after death, and one resurrects in order not to die anymore. But if death precedes resurrection, the resurrection also assures us that the death is real. If the death is entirely consummated, the resurrection will also be the same. One dies only to enter a new life. If one is not resurrected, it is as Paul says, "And if Christ has not been raised, then our proclamation has been in vain and your faith has been in vain" (1 Corinthians 15:14). It is certain therefore that he had one death and he had one resurrection. He also had one spiritual death and one spiritual resurrection; a mystical death and a mystical resurrection, as there was one natural death and one natural resurrection. The natural death happened with the separation of the soul from the body and the resurrection happened with the reunion of the soul with the body.

We understand the spiritual death in two ways. It is a tragedy to separate the soul from her God and to be deprived of grace, and the resurrection happens when the sinful soul enters again into grace. The second is to die to all spiritual light and sentiments. But this is useful for in the resurrection the spirit finds the light in God that she has lost. The mystical death that is spoken of in the passage is the entire separation from all the life of Adam so in the mystical resurrection all that is participates the life of God. There is a division between these two parts of the superior from the inferior. This death does two contrary things and two resurrections that are very different. In regarding the separation of the two parts, it is death that happens first, the resurrection is the reunion of the two parts in God. When this division happens first, the reunion is last. In the second separation, the soul loses the life of Adam and the resurrection happens in Jesus Christ. The life of the Word is substituted in the place of the sins, which is the resurrection. We are assured of this in the testimony of Paul who writes, *So if anyone is in Christ, there is a new creation: everything old has passed away; see, everything has become new!* (2 Corinthians 5:17) The new life is not like the first life subject to death, because Jesus Christ killed death and life became eternal, as it is written *Shall I redeem them from death?* (Hosea 13:14) Then we live the life of Jesus Christ. O Love! It is too much to say. Paul writes about this in his experience, *It is no longer I who live, but it is Christ who lives in me* (Galatians 2:20).

But how does the death and resurrection operate? Jesus Christ is delivered into the hands of sinners and is crucified. Here is the double penalty that causes death to the soul. To be delivered into the hands of sinners like Jesus Christ, is like Paul experienced, "*I am of the flesh sold into slavery under sin*" Romans 7:14. This state is the most terrible of all and in the flesh he is united to the exterior cross. To be delivered to sinners and crucified brings death. But death does not always last and after death follows new life, *after three days*. What are the three days after death? It is the burial according to Paul; the annihilation, when the soul is reduced to the dust of death; but after three days buried and before the total annihilation, he enters into a state of consumed decay, because he rests in the dirt and is gradually consumed and the consumption causes a type of corruption that is compared to rotting. After this he enters into a decay of annihilation where there is no corruption or feeling. In this state there is no pain or pleasure. Then, the soul is resurrected in God, leaving behind the state of consuming death and the lack of life, to enter into a state of eternal life where there is no more pain. He leaves behind a state where there is no pain or pleasure but now enters into abundant life, full of joy, and exempt from evil; a state without a cross and sorrow, now a state with new pleasure. After this new life, the two parts are reunited in God, although late but with an admirable order. Here the inferior remains forever subjected to the superior, and the superior in God, without any resistance to this.

> Now on that same day two of them were going to a village called Emmaus, about seven miles from Jerusalem, 14 and talking with each other about all these things that had happened. 15 While they were talking and discussing, Jesus himself came near and went with them. (Luke 24:13–15)

Jesus Christ is always among those who occupy themselves with him alone. He assures us of this, *For where two or three are gathered in my name, I am there among them* (Matthew 18:20). Yet why is Jesus Christ not in the midst of our conversations? It is because we are concerned only with ourselves. We do not think or talk about him. When we speak we talk only of bagatelles and vanities; this is why we have only bagatelles and vanities. But if we occupy ourselves with God and remain in his company, talk about him, then Oh! We will have the effect of his sweet presence! But instead, we do not speak about him. How will he be present with us if we occupy ourselves with anything but him? Let's think and talk about him and he will be in the middle of us. All life goes on in uselessness if we do not concern ourselves with the One who has consumed his life for us.

> But their eyes were kept from recognizing him. (Luke 24:16)

Many good souls complain that they try to occupy themselves with God, to think only of him, to speak only of him, yet they do not experience the divine presence. Oh, how mistaken they are! They mistake the feeling of the presence for the truth of the presence. Jesus is with them: but *a divine virtue covers their eyes*, that is to say, suspends all light and knowledge so they do not know or distinguish the good that they possess. They do not know they have it because the clarity of the Spirit keeps them from discovering this. This lack of recognition of the good they have is also a good operation; they possess it but they do not know it. It is necessary that faith in the words of Jesus Christ brings a knowledge but that the blindness does not prevent possession. Talk about Jesus Christ; think about him; occupy yourself with Jesus Christ. You will possess Jesus Christ always, even if you do not know it.

> And Jesus said to them, "What are you discussing with each other while you walk along?" They stood still, looking sad. 18 Then one of them, whose name was Cleopas, answered him, "Are you the only stranger in Jerusalem who does not know the things that have taken place there in these days?" He asked them, "What things?" They replied, "The things about Jesus of Nazareth, who was a prophet mighty in deed and word before God and all the people, and how our chief priests and leaders handed him over to be condemned to death and crucified him." (Luke 24:17–20)

Jesus Christ pretends to ignore the conversation of his disciples, but he does this so they will tell him about it. They have pleasure in speaking to him. He is disguised and hidden, and does not make himself known. But when God speaks, we feel it. We must be quiet when we are with and encounter Jesus Christ, but we must speak if he asks us. Our state is silence but we leave the silence, if we are asked to speak. These poor disciples were speaking of the suffering and death of Jesus Christ. They were afflicted by the suffering and death of Jesus Christ. This is what attracted them to the presence of Jesus Christ. If we occupy ourselves with the sufferings of Jesus Christ, and we talk about him, we experience his presence.

When these two disciples talked of Jesus, they said that he *was a prophet mighty in deed and word before God and all the people*. How should this be understood? Jesus Christ as active Word is powerful in words before God because he himself is the Word of the Father. He is powerful in works because in him everything is done and without him nothing is done. He is powerful in words and works before people, that is to say, before simple and common souls, who do not reason and philosophize about everything. He is first powerful in words because his word is an efficacious word that is understood in the foundation of the heart. We must encounter this Word because it is all powerful and it has all power to work in the soul. He is powerful in works, that is to say, to work all things in us and for us, as the Father works in him and for him. Therefore let us allow this working of sovereign power within us. But, alas! The *chief priests*, powerful leaders and authorities prevent him from speaking and working in them and in others, and *condemn him to death*. This condemnation of Jesus Christ to death is done; they did not want his actions, and they stopped them. They did not want him speaking, and they did not want others to listen to him. They crucified him.

> "But we had hoped that he was the one to redeem Israel. Yes, and besides all this, it is now the third day since these things took place." (Luke 24:21)

Israel is an abandoned soul. This soul *hopes always for her deliverance*; but when *three days had passed* since the death, to have been in the tomb with annihilation and corruption, this is when they no longer hope. Nevertheless, hope was never nearer when it appeared the most desperate. We know that only Jesus has the power to *deliver and redeem Israel*: we wait only for deliverance from him: but when a certain state happens, we hope no longer.

> "Moreover, some women of our group astounded us. They were at the tomb early this morning, 23 and when they did not find his body there, they came back and told us that they indeed had seen a vision of angels who said that he was alive. 24 Some of those who were with us went to the tomb and found it just as the women had said; but they did not see him." (Luke 24:22–24)

Christ always allows that the resurrection be announced before the soul in whom he is working discovers this herself. He allows that the *women* are the first, and then the *announcement*. So that we see that he publishes his truth to whom he pleases, and does this frequently to annihilate the learned people, who have been confused by their education, and consider these women ignorant. It must be noted the order that Jesus Christ has in this manifestation. He first discovers the holy women because their love is pure and their faith is strong. They are yielding to believe about that of which they are ignorant. When he announces the truth to them, he tells them to go next to declare this to the apostles so that they seal this truth and make this the judgment of the church. We must not despise the knowledge given to women, to whom he frequently is pleased to reveal his profundities because God is pleased to reveal his secrets to the small ones. These women would be condemned if they did not lay down these lights at the feet of the apostles.

These persons of this state have great difficulty in believing in the resurrection. Because they could not believe the resurrection on the testimony of the women, the resurrection was confirmed to the apostles. The resurrection appears impossible to those who have not experienced it. A person who has not seen the death or heard of the resurrection is astonished and does not believe, as if we showed him dead ashes and say that they will revive. That is the state of the soul when she learns of the resurrection, until the one who works within the soul is manifested.

> Then he said to them, "Oh, how foolish you are, and how slow of heart to believe all that the prophets have declared! 26 Was it not necessary that the Messiah should suffer these things and then enter into his glory?" (Luke 24:25–26)

You upbraid the soul, O God! She has so much trouble believing that a state so poor, small, and despicable can produce such a great good. All evil comes from the lack of faith. *You are slow to believe* and we only believe things when we see them in the world of senses. Oh, if we were quick to believe, what paths would open up to us? We cannot believe that we arrive at a state of happiness through the cross, pains, humiliations, abjections, and confusions. But Jesus Christ assures us, *It is necessary that the Messiah should suffer these things and then enter into glory?* Like him, we enter into happiness through the way of suffering. If we go another way, we will not find happiness.

> Then beginning with Moses and all the prophets, he interpreted to them the things about himself in all the scriptures. (Luke 24:27)

In this passage we learn two truths. First, there is nothing in Jesus Christ that has not been written and predicted in the ancient law and this is not explained in the newness of the resurrection. All should be expressed. Also, there are some states of being that are pointed to in the scripture and are surely true. The state of total nudity and privation leads to the resurrection. Until the privation is complete, we read the scriptures and yet do not make the discovery. When souls arrive in a state of consummation in God and become advanced in the newness of life, the Word is formed within them and he gives them intelligence about the holy scriptures and understanding becomes easy. These interior states of new life are truly found in Jesus Christ. If they are not found in Jesus Christ, they are not true. Jesus Christ truly carried his misery. He remains with us to carry our misery so we do not fall. As our Redeemer, he takes charge of our states of being, our sentiments and feelings. When we experience miseries and weakness, he carries all these states. There is no state of being that is not written about in the holy scriptures. Do we really believe weak creatures that we are, that we have experiences not written about in the scriptures? Our states are there but the light is not always given to us to discover this. We can make imaginary states not in the scriptures.

> As they came near the village to which they were going, he walked ahead as if we were going on. 29 But they urged him strongly, saying, "Stay with us, because it is almost evening and the day is now nearly over." (Luke 24:28–29)

O Love! You often test the love of faithful souls whom you love. You pretend to hide and to pass out of reach, to see if they will stop you and if they love your company. You frequently test your lovers: do you not hide yourself from the bride? And when she believes you are far away, she searches for you with passion, you appear behind the window. Sometimes he pretends to escape, this victorious love, but this is only to attract the heart more strongly and to hold us more strongly. O admirable inventions of love! The heart who believes he wants to abandon her, prays and begs him to stay. She testifies to his passionate love, saying, *I found him whom my soul loves. I held him, and would not let him go* (Song of Solomon 3:4). O adorable Spouse, seeing this loving soul want to hold you, praying and pressing to stay with her. And where do you stay? Within her heart. You are there with her. Then he closes the door to any other. O happiness without parallel, which is agreed upon by her desire and perseverance.

Let us speak of our desire and eagerness for Jesus Christ. When we start, we find little except our growing desire and our growing eagerness for Jesus Christ. God possesses us. The desire is very necessary and there is a state God possesses us with desire. Then we can only desire. This is why we say we always desire, because this assures us that we will have a state of union with God. It is needed that we first desire the repose of possession. We hear that there is a state of pure desire that excludes all other desires. We need to desire God with all that we are because we will have joy and peace in God's possession.

> When he was at table with them, he took bread, blessed and broke it, and gave it to them. 31 Then their eyes were opened, and they recognized him; and he vanished from their sight. (Luke 24:30–31)

They had spent a long time in the company of Jesus Christ without recognizing him. We possess him without knowledge that we possess him. But when *the bread is broken* and the division is made of the two parts, the superior and the inferior, his being is substituted in place of our being, as the substance of Jesus Christ took the place of the bread. Therefore, *they recognized him* and *their eyes were opened*. But as soon as we know and discover him, we lose his sensible and perceptive presence. But when he *disappears* with strength, he remains in substance.

> They said to each other, "Were not our hearts burning within us while he was talking to us on the road, while he was opening the scriptures to us?" (Luke 24:32)

We know that the Word of God is a small and secret fire burning within our soul that brings a profound peace. We hear this Word and it produces an effect within our *heart*. We also hear this through the ministry of the *apostles*. We distinguish the word of God by this certain grace burning in our soul.

> That same hour they got up and returned to Jerusalem; and they found the eleven and their companions gathered together. 34 They were saying, "The Lord has risen indeed, and he has appeared to Simon!" 35 Then they told what had happened on the

road, and how he had been made known to them in the breaking of the bread. 36 When they were talking among themselves, Jesus himself stood among them and said to them, "Peace be with you." (Luke 24:33–36)

This is the extreme joy of the truth of the resurrection of Jesus Christ, who had drawn many out of death and who had delivered many from interior death. Through his resurrection, Jesus Christ manifests himself. He has been drawn out of the state of death and placed in new life. The faith of the resurrection is that which makes mystical resurrection supportable; because finally, as Paul says, *If Jesus Christ is not resurrected, our faith is in vain* (1 Corinthians 15:14). The hope of mystical resurrection, which demands the strongest faith, is founded on the resurrection. He was not just resuscitated but he had died and participated in death and the most mysterious death of them all, the mystical death. I know that the purest love would be content in knowing that God wants this. It is never resuscitation. If it is resuscitation than love, faith and hope are in vain. The hope of the resurrection grounds the faith, and hope, given as a gift, tells us to see our future as good. The goal and object of hope and faith is only love, who loves in simplicity without any other view than love. He loves us in the present. His love lives in our will as a powerful sovereign, but blind because we do not see his love but we taste it. We discern and experience life through the taste of his love and not through our eyes. True love is not seen with the eyes. He loves and it is enough. Those who condemn people who love God for God's self, while not thinking of paradise or hell, or what they desire, are mistaken at this point. They desire heaven as the object of hope, and future promises are the object of their faith. Yet faith and hope are somehow joined together to believe the promises and to have hope. But love is not envisaged in this. She only loves when faith is advanced and reduced to unity and she begins already to become one, little by little to understand and remember, and to fall into unity with his will. Therefore, we do not think of distinct objects and experiences. Instead we fall into the unity of his will. Therefore, we lose distinct objects and find reunion in his will that is powerful and sovereign. Love attracts faith and hope. Falling into God's love does what other powers cannot do. These powers may see God's will but they cannot unite us with God's will. Instead, God's will surpasses these powers and absorbs all other powers. As faith belongs to the understanding and hope to the memory, these two virtues are united and absorbed in only love as the sovereign virtue which takes over and brings them into it. When all is united, faith and hope disappear, and together they become a habit. We rest only in love, who surmounts all, acting in sovereignty and reunited in its only present and future goal. This goal is God who surmounts all and is always present. Heaven and the future glory points only to love and the possession of it. She loves and has joy, and when she does not have joy, she loves.

In heaven there is no faith or hope but all is lost and absorbed in only love. Not because faith, hope, and joy are lost, but because they are a present object and we do not need to look forward to them. But also because, all is united in pure love. We approach union. When the soul is reduced to union, she no longer perceives faith and hope, all is united only in God's will, where we feel joy in God and this experience. The truth extinguishes faith and hope, and even more, and surmounts by love. When we remain in love, we remain in God. When we remain in God, we possess all that is necessary and in this possession we can neither desire or want anything else. Because God's possession is all we can desire. In heaven faith will not be an object of understanding, but we will clearly know. Hope will not be an object in memory, but we will be absorbed entirely in joy. We will look at God directly, pure light, without the need to exercise our memory. When exercising the powers of faith and hope, their object moves and changes, but when we are lost in God's possession we see only love and the perfection in God, where all is reunited in God, and all is found in the same God, who absorbs all in him, taking the soul within him, and transforming light into light and love into love.

This is the ineffable happiness that begins in this life, when all is reunited in only love. The soul is established and remains in this love, because *remaining in love, she remains in God because God is love*. If this is the truth we may never doubt, when we remain in God, God possesses us, and in the possession we never hope or desire any more. We say only that we desire God's possession because in God's possession is perfect ravishment who contains all thoughts and desires. This satisfaction does not mean it cannot grow because this love always grows. The soul is filled according to her capacity and she cannot contain more than she is, and because of this, she cannot desire more. She grows forever in love because God always gives her more and increases her capacity. But this does not cause a vacuum or desire because God fills her to the measure he enlarges her. In filling, he extends and gives her more. She grows continually with ceasing to be full, the same operation that makes the fullness makes the dilation. But this dilation also makes us lose our propriety. Therefore, all is easy and nothing troubles us. There will be no more fall because the soul is always and only in love and lives in the fullness of love. This is the knowledge that David has when he said, *I run the way of your commandments, for you enlarge my understanding* (Psalm 119:32).

This is to say that God does not resuscitate the soul, but it is confirmed in the Christ's resurrection. Peter was not resurrected, and neither were the apostles. Instead, Jesus Christ merited through his death the mystical death, and exempted us to make this real for us but in a different way. He confirmed us in his state of permanent and durable peace, given to us through Jesus Christ so that we never lose this again. He tells us, *Peace be with you* (John 20:21). *It is I; do not fear* (Matthew 14:27). It is I, he says, who revive you and give you peace. It is I. Do not fear that you will be lost. You will never be lost. All the apostles experienced death but differently. Peter experienced a disastrous death with much pain and humiliation. He experienced a profound death. He who had led a flock with a thousand weaknesses, he experienced himself their weakness. The other apostles had less painful and lengthy deaths. Their deaths were shorter and easier. Jesus Christ carried all their suffering. John was different from the other apostles. He died and passed into Jesus Christ. O fortunate apostle! In the moment you die in the arms and in the heart of love. This was a sleep of ecstasy and death. *Come over to me, all ye that desire me, and be filled with my fruits* (Ecclesiasticus 24:26). He passed therefore into Jesus Christ and at the same time, Jesus Christ passed into him. But when did he pass? On the throne of torture. There he died, but in dying he gives and passes his life into John. This is why he assures Mary that John is now her son. But it is not here that we want to expand. We must see that the disciples loved well. The disciple John himself taught us about Jesus Christ's death and resurrection.

> They were startled and terrified, and thought they were seeing a ghost. 38 He said to them, "Why are you frightened, and who do doubts arise in your hearts? 39 Look at my hands and my feet; see that it is I myself. See that it is I myself. Touch me and see; for a ghost does not have flesh and bones as you see that I have." (Luke 24:37–39)

Why does Jesus Christ show his wounds to the apostles as the marks and assurances of the resurrection? The premier reason is to show them that his suffering and death is the only merit of this great good, and that he has exempted them from the long death and ennui and all the circumstances of the mystical death. They are not however exempt from suffering, and they should suffer like him.

Jesus' wounds were preserved after his resurrection as real and visible marks of his death and suffering. These show also the truth of his resurrection and reveal these new advantages. The wounding and misery, which disfigured him at the time of his death, after the resurrection show in him by the same marks his glory. We see the scars, but scars that are not about horror. To the contrary, we know in our own body the resurrection as Jesus Christ was resurrected himself in his body gives to our flesh his benefits that he procured for us in himself.

> And when he had said this, he showed them his hands and his feet. (Luke 24:40)

Why does he show them his hands and his feet? It is for them to see, that since they are resurrected in him and by him, he himself had become their movement and action. We no longer move, act, and live by ourselves, but it is Jesus who moves, acts, and lives in us.

> While in their joy they were disbelieving and still wondering, he said to them, "Have you anything here to eat?" They gave him a piece of broiled fish, and he took it, and ate in their presence. (Luke 24:41–43)

My God! What wonderful experiences are here! The joy of a new soul in whom Jesus Christ lives is wonderful, he moves into him in time during which he *disbelieves* the happiness for which he dares not hope and which he now possesses. He is in a dream-state and remains there in a time filled with admiration and suspension. The soul who tastes this great good is drawn out of himself at the beginning. But afterwards, this great good continues with certainty and without suspension.

Afterwards *he ate*, and Oh! This is mysterious! We see the entire freedom of the soul in resurrected life. She does not do anything because she is forced to do this. She has lost everything. Now she lives in repentance and prayer and all is handed to her with ease. She acts when his duties require actions or for the help to her neighbor. She may do what others do or she may not do what others do. But when she has duties to others, she always does them.

Jesus Christ eats again after his resurrection to show us that the resurrected soul communes with us. If the soul finds this difficult, she is not in the state of resurrection but in the state of death. All is given to her with a wonderful ease. Some people want to say that a soul in resurrected life is not able to communicate but permit me to say that they are wrong in this. The Holy Communion brings this infinite advantage to us. Jesus Christ as God is the way and the life. Losing ourselves in Christ, we find joy in him as the end and the life. I know that when we have joy in Christ, we are not troubled by our infirmity, troubles, and desires because we possess Jesus Christ entirely in the Sacrament and then this is very easy. Jesus Christ wants to eat, to show resurrected souls what he can and must do. It must be noted that at the time of death, we are deprived of life and everything necessary for life's maintenance. But through this privation, we receive life and all things needed. We then serve others in freedom because we are free.

Jesus Christ took it, and ate in their presence to show that the resurrected soul is cleansed from all the external crosses and persecutions. He is in his *presence*. He had been roasted in the fire of tribulation but inside, he receives consolation like a ray of honey that brings him union with God and makes him accept and want everything that had happened to him.

> He took it, and ate in their presence. (Luke 24:43)

He did not eat this to make them see, but we should all experience the fire of tribulations and the interior consolation that brings us union with God.

> Then he said to them, "These are my words that I spoke to you while I was with you—that everything written about me in the law of Moses, the prophets, and the psalms must be fulfilled." (Luke 24:44)

Here is explained and confirmed admirably what has been said, that it is necessary that *everything written* and figured in Jesus Christ must be fulfilled in him. Jesus Christ tells us the mystery written about in Moses, the prophets, and the psalms. In the Law of Moses all the sacrifices prefigure Christ's sacrifice. The law must be perfected and consumed in him. This is why he says *the law of Moses* that he has not come to abolish the law but he has come to fulfill and perfect the law. This has already been explained in Matthew 5:17. Moses, as a pastor, is also a prefiguring of Jesus Christ. Moses came to save Israel and to end the domination of the Pharaoh and the multiplicity of the Egyptians. In the same way, Jesus

Christ has come to destroy the multiplicity of our propriety after we have been freed from sin.

The prophets announce Jesus Christ when they wrote about him and his person. The prophets were the figures of the apostolic state, which Jesus Christ came not to destroy but to establish.

And *David* has written about Jesus Christ in his Psalms. David has pre-figured Jesus Christ both in his life and in his Psalms in an admirable manner. All has been fulfilled in Jesus Christ. But he is not finished yet because he will remain until the end of the centuries in substance and reality. Since all the states of Jesus Christ are contained in the scripture, can we believe that there is not any of the states of Jesus Christ that are not written?

> Then he opened their minds to understand the scriptures. (Luke 24:45)

Those who say that the soul who is resurrected and alive in God is not found in the scriptures are wrong. They take one state for the other. We have a true *intelligence in the scripture* in the resurrected state and it is one that the *Spirit opens* to us.

> And he said to them, "Thus it is written, that the Messiah is to suffer and to rise from the dead on the third day." (Luke 24:46)

Jesus Christ confirms to them again the state of resurrection and how he came to *suffer* and be three days dead in the tomb in decay and perfect annihilation that ordinarily accompany the pure sacrifice of naked faith and perfect abandonment. But this is only known to the soul and these states are succeeded by resurrection.

> "And that repentance and forgiveness of sins to be proclaimed in his name to all nations, beginning from Jerusalem. 48 You are witnesses of these things. 49 And see, I am sending upon you what my Father promised; so stay here in the city until you have been clothed with power from on high." (Luke 24:47–49)

Jesus Christ said that the scriptures mark that *repentance and forgiveness of sins* must be *preached in his name*. This *repentance* is the beginning of the interior state, when we leave sins and the exterior to turn toward God. This is the first thing that must be preached because it is absolutely necessary to leave sins before turning to God, because one is infinitely opposed to the other. This is like a person who has to choose one or the other.

But once this is done, then *forgiveness* is granted by Jesus Christ to mark his goodness and the trust we must have in him. We too must preach the forgiveness and pardon at the same time we preach about repentance. He wants us to preach with strength *to all nations*, but particularly to the faithful who are in the church as *in Jerusalem*. All nations will be instructed in these truths.

Jesus Christ's strong intention is to preach with strength. He wants all the apostles to have a testimony. They are the witnesses of what has happened in him and he wants this announced throughout the world.

But, he adds, so that you may preach these things efficaciously, *I am sending* upon you the gift of the apostolate, *promised by God the Father* and merited by Jesus Christ, a gift that makes and penetrates hearts. However, Jesus says again, so that you receive this gift, you must *stay here in the city*, that is to say, in solitude and retreat, *until you have been clothed with power from on high*. Because it is not enough that the grace be received in the foundation, it is necessary that the grace and the gift be like a vestment that surrounds the exterior so that the teaching and morals support the word.

> Then he led them out as far as Bethany, and, lifting up his hands, he blessed them. 51 While he was blessing them, he withdrew from them and was carried up into heaven. 52 And they worshiped him, and returned to Jerusalem with great joy; 53 and they were continually in the temple blessing God. (Luke 24:50–53)

Jesus Christ, after having taught the apostles by his example and words, *leads them out*, that is to say, draws them absolutely outside of themselves to be lost in him: he wants them outside and *lifting up his hands, he blessed them*. The elevation of the hands of Jesus Christ marks that he gives power to these souls who he wants to be conformed to him in the ministry to which they are called.

Then, *he withdrew from them*, leaving them clothed with his Spirit and his power that saved these souls. *His disciples worshipped and adored him* with a total submission of their wills and a knowledge of the power he had given them, knowing they would remain eternally dependent on him and would be led by his Spirit, *and they went*, says scripture, *with great joy*. Shouldn't they be afflicted to lose Jesus Christ? No, because in losing his presence from their senses, they had the steady presence of his Spirit that filled them with great joy. *If I do not go away, the Advocate will not come to you* (John 16:7). It is necessary that his perceptible presence leaves to give them the purity of his Spirit. This substantial stream of the Spirit of the Word causes a profound joy, which will never be lost. They return again to a retreat and remained *continually in the temple blessing God*. We need to know that the mission and state of the apostolate is given a little time before the exercise of the functions of this state. The soul enjoys for some time an ineffable happiness.

END OF THE GOSPEL OF LUKE

Bibliography

Anonymous. "Supplement to the Life of Madame Guyon." Translated by Nancy Carol James. In *The Pure Love of Madame Guyon*, 85–104. New York: University Press of America, 2014.

Bedoyere, Michael de la. *The Archbishop and the Lady*. New York: Pantheon, 1956.

Blount, Brian K."The Last Word on Biblical Authority." In Brueggemann, William C., William C. Placher and Brian K. Blount. *Struggling with Scripture*. Louisville: Westminster-John Knox Press, 2002

Bossuet, Jacques Benigne. *Quakerism a-la-mode, or A History of Quietism: Particularly that of the Lord Archbishop of Cambray and Madam Guyone*. London: Printed for J. Harris and A. Bell, 1698.

Bremond, Henri. *Apologie pour Fenelon*. Paris: Perrin, 1910.

Caussade, Jean Pierre de. *Abandonment to Divine Providence*. New York: Image Books, 1975.

———. *On Prayer: Spiritual Instructions on the Various States of Prayer According to the Doctrine of Bossuet, Bishop of Meaux*. Translated by Algar Thorold. London: Burns, Oates & Washbourne, 1931.

Conzemius, Viktor. "Quietism" In *Sacramentum Mundi*, Vol 5, 169–72. New York: Herder & Herder, 1970.

Fénelon, Francois de Salignac de La Mothe. *The Archbishop of Cambray's Dissertation on Pure Love, With an Account of the Life and Writings of the Lady, for Whose Sake the Archbishop was Banished from Court*. London: G. Thomson, 1750.

———. *The Complete Fénelon*. Brewster, Massachuetts: Paraclete Press, 2008.

———. *The Maxims of the Saints Explained, Concerning the Interior Life*. Bordeaux, France: 1913.

Gondal, Marie-Louise. *Madame Guyon: un noveau visage*. Paris: Beauchesne 1989.

Gough, James. "Comparative View of the Lives of St. Teresa and M. Guion." In *Life of Lady Guion*, 237–39, Bristol, U.K.: S. Farley, 1772.

———. "Life of Michael de Molinos and Progress of Quietism." In *The Life of Lady Guion*, 308–324. Bristol, U.K.: S. Farley, 1772.

Green, Joel B: "Conversion in Luke-Acts: Divine Action, Human Cognition, and the People of God." Grand Rapids: Baker Academic, 2015,

Guyon, Jeanne de la Mothe. *Autobiography of Madame Guyon*. Vols. 1 and 2. Translated by Thomas Taylor Allen. London: Kegan Paul, Trench, Trubner, 1897.

———. *Les justifications de Mme J.-M.B. de La Mothe-Guyon, ecrites par elle-meme, avec un examen de la IXe et Xe conferences de Cassien touchant l'etat fixe d'oraison continuelle, par M. De Fénelon.* 3 parites, Cologne, 1720.

———. *Les livres du Nouveau Testament avec des explications et reflexions qui regardent la vie interieure.* Pierre Poiret, 1713.

———. *Le Nouveau Testament de Notre-Seigneur Jésus-Christ avec des explications et réflexions qui regardent la vie intérieure.* 12 vols. Cologne: Poiret. 1714–1715.

———. *Les livres de l'Ancien Testament de Notre-Seigneur Jésus-Christ avec des explications et réflexions qui regardent la vie intérieure.* 12 vols. Cologne, 1714–1715.

———. *The Soul, Lover of God.* Translated by Nancy Carol James. New York: University Press of America, 2014.

———. *The Way of the Child Jesus: Our Model of Perfection.* Translated by Nancy Carol James. Virginia: European Emblems, 2015.

Holcombe, William H. *Aphorisms of the New Life: With Illustrations and Confirmations from the New Testament, Fénelon, Madame Guyon, and Swedenborg.* Philadelphia: E. Claxton, 1883.

James, Nancy C. *The Apophatic Mysticism of Madame Guyon.* Michigan: UMI Dissertation Services, 1998.

———. *The Complete Madame Guyon.* Brewster, Massachusetts: Paraclete Press, 2011.

———. *I, Jeanne Guyon.* Jacksonville, FL: Christian Books Publishing House, 2014.

———. *The Pure Love of Madame Guyon.* New York: University Press of America, 2007.

———. *Standing in the Whirlwind.* Cleveland: Pilgrim Press, 2005.

James, Nancy C. and Sharon D. Voros. *Bastille Witness: The Prison Autobiography of Madame Guyon.* New York: University Press of America, 2012.

James, William. *Varieties of Religious Experience.* New York: Collier, 1961.

Johnson, Luke Timothy. *The Gospel of Luke.* Collegeville: the Liturgical Press, 1991,

La Combe, Francois. *A Short Letter of Instruction, Shewing the Surest Way to Christian Perfection.* Translated by J. Gough. In *Life of Lady Guion*, 295–307. Bristol, U.K.: S. Farley, 1772.

Mudge, James. *Fénelon the Mystic.* Cincinnati: Jennings and Graham, 1906.

Poiret, Pierre. "The Theology of Emblems: Preface to the Emblems of Father Hugo and Madame Guyon." Translated by Nancy Carol James. In *The Soul, Lover of God*, xxxiii-xl. New York: University Press of America, 2014.

Ramsay, Chevalier. "Life of Francis de Salignac de la Mothe Fénelon, Archbishop and Duke of Cambray." In *Life of Lady Guion*, Vol. 2, 325–72. Bristol: S. Farley, 1772.

Saint-Simon, Duc de. *Historical Memoirs of the Duc de Saint-Simon.* Vols 1 and 2. Edited and translated by Lucy Norton. New York: McGraw-Hill, 1967.

Underhill, Evelyn. *Mysticism: A Study in the Nature and Development of Man's Spiritual Consciousness*, 12th Ed., Cleveland: World, 1965.

Upham, Thomas C. *Life and Religions Opinions and Experience of Madame de la Mothe Guyon.* 2 vols. New York: Harper & Brothers, 1847.

Wesley, John. *An Extract of the Life of Madame Guion.* London: R. Hawes, 1776.